CHEMISTRY
FOR THE
GRAPHIC ARTS

GATF Graphic Arts Technical Foundation

Chemistry for the Graphic Arts

by
Paul J. Hartsuch, Ph.D.

Graphic Arts Technical Foundation
4615 Forbes Avenue
Pittsburgh, Pennsylvania   15213

Library of Congress Catalog Card Number: 78-58920
International Standard Book Number: 0-88362-051-0

Printed in the United States of America

Reprinted with Minor Revisions   1983

Contents

1. Some Basic Chemistry 1

2. What pH Is and How to Measure It 43

3. Water — An Important Chemical 55

4. Chemistry of the Compounds of Carbon 69

5. Chemistry of Photography 97

6. Lithographic Plates — Introduction 127

7. Lithographic Plates — Negative-Working 145

8. Lithographic Plates — Positive-Working 155

9. Relief and Gravure Image Carriers 179

10. Chemistry of Paper 197

11. Chemistry of Inks 215

12. Chemistry in the Pressroom 249

13. Screen Printing, Heat Transfer Printing, and Collotype 283

14. Tables 291

Index 301

Foreword

Chemical processes are basic to several graphic arts operations and play an important role in many others. For this reason *Chemistry for the Graphic Arts* is considered to be a fundamental text in the Graphic Arts Technical Foundation's family of educational books.

GATF is a focal point of technical information flow for all areas of the graphic arts. It originates information, receives it from many sources, and disseminates it through workshops, seminars, technical services, and publications. Its many books include informational and operational textbooks, troubleshooting guides, and reference works. A particular book may be intended for industry, for schools, or for both.

Chemistry for the Graphic Arts is an informational textbook designed for use both by industry and in the schools. Its author's background remarkably encompasses the many strands desired to be combined in the production of a GATF textbook. During his distinguished career of research, teaching, and publishing, Dr. Hartsuch has been in the forefront of activities that changed lithography from a largely trial-and-error craft to a scientific technology. He was twice associated with GATF (then called Lithographic Technical Foundation) for a total of about fifteen years, first in charge of the chemistry division and at later times as assistant to the research director and as head of technical services.

In his Preface, Dr. Hartsuch acknowledges the many supplementary sources of expert aid he drew upon during the preparation of this book. At GATF, editorial assistance was rendered by Thomas Destree, a technical writer with chemistry specialization; and GATF chemist Dr. Nelson Eldred carefully reviewed the total work.

Finally, the modern style and design of the book have resulted from an editorial and art staff collaboration to produce a standard not for this book alone but for a whole series of GATF educational Books for the Eighties.

Raymond N. Blair
Publications Editor

Preface

My book *Chemistry of Lithography*, prepared for Graphic Arts
Technical Foundation in 1952, was based on a course developed
at the Chicago Lithographic Institute. After that book had
undergone over the years an extensive sequence of revision and
reprintings, GATF requested that I write an essentially new one,
not only updated but expanded in scope. This *Chemistry for the
Graphic Arts* is the result.

Two factors prompted the decision for a new book. First was
the rapid development in recent years of graphic arts chemical
technology. For example, there has been great progress in the
formulation of inks that are fast-setting, either at room
temperature or with the help of infrared or ultraviolet radiation
or electron beams. Heatset inks have been developed that
contain a considerable percentage of water to help reduce air
pollution. Some types of printing plates have disappeared or are
gradually diminishing in use, while several new types have
been introduced.

The second factor was recognition of the importance of
chemistry in other processes besides lithography. The chemistry
of inks and plates or cylinders for letterpress, flexography,
gravure, screen printing, and collotype have been added to make
this book valuable to all segments of the graphic arts.

To help make the information accurate and current, I have
had the advice of many experts in different areas. Their help is
greatly appreciated. Among those to whom I am grateful, the
following deserve special mention:

James Bailey, The X-Rite Company
Harry Baskerville, McGraw Colorgraph Co.
Robert Bassemir, Sun Chemical Corp.
Grant Beutner, RBP Chemical Corp.
Paul Borth, Platemakers Educational and Research Institute
Michael Bruno, graphic arts consultant
William Bureau, P. H. Glatfelter Co.
John Centa, Du Pont Company
Stanley Cygan, Poster Products, Inc.
John Easely, Dow Chemical U.S.A.
Dr. Edward Ewen, Sargent-Welch Scientific Co.
Dr. Karl Fox, Rapid Roller Co.
Merrill Friend, Chemco Photoproducts Co.
Lester Goda, Jr., Eastman Kodak Co.
Robert Harrell, Western Litho Plate and Supply Co.
Scott Harrison, Black Box Collotype
John Herbert, Herbert Products, Inc.

Michael Intrator, Black Box Collotype
William Jackson, Bowers Printing Ink Co.
George Klumb, Culligan Water Institute
Lawrence Lepore, Borden Chemical
Melvin London, London Litho Aluminum Co.
William Magie, Magie Bros. Oil Co.
William Mason, Du Pont Company
William McGraw, Du Pont Company
Norman Pozniak, Dow Chemical U.S.A.
James Radford, 3M Company
Laurence Rehm, Chicago Rotoprint Co.
John Riley, W.R. Grace & Co.
William Rocap, Jr., Meredith Publishing Co.
John Sampson, Central Solvents Chemical Co.
Terry Scarlett, GPI Division, Sun Chemical Corp.
Paul Schretter, Poster Products, Inc.
Ted Schwartz, Azoplate Division, American Hoechst Corp.
Dolph Simons, The Simco Company
Peter Terry, Naz-Dar Company
William Tousignant, RBP Chemical Corp.
Douglas Tuttle, Pamarco Incorporated
Robert Walsh, Agfa-Gevaert Incorporated
Charles Williams, Sargent-Welch Scientific Co.
Gary Winters, Inmont Corporation

1 Some Basic Chemistry

Chemistry is concerned with change. Chemical change involves the basic composition and structure of materials. In a *chemical reaction*, some materials disappear, and some other material or materials are formed. We say that the original materials react chemically with each other. They are called the *reactants*, and what is produced as a result of the reaction is the product or *products*.

Chemistry is involved in many areas of the graphic arts. When an ink dries, or sets, chemical changes sometimes occur. The development and fixing of photographic films and papers consist of several chemical reactions. Chemistry is involved in the action of light and developers on the coatings of offset and relief plates. When a metal relief plate is etched, a chemical reaction takes place. These examples represent only a few of the kinds of chemical change that are considered in this book.

In general, chemical reactions follow certain rules. Some things are possible, and some are not; the more you know about these rules, the better you can predict whether two materials are apt to react with each other. For example, it is impossible to change aluminum into iron, or iron into gold. A copper gravure cylinder can be etched with a water solution of ferric chloride, but copper will not react with acids such as hydrochloric or sulfuric. On the other hand, a magnesium relief plate can be etched with hydrochloric acid. Chemistry attempts to make sense of these things and many more.

One thing should be made clear right away. When a chemical reaction occurs, the total amount of matter remains exactly the same; matter cannot be created or destroyed. Of course the reactants do disappear, but products are formed in their place. The weight of the products is exactly the same as the weight of the reactants that disappeared. This fact is known as the *law of the conservation of mass*.

You might disagree with this. Thus you might say, "When coal burns, a chemical reaction is certainly taking place, and all that is left is a small amount of ash. The rest has disappeared." It appears that matter has been destroyed. However, such is not the case. When coal burns, gaseous products such as water vapor and carbon dioxide are formed. These have weight even though they are invisible. The total weight of the ash plus the gaseous products is exactly the same as the weight of the coal and air that reacted during burning.

The drying of an ink that contains a drying-oil varnish is another example. As such an ink dries on paper, it reacts with the oxygen in the air. At the same time, several gaseous products are liberated from the ink and go into the air (some of these gases are responsible for the odor you smell on sheets with dried ink). The net result is that the ink on the paper gains a little weight; the weight of the oxygen that enters the ink film is greater than the weight of the gaseous materials liberated from the ink. But if you carry out this drying process in a closed container, you find that the total weight remains unchanged. The various kinds of matter are different at the end of the drying process than at the start, but the total amount of matter remains the same.

Understanding this fundamental law of nature will help greatly when various chemical reactions are discussed. It is also necessary to know some other elements of basic chemistry before we can plunge into the chemistry of the drying of inks, of photographic processes, and of offset and relief plates and gravure cylinders.

Materials

Anything that has weight is a *material*. Paper, ink, aluminum for offset plates, and photographic developer are all materials. Even gases like air or carbon dioxide are materials. They all have weight. "Material" is the most general term that can be applied to anything.

Gases, Liquids, and Solids

Materials exist in three states, called *gas, liquid*, and *solid*. The term "gas" in chemistry means much more than illuminating gas; it refers to any material that is not in a liquid or solid state.

You are familiar with the states of many materials at room temperature. Thus aluminum, iron, and table salt are solids. Water, alcohol, and naphtha are liquids; air is a gas. These particular materials are respectively solids, liquids, and gas at room temperature and the pressure of the atmosphere; but a change in temperature or pressure, or both, may cause a material to change to another state. Water is a good example. If the temperature is lowered enough, liquid water changes to a solid (ice). If the temperature is raised enough, water changes in a gas (water vapor). If iron is heated high enough, it changes to a liquid. Ammonia is a gas at 77°F (25°C) and one atmosphere pressure. But it becomes a liquid at 77°F (25°C) and 10 atmospheres pressure. Here a change in pressure produces a change from gas to liquid, with no change in temperature. Even a gas like oxygen can be changed to a liquid, but (at one atmosphere pressure) it must be cooled to −297°F (−183°C) to accomplish the change. (It can be accomplished with less cooling by increasing the pressure.)

It is important to know when a chemical change is taking place, and when some change is occurring that does not involve a chemical reaction. When a material changes from a solid to a liquid, or from a liquid to a gas, or the reverse, this is *not* a chemical reaction. Water is still water, whether it is the solid, liquid, or gaseous state. The same is true of any other material.

Substances and Mixtures

A material is either a substance or a mixture. A *substance* may be defined as a material that has a constant, fixed composition by weight. If a substance is analyzed, you always find the same percentage by weight of the things that make up the substance. A substance, then, is a pure material. Pure water and pure salt are substances. So are pure metals, such as iron, copper, magnesium, and aluminum.

Besides having a fixed composition by weight, substances have a fixed melting point and a fixed boiling point (at one atmosphere pressure). It is necessary to fix the pressure, since the boiling point of a substance changes as the pressure changes. As the pressure increases, the boiling point increases.

If two or more substances are mixed, the result is a *mixture*. A mixture does not have a definite composition, as the substances may be mixed in different proportions, within limits. But it is often not possible to tell by looking at a material whether it is a substance or a mixture.

Many of the materials used in the graphic arts are mixtures. Inks are a mixture of several substances. Gasoline, naphtha, and other petroleum materials are a mixture. A solid dissolved in a liquid is a mixture, called a solution. For example, a photographic fixing bath is a solution of sodium thiosulfate ("hypo") and a hardening agent in water.

The air we breathe is a mixture of gaseous substances, including oxygen, nitrogen, carbon dioxide, water vapor, argon, and very small amounts of other substances (see Appendix). By cooling air to a very low temperature, it can be changed to a liquid, and then distilled by what is called fractional distillation, to separate it into oxygen, nitrogen, and argon. Fractional distillation is done commercially on a large scale. It is possible to buy tanks of oxygen for use in hospitals, certain welding operations, etc. Nitrogen is also available in tanks and is used in one process that claims to dry ultraviolet (UV) inks in an atmosphere of nitrogen, with lower energy than is required when UV inks dry in the presence of air.

Elements and Compounds

So far, materials have been divided into substances and mixtures. In turn, substances are divided into two classes, called elements and compounds. Substances get their characteristics from basic particles of which they are composed called atoms (described in more detail at a later point). *Elements* are substances made up of only one type of atom. Many familiar substances are elements. These include all the pure metals, and substances such as oxygen, hydrogen, iodine, nitrogen, and sulfur. There are now 105 known elements, but in the chemistry of the graphic arts we will be concerned with only a few of them.

A chemical *compound* consists of two or more elements chemically combined in a fixed proportion by weight. As an example, the compound magnesium nitrate consists of 16.4% magnesium, 18.9% nitrogen, and 64.7% oxygen by weight. In this case, the three elements—magnesium, nitrogen, and oxygen— have combined to form the compound called magnesium nitrate.

Many chemical compounds occur in nature. Water is a chemical compound of the elements hydrogen and oxygen. Common table salt has the chemical name sodium chloride and is a compound of the elements sodium (a metal) and chlorine. There are whole mountains of limestone, which is principally the compound calcium carbonate. Calcium carbonate consists of a chemical combination of calcium (a metal), carbon, and oxygen, all of which are elements.

Some chemical compounds do not occur in nature, but chemists have devised ways to chemically combine naturally occurring elements and compounds in new ways. To do this, they must of course bring two or more compounds or elements together, and then get them to react with each other. Often these materials are not eager to react, and the reaction is forced by the use of various techniques such as heat, electric current, or light of particular wavelengths.

Only a relatively few of the elements occur as such in nature. Among the common ones are oxygen, nitrogen, helium, neon, argon, sulfur, and gold. Most of the common metals, such as iron, lead, zinc, aluminum, and copper, occur in nature only as compounds. By one method or another, these compounds are broken down to produce the metals in their elementary state (as free elements). Many big companies are engaged in the production of iron and steel, aluminum, magnesium, and other metals from compounds of these metals.

Just as there are only twenty-six letters in the alphabet, but thousands of words that have been formed from them, so there are 105 elements, but over a million compounds that have been formed from them.

Here is a chart that shows the relationship between materials, substances, mixtures, elements, and compounds:

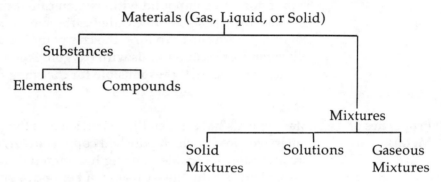

Metals and Nonmetals

Elements may be divided into *metals* and *nonmetals*. Table I lists the common metals and nonmetals, many of which will be mentioned later. The abbreviation after the name of the element, such as Al for Aluminum, is called the *symbol* of the element. Such symbols are handy when it comes to writing equations for chemical reactions.

Table I: Common Metals and Nonmetals, with Symbols

Metals		Nonmetals
Aluminum, Al	Mercury, Hg	Bromine, Br
Barium, Ba	Molybdenum, Mo	Carbon, C
Cadmium, Cd	Nickel, Ni	Chlorine, Cl
Calcium, Ca	Platinum, Pt	Fluorine, F
Chromium, Cr	Potassium, K	Iodine, I
Cobalt, Co	Silver, Ag	Nitrogen, N
Copper, Cu	Sodium, Na	Oxygen, O
Gold, Au	Tin, Sn	Phosphorus, P
Iron, Fe	Titanium, Ti	Silicon, Si
Lead, Pb	Tungsten, W	Sulfur, S
Magnesium, Mg	Zinc, Zn	
Manganese, Mn		

It is quite common for metals to react with nonmetals to form a compound. Sometimes a metal is already combined in nature with some nonmetal; iron oxide, for example, is a compound of iron and the nonmetal oxygen. Keep in mind that this is only a general rule, because a metal may not react with all of the nonmetals. Platinum and gold, for example, are very unreactive. Metals will not react with other metals under most conditions. However, under certain conditions, so-called "intermetallic compounds" are formed as alloys of two metals, but these are not compounds as normally defined.

Some of the nonmetals will react with each other. Thus carbon forms a compound with oxygen called carbon dioxide and also forms another one called carbon monoxide. Carbon combines with sulfur to form the compound carbon disulfide. Nitrogen forms compounds with oxygen. Some of these oxides of nitrogen are partly responsible for the smog that forms occasionally over our big cities.

Properties of Metals

Many metals have a metallic luster, such as the characteristic reflective glow of clean polished copper, silver, or gold. Many are malleable—capable of being hammered into thin sheets. Also, many are ductile—capable of being drawn into a wire. In addition, many are fair-to-excellent conductors of electricity and heat.

The things mentioned above are *physical properties* of metals. Nonmetals and compounds also have physical properties, though they are usually quite different from those of metals. Other physical properties include color, crystalline form, density, melting point, boiling point, refractive index, surface tension, tensile strength, and thermal expansion. The term "physical properties" is used because these qualities are not concerned with the chemical reaction of a material with another material. When you study such chemical reactions, you are involved with the *chemical properties* of the material.

Not all metals have the physical properties listed above. Some are too soft to be drawn into wire. And, of course, mercury, which under normal conditions is a liquid metal, cannot be hammered into sheets or drawn into wire. In order to understand why certain elements were listed as metals in Table I, we need to know something about atomic structure.

Atoms

All elements are believed to consist of very tiny particles called *atoms.* A piece of aluminum weighing one ounce consists of 6.35×10^{23} atoms, which is another way of saying that it consists of 635,000,000,000,000,000,000,000 atoms! This means that the weight of a single atom is very, very small. Yet each aluminum atom reacts chemically the same as every other aluminum atom.

The reason sulfur or oxygen is different chemically from aluminum is that sulfur and oxygen atoms are different from aluminum atoms. Indeed, the atoms of all the elements differ from one another in their weights. They also differ in the structure of the atoms, and this difference is very important because the structure of the atoms determines to a considerable extent how those atoms react chemically.

Structure of Atoms

The atoms of all elements are made up of still tinier particles, called protons, neutrons, and electrons. The interesting thing is that the atoms of *all* elements consist of some combination of protons, neutrons, and electrons. What makes the atoms of one element different from the atoms of another element is the number of protons, neutrons, and electrons in one atom of the element.

The atoms of all elements consist of two main parts—the center, or nucleus, consisting of protons and neutrons, and electrons outside of the nucleus that are moving rapidly around it. These three kinds of particles differ in their mass and electrical charge, as follows:

Proton—"unit" mass and "unit" positive electrical charge
Neutron—"unit" mass and no electrical charge
Electron—"unit" negative electrical charge

The mass of an electron is negligible compared with the mass of the proton and the neutron, and for most practical purposes can be considered to be zero.

It doesn't matter what a "unit" of mass is. All that is important is that the proton and the neutron have the same mass. The negative electrical charge can neutralize a positive electrical charge of equal amount. The negative charge on an electron is of the same amount as the positive charge on a proton; they neutralize each other. Thus an atom with, say, eleven protons in the nucleus and eleven electrons outside of the nucleus is an atom with no net electrical charge. The neutrons in the nucleus have no effect on this electrical charge, since they do not have any charge.

It is possible to give a number to every element, starting with one and going up to 105. This number is called the atomic number and is equal to the number of protons in the nucleus of the atoms of that element. For example, the metal element sodium has the atomic number 11. This means that all sodium atoms have eleven protons in the nucleus. And, since atoms have no net electrical charge, all sodium atoms have eleven electrons rotating around the nucleus. These amounts complete the structure of sodium atoms, except for the number of neutrons in the nucleus.

The total weight of any atom is equal to the sum of the weights of the protons and neutrons in the nucleus. (Remember, the weight of the electrons is negligible.) The *mass number* of a particular kind of atom is the sum of the protons and the neutrons in the nucleus. The mass number of sodium is 23. Since there are eleven protons in the nucleus of sodium atoms, twenty-three minus eleven gives twelve neutrons in the nucleus.

The complete symbol for sodium is:

$$\text{Mass No.} \longrightarrow \quad \text{Atomic No.} \longrightarrow \quad {}^{23}_{11}\text{Na}$$

and the structure of a sodium atom is:

nucleus	extranuclear electrons
11 p	11 e
12 n	

Only one more thing is needed to complete the structure of sodium, and other, atoms. The extranuclear electrons have different energies and exist in different energy "levels." Two electrons are the maximum number that can be accommodated in Energy Level 1. Level 2 can hold a maximum of eight electrons. Level 3 holds a maximum of eight electrons with the lighter atoms, but with the heavier elements it holds up to eighteen.

There are eleven extranuclear electrons in sodium atoms. Two of these are in Level 1, eight (the maximum) in Level 2, leaving one electron in Level 3.

Atomic structure of a sodium atom.

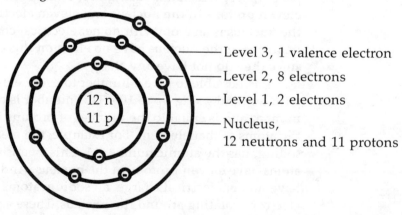

———— Level 3, 1 valence electron

———— Level 2, 8 electrons

———— Level 1, 2 electrons

———— Nucleus,
12 neutrons and 11 protons

The number of electrons in the *outermost* energy level is especially important. These are the most loosely bound electrons, and they can be lost (or shared) when atoms of one element combine with atoms of another element. These electrons that can participate in forming chemical bonds are called *valence electrons.* Sodium atoms, for example, have only one valence electron.

With a little practice, and by using the rules given above, you can show the structure of the atoms of any element—at least up to element No. 20—if you know its atomic number and its mass number. Thus the structure of $^{32}_{16}S$ (sulfur) is:

nucleus	extranuclear electrons		
	Level 1	Level 2	Level 3
16p	2e	8e	6e
16n			

The atomic number of sulfur is 16, so there are sixteen protons in the nucleus and also sixteen extranuclear electrons. Of these sixteen electrons, two exist in Level 1 and eight in Level 2, leaving six (sixteen minus ten) in Level 3. Since the mass number is 32, there must be thirty-two minus sixteen, or sixteen, neutrons in the nucleus.

Atomic structure of a sulfur atom.

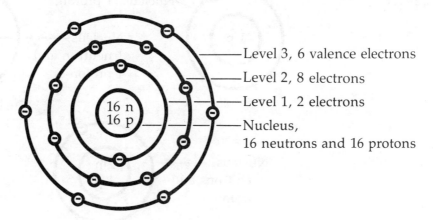

————Level 3, 6 valence electrons

————Level 2, 8 electrons

————Level 1, 2 electrons

————Nucleus, 16 neutrons and 16 protons

16 n
16 p

Atoms of a particular element *must* have as many protons in the nucleus and as many extranuclear electrons as the atomic number of that element. However, sometimes atoms of a particular element do not all have the same weight (mass). Some may have more neutrons in the nucleus than others. Atoms which have the same atomic number, but have different numbers of neutrons in the nucleus, are known as *isotopes* of the same element.

Hydrogen is the lightest of all of the elements, and it has an atomic number of 1. Most hydrogen atoms also have a mass number of 1. Thus the structure of $_1^1H$ is:

| nucleus | extranuclear electron |
| 1p | 1e |

So hydrogen atoms have *one* valence electron.

A very small percentage of hydrogen atoms have a mass number of 2. These are called deuterium atoms (previously, "heavy hydrogen"). The structure of deuterium, $_1^2H$, is:

nucleus	extranuclear electron
1p	1e
1n	

Deuterium is still hydrogen since there is one proton in the nucleus, but the atoms of deuterium are twice as heavy as those of $_1^1H$. Another isotope of hydrogen, tritium, has two neutrons in the nucleus.

Isotopes of hydrogen.

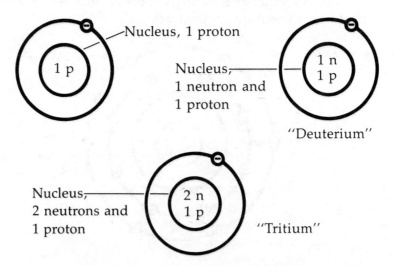

Many elements consist of isotopes, while others consist of atoms that have only one weight. Table II gives the structure of the atoms of elements with atomic numbers from 1 through 20. Keep in mind that the electrons in the outermost energy level are the valence electrons. Thus carbon has four valence electrons, nitrogen has five, oxygen has six, and chlorine has seven. This difference in the number of valence electrons makes one element react differently from another.

Table II: Structure of Principal Atoms of Elements 1-20

Element	Atomic No.	Mass No.	Nucleus Protons	Nucleus Neutrons	Extranuclear Electrons Level No. 1	2	3	4
Hydrogen	1	1	1	0	1			
Hydrogen	1	2	1	1	1			
Helium	2	4	2	2	2			
Lithium	3	6	3	3	2	1		
Lithium	3	7	3	4	2	1		
Beryllium	4	9	4	5	2	2		
Boron	5	11	5	6	2	3		
Carbon	6	12	6	6	2	4		
Nitrogen	7	14	7	7	2	5		
Oxygen	8	16	8	8	2	6		
Fluorine	9	19	9	10	2	7		
Neon	10	20	10	10	2	8		
Sodium	11	23	11	12	2	8	1	
Magnesium	12	24	12	12	2	8	2	
Magnesium	12	25	12	13	2	8	2	
Magnesium	12	26	12	14	2	8	2	
Aluminum	13	27	13	14	2	8	3	
Silicon	14	28	14	14	2	8	4	
Phosphorus	15	31	15	16	2	8	5	
Sulfur	16	32	16	16	2	8	6	
Chlorine	17	35	17	18	2	8	7	
Chlorine	17	37	17	20	2	8	7	
Argon	18	40	18	22	2	8	8	
Potassium	19	39	19	20	2	8	8	1
Calcium	20	40	20	20	2	8	8	2

Families of Elements

If elements that react similarly can be grouped, the learning process is simplified. When such a grouping is made, it is found that the atoms of all of the elements in a particular group, or family, have the same number of valence electrons. Four important families of elements are:

● **Alkali metals.** The common metals in this family are lithium, sodium, and potassium. The atoms of all these elements have *one* valence electron.

● **Alkaline earth metals.** The common metals in this family are beryllium, magnesium, calcium, strontium, and barium. The atoms of all of these elements have *two* valence electrons.

One of the things to notice is that the atoms of most metals have one or two valence electrons. One metal, aluminum, consists of atoms with three valence electrons. So it can be stated that elements classed as metals usually consist of atoms that have one, two, or at most three valence electrons. The heavy metals lead and tin are exceptions. Their atoms have four valence electrons.

● **Halogens.** The halogens are nonmetals and include fluorine, chlorine, bromine, and iodine. The atoms of all these elements have *seven* valence electrons.

● **Noble gases.** The noble gases include helium, neon, argon, krypton, and xenon. In the atoms of all of the noble gases, the outermost energy level is filled with all of the electrons it can hold. Helium has two electrons in Level 1, all that Level 1 can hold. As a general rule, the others have eight electrons, and that is all that the outermost energy level can hold.

Since the outermost energy levels of the atoms of the noble gases are filled, one can say that these atoms do not have any valence electrons. Therefore, the noble gases are extremely inert. Until 1962, no compounds of these gases had ever been produced.

Where does all this information lead us? It has already been mentioned that the valence electrons are the most loosely bound ones and can be lost (or shared) when atoms of one element combine with atoms of another element. The electrons really aren't lost. They are merely transferred to the atoms of the other element. When this happens, the atoms of *both* elements have electrons in the outermost energy level that are the same in number as those of the nearest noble gas. This fact, combined with subsequent information, explains why certain atoms react with certain others.

Atomic Weights   As you have seen, the atoms of different elements differ in weight. Since the actual weight of atoms is such a very small figure, chemists have adopted the practice of using the relative weights of the atoms of elements. These are called the *atomic weights* of the elements even though they are expressed in relative, or unitless, numbers.

Atomic weights can be used to figure weight relations in chemical reactions. By their use, you can calculate what weight of one substance will react with a given weight of another substance, and what the weights will be of the substances that are produced.

In originally making a table of atomic weights, it was necessary to pick one element as the standard. For many years, oxygen was used as the standard and was assigned an atomic weight of 16.000. The number 16 was chosen so that the lightest element, hydrogen, would have an atomic weight close to one. By using chemical combining weights, it was possible to determine the relative weights of other elements, compared with 16 for oxygen.

The table of atomic weights was used by chemists for many years before it was discovered that many elements consist of two or more isotopes. This discovery helped to explain why the atomic weights of the elements are not even multiples of the atomic weight of hydrogen. Actually the exact atomic weights are based on the combining weights of elements in chemical reactions which involve billions and billions of atoms. So, for example, the atomic weight of chlorine (35.5) represents the average weight of chlorine atoms compared with 16.000 for the average weight of oxygen atoms. It is such average weights that determine the proportions by weight of substances that are involved in a chemical reaction. The approximate atomic weights of many of the more common elements are given in Table III.

Table III: Selected Characteristics of Common Elements

Element	Symbol	Atomic Number	Atomic Weight	No. of Valence Electrons
Aluminum	Al	13	27.0	3
Argon	Ar	18	39.9	0
Barium	Ba	56	137.3	2
Boron	B	5	10.8	3
Bromine	Br	35	79.9	7
Cadmium	Cd	48	112.4	2
Calcium	Ca	20	40.1	2
Carbon	C	6	12.01	4
Chlorine	Cl	17	35.5	7
Chromium	Cr	24	52.0	1 (T)
Cobalt	Co	27	58.9	2 (T)
Copper	Cu	29	63.5	1 (T)
Fluorine	F	9	19.0	7
Gold	Au	79	197.0	1 (T)
Helium	He	2	4.0	0
Hydrogen	H	1	1.008	1
Iodine	I	53	126.9	7
Iron	Fe	26	55.8	2 (T)
Krypton	Kr	36	83.8	0
Lead	Pb	82	207.2	4

(continued on next page)

Table III: Selected Characteristics of Common Elements (continued)	Element	Symbol	Atomic Number	Atomic Weight	No. of Valence Electrons
	Magnesium	Mg	12	24.3	2
	Manganese	Mn	25	54.9	2 (T)
	Mercury	Hg	80	200.6	2
	Molybdenum	Mo	42	95.9	1 (T)
	Neon	Ne	10	20.2	0
	Nickel	Ni	28	58.7	2 (T)
	Nitrogen	N	7	14.01	5
	Oxygen	O	8	16.00	6
	Phosphorus	P	15	31.0	5
	Platinum	Pt	78	195.1	1 (T)
	Potassium	K	19	39.1	1
	Silicon	Si	14	28.1	4
	Silver	Ag	47	107.9	1 (T)
	Sodium	Na	11	23.0	1
	Sulfur	S	16	32.1	6
	Tin	Sn	50	118.7	4
	Titanium	Ti	22	47.9	2 (T)
	Tungsten	W	74	183.8	2 (T)
	Xenon	Xe	54	131.3	0
	Zinc	Zn	30	65.4	2

(T) = "transition" element.

In recent years, the expansion of the metric system known as "SI" (for Systeme International) has provided a new standard for atomic weights. It is based on using 12.000 for the atomic weight of the principal isotope of carbon, with a mass number of 12. This new definition changes the former atomic weights by only 0.0045%. Although this is a small amount, it is important in the most precise scientific calculations.

Molecules of Certain Elements

If two or more atoms, either alike or different, are held tightly together, the combination is called a *molecule*. Most elements consist of single atoms, but in a few cases, two atoms of an element join to form a molecule of the element. Hydrogen, for instance, exists as molecules having two hydrogen atoms each. The molecular formula is H_2.

Why does hydrogen form such molecules? Any atom prefers to have a completed level of outer electrons, which makes it more like the noble gases. Hydrogen has one valence electron, and the first energy level is complete with two electrons. When two hydrogen atoms join to form a molecule of hydrogen, they share two electrons, and this makes them more like the nearest noble gas, helium, which has a completed energy level of two electrons. A pair of electrons shared between two atoms, whether the two atoms are of the same element of two different elements, is called a *covalent bond.* Valence electrons can be expressed as small black dots. Thus a hydrogen atom is written H˙, and a molecule of hydrogen is written H:H. The sharing of two electrons between two hydrogen atoms is the chemical force that holds the molecule together.

Two hydrogen atoms forming a molecule of hydrogen.

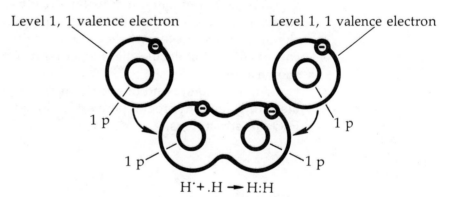

Level 1, 1 valence electron   Level 1, 1 valence electron

1 p   1 p

1 p   1 p

H˙ + .H → H:H

Fluorine, chlorine, bromine, and iodine have seven valence electrons. The noble gas nearest to each of them has completed energy level of eight electrons. Again, two atoms of these elements can share two electrons between them so that each atom, in effect, has a completed energy level of eight electrons. Chlorine, for example, can be written $:\ddot{C}l\cdot$. When two of these combine to give a Cl_2 molecule, the structure is $:\ddot{C}l:\ddot{C}l:$. In a similar way, atoms of the other halogens combine to form diatomic molecules—F_2, Br_2, and I_2. Other elements that also form diatomic molecules include oxygen, O_2, and nitrogen, N_2.

Molecules of Compounds

If atoms of different elements combine chemically, molecules of a compound are formed. The atoms in thousands of different kinds of molecules are held together by covalent bonds (see previous section on Molecules of Certain Elements). A simple example is the compound water, which consists of H_2O molecules. The shorthand expression H_2O means that one molecule of water consists of two atoms of hydrogen combined with one atom of oxygen. We say that the *molecular formula* of water is H_2O.

Oxygen atoms have six valence electrons and would like to have eight to complete the second energy level. (The nearest noble gas, neon, has a completed second energy level of eight electrons.) One hydrogen atom has only one valence electron. So it takes *two* hydrogen atoms to combine with one atom of oxygen to form one molecule of H_2O. A pair of electrons is shared between the oxygen atom and each hydrogen atom. We can picture this as follows:

$$2H\cdot \text{ plus } \cdot \ddot{O}\colon \text{ gives } H\colon\!\ddot{O}\colon$$
$$\phantom{2H\cdot \text{ plus } \cdot \ddot{O}\colon \text{ gives } }H$$

A tremendous amount of water already exists in oceans, rivers, and lakes, so it is not necessary to produce it by a chemical reaction. Nevertheless, all naturally occurring water consists of H_2O molecules held together by covalent bonds, as shown above.

Another compound of hydrogen and oxygen is the bleaching agent hydrogen peroxide, which has the formula H_2O_2. Its structure is:

$$\begin{array}{c} H \\ \colon\!\ddot{O}\!\colon\!\ddot{O}\colon \\ H \end{array}$$

In molecules of hydrogen peroxide, each oxygen atom shares two electrons with one hydrogen atom; in addition the two oxygen atoms share two electrons with each other. Such an arrangement is less stable than the H_2O arrangement, and this is what makes hydrogen peroxide a reactive bleaching agent.

The Difference between a Mixture and a Compound

A mixture of hydrogen and oxygen gases consists, of course, of hydrogen and oxygen. The compound water also consists of hydrogen and oxygen. Water consists of molecules of H_2O with the hydrogen and oxygen atoms chemically combined. A mixture of hydrogen and oxygen gases consists of H_2 molecules and O_2 molecules. These molecules are in continuous motion and are continuously bumping into each other, but they remain as H_2 and O_2 molecules. Furthermore, since they are a mixture, the two gases can be present in any proportion and not necessarily in the proportion required to produce molecules of H_2O. So there is a vast difference between a mixture and a compound.

Suppose we have a mixture of 4 grams of H_2 molecules and 32 grams of O_2 molecules. This is the correct proportion by weight required to form H_2O molecules, since hydrogen molecules are much lighter than oxygen molecules. These molecules want to react with each other but they can't until they are "activated." Activation requires an electrical spark or a lighted match, which provides what is called the *energy of activation*. Then the gases react so rapidly that there is an explosion. It can be expressed as follows: Four grams (0.14 ounces) H_2 react with 32 grams (1.12 ounces) O_2 to produce 36 grams (1.26 ounces) H_2O plus 569,400 joules (420,000 foot-pounds) of heat. This reaction is another example of the law of the conservation of mass. The weight of H_2 and O_2 that disappear (4 grams plus 32 grams) is *exactly* the same as the weight of water (36 grams) that is formed.

The reaction also liberates a large quantity of heat. All chemical reactions proceed either with emission or absorption of energy of one kind or another. Sometimes the amount is small and not noticed, while in other cases it is considerable.

If a material is dissolved in water that will enable it to carry an electric current, and two carbon electrodes are inserted into the water, it is possible to pass an electric current through the water and *decompose* the water molecules. Hydrogen gas is formed at one electrode and oxygen gas at the other electrode. Energy is being consumed to *reverse* the chemical reaction just discussed. It is found that the electrical energy required to form 4 grams of H_2 and 32 grams of O_2 is 569,400 joules. This is an example of the *law of the conservation of energy*, which states that energy cannot be created or destroyed. In this case, the amount of energy released when water is formed from H_2 and O_2 is exactly equal to the amount of energy absorbed to convert the water back to H_2 and O_2.

The energy involved in changing a substance from one state to another is an example of the law of the conservation of energy. For instance, heat must be absorbed to change 18 grams (0.63 oz.) of ice into liquid water, at 0°C (32°F). This is called the *molar heat of fusion*. More heat must be absorbed to raise the temperature of the liquid water to 100°C (212°F), the boiling point. A considerable amount of heat is then absorbed at 100°C to convert the water into steam. This is called the *molar heat of vaporization*. Now, if this process is reversed, exactly the same amount of heat is evolved that was originally absorbed in each step.

Ions and Ionic Solids

The atoms in the molecules of many compounds are held together by covalent bonds. If such a compound is soluble in water, it may break apart to form electrically charged particles that are called *ions*. One kind of ion carries a positive charge and the other a negative charge. Thus the common *nitrate* ion is NO_3^-: the combination of three oxygen atoms and one nitrogen atom has an electrical charge of -1. In such cases, negative ions are always balanced by positive ions so the net electrical charge is zero.

Remember that atoms of elements are uncharged, with as many extranuclear electrons as there are protons in the nucleus. We can say, however, that certain atoms are not satisfied with the number of valence electrons in the outer energy level. In this case, they can become more satisfied by either losing or gaining electrons, depending on the particular kind of atom. Let's use table salt, sodium chloride, NaCl, for an example. Sodium atoms have one valence electron and are more satisfied if they don't have any. Chlorine atoms have seven valence electrons, and are more satisfied if they have eight, which is a completed energy level. As a consequence, each sodium atom donates its valence electron to a chlorine atom. Since the electron donated carries a negative charge, the chlorine atom is changed to a Cl^- ion, called a *chloride* ion. The sodium atom minus an electron becomes a Na^+ ion.

Sodium atom donating electron to chlorine atom.

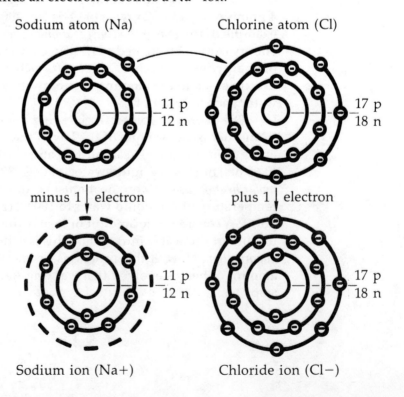

Sodium atom (Na)   Chlorine atom (Cl)

11 p
12 n   17 p
18 n

minus 1 | electron   plus 1 | electron

11 p
12 n   17 p
18 n

Sodium ion (Na+)   Chloride ion (Cl−)

The tendency for this electron transfer is so great in the case of sodium chloride, NaCl, that even solid sodium chloride consists of a network of sodium and chloride ions; even in the solid state there are no molecules of NaCl. So when NaCl dissolves in water, the Na^+ and Cl^- ions merely separate and start moving around among the water molecules. A solid compound with this characteristic is called an *ionic solid*.

The compound calcium chloride has the formula $CaCl_2$. Calcium atoms have two valence electrons. When calcium chloride dissolves in water, each calcium atom can give an electron to each of two chlorine atoms. The calcium atom minus two electrons becomes the Ca^{++} ion. A solution of calcium chloride in water consists of billions of Ca^{++} ions and twice as many Cl^- ions. This of course makes the solution electrically neutral.

In a similar way, aluminum atoms, which have three valence electrons, can transfer the electrons to three chlorine atoms, so a solution of aluminum chloride in water consists of billions of Al^{+++}, and three times as many Cl^-.

The same procedure occurs with more complicated compounds. Magnesium nitrate has the formula $Mg(NO_3)_2$. This means that one magnesium atom is combined with two nitrate groups, NO_3. Magnesium atoms have two valence electrons. When magnesium nitrate is dissolved in water, each magnesium atom contributes an electron to each of two nitrate groups. The result is a solution with billions of magnesium ions, Mg^{++}, and twice as many nitrate ions, NO_3^-.

The matter becomes even more complicated with the *transition elements* (identified with "T" in Table III). These all have one or two valence electrons, and therefore are all metals. Examples are iron, copper, silver, and gold. What makes the transition elements special is that they can lose not only their valence electrons, but they can also lose an electron from the energy level next to the outermost energy level.

Copper, for example, can form *cuprous* chloride, CuCl, where the one valence electron of copper atoms is involved. Or it can form *cupric* chloride, $CuCl_2$. In water solution, each $CuCl_2$ molecule gives a cupric ion, Cu^{++}, and two chloride ions, Cl^-. In this case, each copper atom has lost its one valence electron and also one from the energy level next to the outermost one. In the same way, iron atoms can lose their two valence electrons to form ferrous ions, Fe^{++}. Or they can lose three electrons to form ferric ions, Fe^{+++}. So one chloride compound is ferrous chloride, $FeCl_2$, and another is ferric chloride, $FeCl_3$.

It is convenient to have a table of the common ions; Table IV lists the ions with their positive or negative charge. It must be kept in mind that these ions cannot exist alone. In any water solution, or in any ionic solid, there must be exactly as many positive charges as negative. Certain ions, such as oxygen ions, O^{--}, do not exist. Oxygen forms compounds with other elements that are held together by covalent bonds. It is merely convenient to consider oxygen as having a -2 charge when writing formulas for compounds of oxygen with another element.

Table IV(a): Selected Positively Charged Ions

Name	Symbol	Name	Symbol
Aluminum	Al^{+++}	Silver	Ag^+
Ammonium	NH_4^+	Sodium	Na^+
Barium	Ba^{++}	Tin (II), or stannous	Sn^{++}
Calcium	Ca^{++}	Tin (IV), or stannic	Sn^{++++}
Chromium (II), or chromous	Cr^{++}	Zinc	Zn^{++}
Chromium (III), or chromic	Cr^{+++}		
Cobalt	Co^{++}		
Copper (I), or cuprous	Cu^+		
Copper (II), or cupric	Cu^{++}		
Hydrogen, or hydronium	H^+, H_3O^+		
Iron (II), or ferrous	Fe^{++}		
Iron (III), or ferric	Fe^{+++}		
Lead	Pb^{++}		
Lithium	Li^+		
Magnesium	Mg^{++}		
Manganese (II), or manganous	Mn^{++}		
Mercury (I), or mercurous	Hg_2^{++}		
Mercury (II), or mercuric	Hg^{++}		
Nickel (II), or nickelous	Ni^{++}		
Nickel (III), or nickelic	Ni^{+++}		
Potassium	K^+		

Table IV(b):	Name	Symbol
Selected	Acetate	CH_3COO^-
Negatively	Aluminate	AlO_2^-
Charged Ions	Bromide	Br^-
	Carbonate	CO_3^{--}
	Chlorate	ClO_3^-
	Chloride	Cl^-
	Chlorite	ClO_2^-
	Chromate	CrO_4^{--}
	Citrate	$C_6H_5O_7^{---}$
	Cyanide	CN^-
	Dichromate	$Cr_2O_7^{--}$
	Dihydrogen phosphate	$H_2PO_4^-$
	Ferricyanide	$Fe(CN)_6^{---}$
	Ferrocyanide	$Fe(CN)_6^{----}$
	Fluoride	F^-
	Hydrogen carbonate, or bicarbonate	HCO_3^-
	Hydrogen sulfate, or bisulfate	HSO_4^-
	Hydrogen sulfide, or bisulfide	HS^-
	Hydrogen sulfite, or bisulfite	HSO_3^-
	Hydroxide	OH^-
	Hypochlorite	ClO^-
	Iodide	I^-
	Metaborate	BO_3^{---}
	Metasilicate	SiO_3^{--}
	Monohydrogen phosphate	HPO_4^{--}
	Nitrate	NO_3^-
	Nitrite	NO_2^-
	Oxalate	$C_2O_4^{--}$
	Oxide	O^{--}
	Perchlorate	ClO_4^-
	Permanganate	MnO_4^-
	Phosphate	PO_4^{---}
	Sulfate	SO_4^{--}
	Sulfide	S^{--}
	Sulfite	SO_3^{--}
	Tartrate	$C_4H_4O_6^{--}$
	Tetraborate	$B_4O_7^{--}$
	Thiocyanate	CNS^-
	Thiosulfate	$S_2O_3^{--}$

Formulas of Compounds

It has already been explained why the formula of sodium chloride is NaCl, calcium chloride is $CaCl_2$, and aluminum chloride is $AlCl_3$. Formulas for many other compounds can be written by using the proper combination of the positive and negative ions given in Table IV, based on the fact that the molecules of any compound are *uncharged*. The total positive charge of the positive ions must be the same as the total negative charge of the negative ions. Here are some examples:

● **Sodium sulfate.** Formula is Na_2SO_4. (Two sodium ions each with a $+1$ charge are needed to balance the -2 charge of the sulfate ion.)

● **Ammonium chloride.** Formula is NH_4Cl.

● **Potassium dichromate.*** Formula is $K_2Cr_2O_7$. (Two potassium ions each with a $+1$ charge are needed to balance the -2 charge of the dichromate ion.)

● **Calcium phosphate.** Formula is $Ca_3(PO_4)_2$. (Three calcium ions each with a $+2$ charge are needed to balance with two phosphate ions each with a -3 charge.)

● **Iron (III) oxide.** Formula is Fe_2O_3. (Two ferric ions each with a $+3$ charge are balanced with three oxygens, with an assumed charge of -2 each.)

Table IV can be used to assist in writing the formulas of other compounds.

Most of the chemical elements occur in nature as compounds. The principal ore of silver is silver sulfide, Ag_2S. Zinc occurs in nature as zinc sulfide, ZnS. Aluminum occurs as bauxite, $Al_2O_3 \cdot 2H_2O$. The dot in the center of the preceding formula marks the division between different molecules in combination. In bauxite, two molecules of water are combined with one molecule of aluminum oxide, Al_2O_3. Calcium occurs in nature as calcium carbonate, $CaCO_3$, and also as calcium phosphate, $Ca_3(PO_4)_2$.

When some compounds dissolved in water form solid crystals as the solution is evaporated or cooled, they carry with them a certain amount of water, called *the water of crystallization*. Thus the formula for crystals of sodium carbonate is:

$$Na_2CO_3 \cdot 10\ H_2O$$

This is called *hydrated* sodium carbonate because of the associated water molecules. It is often possible to drive off this water by heating the crystals or sometimes merely exposing them to fairly dry air. Then the crystalline form disappears and

*Printers often call this "bichromate."

the compound becomes a powder, called an *anhydrous* compound. The hydrated and anhydrous forms behave the same in a chemical reaction. The only difference is that a greater weight must be used of the hydrated form because of the water present in it.

Sometimes when two compounds are dissolved in the same water, and the solution is evaporated or cooled, solid crystals will be formed that contain both compounds. The *alums* are examples of this. Here is the formula of a common alum:

Potassium aluminum alum, $K_2SO_4 \cdot Al_2(SO_4)_3 \cdot 24\ H_2O$

The two compounds K_2SO_4 and $Al_2(SO_4)_3$ do not combine chemically. They simply crystallize out together. When the crystals are dissolved in water, all you have is a mixture of the two compounds.

Inorganic and Organic Compounds

Most of the compounds that have formulas that can be written with the aid of Table IV are called *inorganic compounds. Organic compounds* are compounds of the element carbon with other elements. In fact, all compounds containing carbon are organic, with the exception of carbon dioxide, CO_2; carbon monoxide, CO; and a few compounds such as sodium carbonate, Na_2CO_3 and sodium cyanide, $NaCN$. There are so many organic compounds, and so many types, that they are covered in a separate chapter.

Oxidation and Reduction

Oxidation and reduction are two interdependent chemical concepts; it is impossible to have one without the other. An *oxidation-reduction reaction* is one in which some atoms lose electrons to other atoms. The atoms that lose electrons are said to be *oxidized;* the atoms that gain electrons are said to be *reduced.* For example, when oxygen from the air combines with iron to form iron oxide, or rust, the iron is oxidized (it loses electrons to the oxygen), and the oxygen is reduced (it gains electrons from the iron). However, "oxidation" (the taking of electrons from some atoms by others) does not always involve oxygen.

To determine if any oxidation-reduction reaction has occurred, it is necessary to define "oxidation number." The *oxidation number* is the number of electrons that must be lost or gained by an atom in a combined state to convert it to its elemental form. The oxidation number of an uncombined element is therefore 0.

Water, H_2O, was established as the reference compound for determining oxidation numbers of elements in compounds. The arithmetic sum of the oxidation numbers of any compound must equal zero, because a compound has no net charge. Therefore, oxygen was given the oxidation number of -2, and hydrogen was given the oxidation number of $+1$. The oxidation numbers of other atoms in combined form are calculated in relation to the oxidation number of oxygen and hydrogen. Now we can say that oxidation occurs when there is an *increase* in the oxidation number of some element, and reduction occurs when there is a *decrease* in the oxidation number of another element.

When magnesium burns in air, the compound magnesium oxide, MgO, is formed. In this reaction, the oxidation number of oxygen has gone from zero (free oxygen) to -2 in MgO. So oxygen has been *reduced*. At the same time, the oxidation number of magnesium has gone from zero (Mg metal) to $+2$ in MgO. So magnesium has been oxidized. A substance that oxidizes something else is called an *oxidizing agent*. And a substance that reduces something else is called a *reducing agent*.

The atoms in multiatomic ions, such as sulfate, SO_4^{--}, can be assigned an oxidation number. For multiatomic ions, the sum of the oxidation numbers must equal the charge of the ion. In this case, the oxidation number of the four oxygen atoms is $4 \times (-2)$, or -8. Since the sulfate ion has a charge of -2, the sulfur atom in it must have an oxidation number of $+6$. Using the same kind of arithmetic, the oxidation number of sulfur in the sulfite ion, SO_3^{--}, is $+4$. This means that a compound with sulfite ions must be oxidized to convert it to a sulfate compound. In the same way, a nitrite ion, NO_2^-, must be oxidized to convert it to a nitrate ion, NO_3^-.

Sodium hypochlorite, NaOCl, is a good oxidizing agent. This means that some atom in this compound must be reduced. This is the Cl atom. In NaOCl, the Cl has an oxidation number of $+1$. When this compound oxidizes something else, the Cl changes to chloride ion, Cl^-. So there has been a reduction in the oxidation number of Cl from $+1$ to -1. That is, the Cl in NaOCl has been reduced.

More examples of oxidation and reduction will be given as we proceed.

Acids

An acid can be defined as a compound that can release hydrogen ions, H^+, when dissolved in water. Here are the names and formulas of some common acids:

Acetic acid	CH_3COOH
Carbonic acid	H_2CO_3
Citric acid	$H_3C_6H_5O_7$
Hydrochloric acid	HCl
Hydrocyanic acid	HCN
Hydrofluoric acid	HF
Hydrogen sulfide	H_2S
Metaboric acid	H_3BO_3
Nitric acid	HNO_3
Oxalic acid	$H_2C_2O_4$
Phosphoric acid	H_3PO_4
Sulfuric acid	H_2SO_4
Sulfurous acid	H_2SO_3
Tartaric acid	$H_2C_4H_4O_6$

All of the formulas of these acids can be written by combining hydrogen ions with the appropriate negative ions given in Table IV.

Properties of Acids

Some of the properties of acids are that they:

1. React with certain metals, such as zinc, magnesium, and iron.

2. Conduct an electric current when dissolved in water.

3. Taste sour, in dilute solution. (Be careful! Some acids are very powerful, and some—like HCN—are very poisonous.)

4. Turn blue litmus paper red. (There is a dye in this paper that turns red when the paper is immersed into an acid solution.)

5. React chemically with other substances called bases.

Since all acids supply hydrogen ions in a water solution, it is assumed that their acid properties are due to the hydrogen ions. Actually, most hydrogen ions are simply protons (except for heavy hydrogen ions). It is generally believed that a proton becomes attached to a molecule of water; the resulting ion, H_3O^+, is called the *hydronium* ion. For example, we can write:

$$HCl\,(aq)\ +\ H_2O\ \longrightarrow\ H_3O^+(aq)\ +\ Cl^-(aq)$$

The "aq" means that this reaction takes place in an aqueous (water) solution. When HCl, which is a gas, is dissolved in water, the HCl molecules ionize to form hydronium ions and chloride ions. The hydrochloric acid that is sold commercially is a concentrated solution of HCl in water.

Sometimes we will talk about the hydrogen ion concentration of a solution, but it should be kept in mind that the hydrogen ions are combined with water molecules to form hydronium ions.

Strong and Weak Acids

Some acids are "strong," and unless only a little of the acid is dissolved in a lot of water, they will attack the mouth tissues. Others are "weak." A typical example of a weak acid is acetic acid, which is the acid present in vinegar. A strong acid may attack some metals rapidly, while a weak acid will react very slowly or not at all.

The difference is due to the percentage of the acid molecules that ionize when the acid is dissolved in water. If most of the molecules ionize, the acid is strong. If only a small percentage of the molecules ionize, then the acid is weak. Acids vary in their strength. Here is a table showing the percent ionization of some common acids.

Hydrochloric acid (HCl)	about 100%
Nitric acid (HNO_3)	about 100%
Sulfuric acid (H_2SO_4)	about 100%
Oxalic acid ($H_2C_2O_4$)	17.6%
Phosphoric acid (H_3PO_4)	8.3%
Tartaric acid ($H_2C_4H_4O_6$)	3.3%
Hydrofluoric acid (HF)	2.6%
Acetic acid (CH_3COOH)	0.43%
Carbonic acid (H_2CO_3)	0.06%
Metaboric acid (H_3BO_3)	0.003%

Thus acids vary widely in the extent that they ionize when dissolved in water. The above figures apply only to a certain concentration of the acids. At this concentration, 99.57% of acetic acid molecules, for example, remain in solution as molecules, and only 0.43% ionize to give H_3O^+ and CH_3COO^- ions. This percent ionization means that the hydronium (hydrogen) ion concentration of the acetic acid solution is very much less than if an equivalent amount of hydrochloric acid is dissolved in water.

Bases

A modern definition of a base is a substance that produces hydroxide ions, OH^-, when dissolved in water or a substance that can react with the hydrogen ions of an acid. Typical bases are: sodium hydroxide, NaOH; potassium hydroxide, KOH; calcium hydroxide, $Ca(OH)_2$; sodium carbonate, Na_2CO_3; sodium phosphate, Na_3PO_4; and ammonia, NH_3.

Properties of Bases

Some of the properties of bases are that they:

1. Taste bitter
2. Feel "slippery"
3. Conduct an electric current when dissolved in water
4. Turn red litmus paper blue
5. React chemically with acids

Reactions of Acids with Bases; Chemical Equations

Chemists express chemical reactions with *equations*. Here is a typical one:

$$HCl \ + \ NaOH \longrightarrow NaCl \ + \ H_2O$$

This means that a molecule of HCl (acid) reacts with a molecule of NaOH (base) to form a molecule of sodium chloride, NaCl, and a molecule of water, H_2O. This isn't exactly what happens, but is a convenient equation for calculating what *weight* of HCl will react with a given *weight* of NaCl.

If the atomic weights in HCl, approximately 1.0 and 35.5, are added, the total 36.5, is called the *molecular weight* of HCl. In the same way, the atomic weights 23, 16, and 1 are added to give a total of 40, the molecular weight of NaOH. The molecular weight of NaCl is 58.5 and H_2O is 18. These are only numbers, but they show the relative reacting weights of HCl and NaOH, and the relative weights of the products of the reaction, NaCl and H_2O. The quantity of substance having a weight in grams numerically equal to the molecular weight of the substance is called a mole. Now we can write:

$$HCl \ + \ NaOH \longrightarrow NaCl \ + \ H_2O$$

HCl	NaOH	NaCl	H₂O
36.5 g	40.0 g	58.5 g	18 g
1 mole	1 mole	1 mole	1 mole

HCl and NaOH do not have to be mixed in this proportion, but if you want them to react and not have some of one or the other left over, you must mix them in the proportion of 36.5 grams of HCl to 40.0 grams of NaOH. If these weights are used, then 36.5 plus 40.0 g, or 76.5 g, of the reactants disappear, and 58.5 plus 18.0 g, or 76.5 g, of new substances (called products) are formed. This is an example of the law of the conservation of mass, and any equation that is written must show such an equality or it is not "balanced."

To show this, let's consider the reaction between nitric acid, HNO_3, and sodium carbonate, Na_2CO_3. The reaction is:

$$HNO_3 \; + \; Na_2CO_3 \longrightarrow NaNO_3 \; + \; CO_2 \; + \; H_2O$$

You have to *know* what the reactants are and what the products are in order to write the correct formula for what goes in and what results. But the equation as written is not balanced with respect to relative quantities, since it shows two sodium atoms disappearing and only one remaining as a product. This imbalance can be remedied if *two* molecules of $NaNO_3$ are formed. However, there are now two NO_3 groups. This new imbalance can be corrected if *two* molecules of HNO_3 react. So the balanced equation is:

$$2HNO_3 \; + \; Na_2CO_3 \longrightarrow 2NaNO_3 \; + \; CO_2 \; + \; H_2O$$

2HNO₃	Na₂CO₃	2NaNO₃	CO₂	H₂O
126 g	106 g	170 g	44 g	18 g
2 moles	1 mole	2 moles	1 mole	1 mole

The weights can be verified by adding the atomic weights as they are given in Table III. To see if the equation is balanced, you can check the number of each kind of atom on each side. In this case, there are one carbon, two hydrogen, two nitrogen, two sodium, and nine oxygen atoms on each side. Also the total weight of reactants (232 g) is the same as the total weight of products (232 g). Every equation that is written must show a similar balance between the reactants that disappear and the products that are formed.

The reactions between HCl and NaOH and between HNO_3 and Na_2CO_3 are typical of acid-base reactions. The acid is said to *neutralize* the base, and the base is said to neutralize the acid.

Sometimes an acid-base reaction can be carried only part way. If only one mole of nitric acid reacts with one mole of sodium carbonate, the reaction is:

$$HNO_3 \; + \; Na_2CO_3 \longrightarrow NaNO_3 \; + \; NaHCO_3$$

HNO₃	Na₂CO₃	NaNO₃	NaHCO₃
63 g	106 g	85 g	84 g
1 mole	1 mole	1 mole	1 mole

Equations like this are fine if you want to determine what weight of a particular acid will react with a certain weight of a particular base. It is not necessary to use molar weights. You may, for example, want to neutralize 500 grams of NaOH with the acid HCl. To do this will require:

$$500 \text{ g NaOH} \quad \cdot \quad \frac{(36.5 \text{ g/mole HCl})}{(40.0 \text{ g/mole NaOH})} \quad = \quad 456.3 \text{ g HCl}$$

To understand the mechanism of typical acid-base reactions, you need another kind of equation. Substances such as HCl, HNO_3, and Na_2CO_3 are almost completely ionized in an aqueous solution. So what really happens when HCl reacts with NaOH is:

$$H^+ \quad + \quad OH^- \quad \longrightarrow \quad H_2O$$

In other words, hydrogen ions from the HCl react with OH^- ions from the NaOH to form molecules of water. The Na^+ and Cl^- ions are present at the start and are still present after the reaction has taken place. Therefore, they do not enter into the reaction.

In the graphic arts, the subject of relative weights of reacting chemicals is the more important consideration, so we will use molecules in equations even though they do not react as such.

Hydrolysis   When some compounds, such as sodium acetate, CH_3COONa, or ammonium chloride, NH_4Cl, or sodium phosphate, Na_3PO_4, or sodium carbonate (washing soda), Na_2CO_3, are dissolved in water, the resulting solution is either alkaline or acid. This is due to a reaction, called *hydrolysis*, between ions of the compound and water. Here are equations to show what happens during a hydrolysis reaction:

For sodium acetate: $CH_3COO^- + H_2O \longrightarrow CH_3COOH + OH^-$ (In this case the OH^- ions make the solution alkaline.)

For ammonium chloride: $NH_4^+ + H_2O \longrightarrow NH_4OH + H^+$ (In this case the H^+ ions make the solution acid.)

For sodium phosphate: $PO_4^{---} + H_2O \longrightarrow HPO_4^{--} + OH^-$

For sodium carbonate: $CO_3^{--} + H_2O \longrightarrow HCO_3^- + OH^-$ (Solutions of sodium phosphate and sodium carbonate are both alkaline, due to the formation of hydroxide ions, OH^-.)

It is important to understand that many chemical reactions do not proceed to completion. Instead, what is called an *equilibrium* is reached. At equilibrium, some of the reacting substances are still present, along with the products that are formed. Such an equilibrium mixture could be left for a long time and would still contain the same percentage of reactants and product. Often it is possible to change these percentages by adding an excess of one of the reactants, by heat, or by pressure. Then a new equilibrium is reached, with different percentages of reactants and products.

The hydrolysis reactions above provide good examples of equilibrium. With some of them, less than 0.1% of the total amount of ions in the solution react with water. Then the solution reaches an equilibrium and nothing more happens. But even this small amount of reaction is enough to generate a small concentration of either H^+ or OH^- ions, making the solution either slightly acid or slightly alkaline.

Keep in mind, first, that chemical reactions do not always go to completion. Furthermore, nothing but experience can tell how *fast* a particular reaction will go. Some, like those that occur when water is used for the solvent, take place very rapidly. Others take place quite slowly. It takes several hours for some inks to dry; the hardening of light-sensitive coatings on lithographic and relief plates requires about one to three minutes.

Solubility of Compounds in Water

If any solid compound is poured into a quantity of water, some of it will dissolve in the water. If such a mixture is stirred for a long time at a particular temperature, the amount of the compound that dissolves will reach a fixed concentration in the water and no more will dissolve. A solution in such an equilibrium is called a *saturated solution*. We say that the compound has a certain *solubility* in water. Tables are available that list the solubility of many compounds. The concentration can be expressed in different ways, but a common expression of concentration is the grams of the compound that can be dissolved in 100 grams of water. The temperature must also be given, since many compounds have a greater solubility as the temperature is increased, and some have a lower solubility.

The situation is somewhat different if a liquid is mixed with water. Some liquids, like ethyl alcohol (drinking alcohol), are completely soluble in, or miscible with, water. With others, only a certain amount dissolves in the water; at the same time a certain amount of water may dissolve in the liquid.

Compounds vary widely in their solubility in water. Only 0.615 grams of $Ca(OH)_2$ will dissolve in 100 grams of water at 20°C, but the amount is 11 grams for Na_3PO_4 and 36 grams for NaCl at the same temperature. Some compounds dissolve so little in water that they are called "insoluble." Even the "insoluble" compounds have a very small solubility. The solubility of silver chloride, AgCl, is 1.5×10^{-4} gram per 100 grams of water. (Silver chloride is used in the light-sensitive emulsion of photographic films and papers.)

Since compounds are formed by a combination of positive and negative ions, it is possible to construct a table that lists, in general, the solubility of many compounds by referring to various combinations of positive and negative ions. Table V is such a table. It makes a useful reference table.

To determine if ammonium chloride, NH_4Cl, is soluble in water, we look for the NH_4^+ ion in the column of positive ions and find that *all* compounds of NH_4^+ with negative ions are soluble. So ammonium chloride must be fairly soluble in water. To determine if ferric chloride, $FeCl_3$, is soluble in water, we look for Cl^- in the column of negative ions. The positive-ion column shows that compounds of Cl^- with silver, lead, mercurous mercury, and cuprous ions have low solubility, while all other chloride compounds are soluble. This means that $FeCl_3$ is soluble. Other compounds can be checked in a similar way for their solubility in water. Use Table V to check the correctness of the following: $Mg(OH)_2$, low solubility; $BaSO_4$, low; KBr, soluble; and $CaCO_3$, low.

Reaction of Two Compounds Dissolved in Water to Form a Precipitate

Suppose we dissolve some of a soluble compound in one quantity of water. Next, let's dissolve some of another soluble compound in another quantity of water. Finally, we will pour one solution into the other. One of two things will happen: either the mixture of the two solutions will remain perfectly clear; or a cloudiness will appear, and sooner or later a solid will settle to the bottom of the container. This sediment is called a *precipitate*.

When two such solutions are mixed, a precipitate will form and settle out if the positive ions of one compound can combine with the negative ions of the other compound to form a new compound that has low solubility in water. Suppose one solution contains silver nitrate, $AgNO_3$, and the other contains potassium chloride, KCl. Both of these compounds are fairly soluble in water. However, when they are mixed, the silver ions of the silver nitrate combine with the chloride ions of the potassium chloride to form silver chloride, which is very insoluble in water. The ionic equation is:

$$Ag^+ \ + \ Cl^- \longrightarrow AgCl \text{ (solid)}$$

If one solution contains water-soluble lead acetate, $Pb(CH_3COO)_2$, and the other contains water-soluble magnesium sulfate, $MgSO_4$, a precipitate of water-insoluble lead sulfate, $PbSO_4$, forms when the two solutions are mixed. The ionic equation is:

$$Pb^{++} \ + \ SO_4^{--} \longrightarrow PbSO_4 \text{ (solid)}$$

Table V: Approximate Solubility of Common Compounds in Water	Negative Ions	Positive Ions	Compound of Positive and Negative Ions
	Almost all }	{ NH_4^+ Li^+, Na^+, K^+	soluble
	NO_3^- CH_3COO^- }	{ Almost all	soluble
	OH$^-$	Li^+, Na^+, K^+, NH_4^+, Sr^{++}, Ba^{++}	soluble
		all other positive ions	slightly soluble
	Cl^- Br^- I^-	Ag^+, Pb^{++}, Hg_2^{++}, Cu^+	slightly soluble
		all others	soluble
	SO_4^{--}	Ca^{++}, Sr^{++}, Ba^{++}, Pb^{++}	slightly soluble
		all others	soluble
	PO_4^{---} CO_3^{--} SO_3^{--}	Li^+, Na^+, K^+, NH_4^+	soluble
		all others	slightly soluble

(Compounds vary greatly in their solubility in water, but those that are fairly soluble are listed as "soluble," and those with low to very low solubility are listed as "slightly soluble.")

On the other hand, if a rearrangement of the positive and negative ions of two compounds would give two other compounds that are also soluble in water, then nothing happens. The mixture of the two solutions merely contains two kinds of positive ions and two kinds of negative ions. In this case, the mixture remains perfectly clear.

Why Many Solutions Conduct an Electric Current

Compounds that form positive and negative ions when the compounds are dissolved in water form solutions that can conduct an electric current. Such compounds are called *electrolytes*. There are both strong electrolytes and weak electrolytes. A strong electrolyte is a compound that ionizes almost completely when dissolved in water. Strong acids, for example, are strong electrolytes. If only a small percentage of the molecules of a compound ionize when the compound is dissolved in water, then it is a weak electrolyte (meaning that the solution does not conduct current as well). Weak acids, for example, are also weak electrolytes. Other compounds, such as sugar, do not ionize when dissolved in water. A solution of sugar does not conduct current any better than water, which is a very poor conductor. Substances like sugar are called *nonelectrolytes*.

In order to get a solution to carry electricity, it is necessary to immerse two *electrodes* into the solution; one electrode is connected to the positive pole of a battery, and the other is connected to the negative pole of the battery. If an electrolyte is dissolved in water, a current will flow. The current flows through the solution because the positive ions of the electrolyte move toward the negative electrode and the negative ions move toward the positive electrode. In the wires that go from the electrodes to the battery, the current is due to a flow of negatively charged electrons through the wires.

Illustrated is a complete electrical circuit that includes a battery and an electrolysis cell that consists of two electrodes immersed in a cupric chloride, $CuCl_2$, solution. The Cu^{++} ions move toward the negative electrode and the Cl^- ions move toward the positive electrode.

At each electrode, a reaction takes place. Here are the ionic equations:

Positive electrode: $2Cl^- \longrightarrow Cl_2 \text{ (gas)} + 2e^-$

Negative electrode: $Cu^{++} + 2e^- \longrightarrow Cu° \text{ (metallic Cu)}$

The Cl^- ions lose electrons (e^-), and therefore oxidation takes place. The Cu^{++} ions gain electrons, and therefore reduction takes place. This is a case where oxidation and reduction occur simultaneously but at different places.

A battery can be considered to be an electron pump. It pulls in the electrons liberated when chloride ions change to chlorine gas, then pumps the electrons around to the negative electrode to supply the electrons necessary to reduce cupric ions to metallic copper.

Electrolysis of cupric chloride.

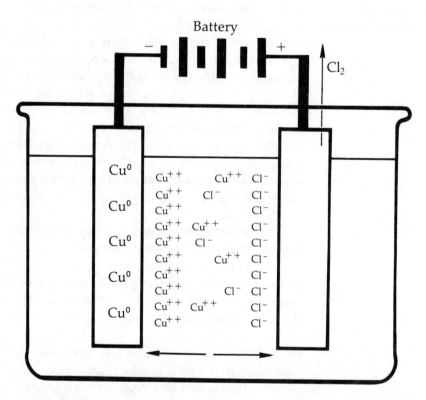

Electrolysis cells can be used to produce some metals in the pure metallic state. In the electrolytic method for the recovery of silver from a photographic hypo fixing bath, a current is passed through the bath, depositing pure silver onto the negative electrode: silver ions in the bath are reduced to uncharged silver atoms, or metallic silver.

Relative Activity of Metals

Some metals are more *active* than others. For instance, some metals will react readily with the oxygen in the air (in the presence of some water or water vapor) to form *oxides* of the metals. Others have very little tendency to do this. Some metals will react rapidly with strong acids, while others react very slowly or not at all. So metals vary in how active they are.

If metallic zinc is placed in a water solution of silver nitrate, the following ionic reaction occurs:

$$Zn° \text{ (metallic zinc)} \quad + \quad 2\,Ag^+ \text{ (in solution)} \longrightarrow$$
$$Zn^{++} \text{ (in solution)} \quad + \quad Ag° \text{ (metallic silver)}$$

Some of the zinc metal goes into solution as zinc ions, and the silver ions in solution are precipitated as solid metallic silver.

A similar reaction is used to recover silver from a hypo fixing bath. In this reaction, zinc atoms lose electrons, and therefore zinc is oxidized. The silver ions gain electrons, so the silver ions are reduced. From this result, one concludes that zinc is a more active metal than silver. Zinc prefers to be in the oxidized state of zinc ions, in contrast with silver, which prefers to be in the metallic state. Further evidence: if a piece of silver is placed into a solution of zinc nitrate, nothing happens.

Based on experiments with other combinations of metals and experiments with electrical cells involving two different metals, a table that lists metals according to their relative activity can be developed. Table VI is such a list.

In general, the tendency of metals to react with oxygen decreases the lower the metal is in the list. Also the tendency to react with acids decreases. Sheets of magnesium are used to make magnesium relief plates. A solution of hydrochloric acid, HCl, is used to etch away the metal in the nonprinting areas. The molecular equation for this reaction is:

$$Mg° \quad + \quad 2HCl \longrightarrow MgCl_2 \quad + \quad H_2$$

The metallic magnesium is oxidized to Mg^{++} ions, and the H^+ ions of HCl are reduced to hydrogen gas, H_2.

Table VI: Relative Activity of Metals	Potassium Barium Calcium Sodium	}	Very active metals; react very rapidly with acids, and even react with water
	Magnesium Aluminum Zinc	}	Fairly active metals
	Chromium Iron Cadmium Cobalt Nickel Tin Lead	}	Moderately active metals; usually less active than magnesium, aluminum, and zinc
	Copper Mercury Silver	}	Rather inactive metals; react only with an "oxidizing" acid such as strong nitric acid
	Gold Platinum	}	Very inactive metals; called "noble" metals

The metal copper is much lower in the list of Table VI, which means that copper is much less active than magnesium. Copper will not react with hydrochloric acid. It is necessary to use nitric acid, which is sometimes called an oxidizing acid. When nitric acid dissolves copper in the nonprinting areas of a copper photoengraving, oxides of nitrogen, such as NO and NO_2, are evolved as gases, instead of hydrogen.

While the list of Table VI is useful, some metals at times appear to be less active than their position in this list would indicate. For instance, aluminum is the most widely used metal for lithographic printing plates. In Table VI, aluminum is listed as a "fairly active metal." Yet aluminum reacts very slowly with hydrochloric acid. In fact, concentrated nitric acid can be shipped in an aluminum tank car. Why don't these acids affect the aluminum? The answer is that ordinary aluminum, as used for lithographic plates—or aluminum cans—is covered with a tightly adhering film of aluminum oxide; the surface of the aluminum is already oxidized. This film keeps more oxygen or certain acids from reaching the active aluminum underneath the film.

Hydrofluoric acid, HF, is able to react with the film of aluminum oxide, to form aluminum fluoride, AlF_3, and water. Then the HF can attack the aluminum, dissolving it to form aluminum fluoride. The other product is hydrogen gas, H_2.

Corrosion of Metals in Contact with Each Other

If two different metals are fastened together and exposed to a humid atmosphere, immersed in water, or immersed a dilute solution of an electrolyte in water, then one of the two metals will usually corrode (oxidize) at the expense of the other metal. As you might expect, the metal that corrodes is the one that is higher in the list of Table VI.

The corrosion of metals in contact with each other is the principle of the protection of iron objects by galvanizing. Galvanizing is accomplished by dipping the iron object into a bath of molten zinc. When galvanized objects are subjected to the weather, the zinc, rather than the iron, gradually oxidizes.

Iron is often covered with a thin layer of tin to produce tinplate. By reference to Table VI, it appears that tin is less active than iron, which means that iron is more apt to oxidize than tin. In this case, the tin offers protection only if it covers all of the iron.

The principle of an active metal protecting a less-active metal is used to help keep steel storage tanks from corroding. One method is to bury large pieces of magnesium at intervals around the storage tank, and connect the magnesium with a cable to the tank. Under moist conditions, the magnesium gradually oxidizes. The oxidization keeps the steel of the tank from corroding, or at least it greatly retards corrosion of the steel.

Certain active metals, particularly alloys of iron with other metals such as chromium and nickel, can be rendered passive by treatment with various chemicals or by electrolysis. The position of a metal or alloy in the active state is considerably higher on such a list as that of Table VI than the position of the same metal or alloy in the passive state. No explanation is offered here for these two states because differing theories exist about them.

Radioactivity and Atomic Energy

Atomic energy is a fascinating subject that will add to your understanding of modern chemistry. It even has some direct applications in the graphic arts to a minor extent.

In the chemical reactions discussed earlier in this chapter, neutral atoms were sometimes converted to electrically charged ions, or the reverse. Some atoms combined with others to form compounds held together by covalent bonds. In neutralization reactions, the hydrogen ions of an acid combine with various ions to form molecules of water or other ions such as HCO_3^- or HPO_4^{--}. In all of these reactions, each kind of atom remained the same. With the exception of whether the atoms were uncharged or charged, hydrogen remained hydrogen, oxygen remained oxygen, chlorine remained chlorine, etc.

Now we consider the world of radioactive materials, where atoms of one element change into atoms of another element, or where atoms of the same element change in atomic weight.

Let's start with naturally radioactive radium, whose atomic number is 88. There are several isotopes of radium. The atoms of one of these, with mass number 226, continually emit alpha particles, which are helium ions. As a result, what is left is no longer radium atoms but atoms of *another* element, radon, with an atomic number of 86 and a mass number of 222.

This process happens to radium atoms one at a time. In any given length of time, only a certain number of atoms will disintegrate. It is possible to talk about the "half-life" of any radioactive species. This is the time required for half the atoms of any quantity of the element to disintegrate. The half-life of radium 226 is 1,620 years. In this time, half of a sample of radium will be gone—changed into radon. In the next 1,620 years, half of what had been left will be gone. This process will repeat indefinitely. Many radioactive elements are known whose half-lives vary from a few seconds up to thousands of years.

Several other elements are naturally radioactive and emit alpha particles. These include bismuth 211, polonium 208, and uranium 238.

It is possible to bombard elements—with high-speed neutrons, for example—and make them radioactive. Over 2,000 such radioactive isotopes have been produced. Many of these emit *beta* particles when they disintegrate. Beta particles are simply negatively charged electrons. What happens is that one of the neutrons in the nucleus of one of these atoms is converted to a proton and an electron. The proton remains in the nucleus, but the electron is ejected and is called a beta particle. This leaves the nucleus with one more proton than before. So it is now a nucleus of an atom of a different element with an atomic number one greater.

A good example of such transformation is given by a radioactive isotope of phosphorus. Since the atomic number of phosphorus is 15, a phosphorus atom must have 15 protons. Ordinary phosphorus has a mass number of 31, but it is possible to produce phosphorus with a mass number of 32. Phosphorus

32 is radioactive, emitting beta particles, and has a half-life of 14.5 days. As phosphorus 32 atoms disintegrate, the following reaction occurs:

$^{32}_{15}$P disintegrates to give $^{32}_{16}$S $+ \, ^{0}_{-1}$e. The last term, e, is the electron that is emitted as a beta particle; it has a mass number of 0 and a charge of -1. Phosphorus atoms are actually changing into sulfur atoms! (The actual atomic weight remains almost the same.)

A very small quantity of H_3PO_4 containing radioactive phosphorus 32 atoms can be mixed with a larger quantity of ordinary H_3PO_4 to serve as a "tracer." Whatever happens to the ordinary H_3PO_4 will also happen to the phosphoric acid containing the phosphorus 32 atoms. For example, a lithographic plate is scrubbed with a dilute solution of phosphoric acid, and the acid is then rinsed from the plate with water several times. Has any phosphoric acid remained attached to the surface of the plate? This determination would be very difficult to make by other means, but by the use of a Geiger counter you can ascertain if beta particles are coming off the litho plate. If any are detected, they indicate that some phosphoric acid remains adsorbed to the surface of the plate, even after several rinsings with water.

In the radioactive changes mentioned above, some energy charges are involved, but they are very small. There are other changes that involve tremendous amounts of energy.

Most uranium atoms have a mass number of 238; a small percentage have a mass number of 235. When uranium 235 is separated from uranium 238 and is bombarded by neutrons, the neutrons first combine with the nucleus of the uranium 235 atoms. Then the atoms split apart to form atoms of two other elements, such a barium and krypton, whose atomic numbers total 92. In this process, three neutrons are evolved for every one neutron that initially combined with a uranium 235 nucleus. In addition, a large amount of energy is liberated. The neutrons evolved react with the nuclei of more uranium 235 atoms. Since three neutrons are evolved for every one that reacts, this process builds up extremely rapidly and, if uncontrolled, results in an atomic explosion because a tremendous amount of energy is liberated almost instantaneously, as in a bomb. When 235 grams (one mole) of uranium 235 reacts, about 4.5×10^{12} calories of energy are released. It is difficult to visualize how much energy this is; if controlled, it would be enough to operate an average automobile for about 100 years.

In a nuclear reactor (nuclear power plant), this reaction is controlled by the use of rods in cadmium metal located between rods that contain uranium 235. Cadmium is a good adsorber of neutrons, and the amount of cadmium used is just enough so that some neutrons are left to keep the uranium 235 splitting reaction going at a steady rate. The result is a continuous evolution of energy that can be used to generate electrical power.

Earlier in this chapter the law of the conservation of mass was presented which states that no mass (weight) can be lost or gained in chemical reactions. Also discussed was the law of the conservation of energy, which states that energy cannot be created nor destroyed. Both of these laws are essentially true for ordinary chemical reactons. However, Einstein postulated in 1905 that mass and energy are related. He theorized that if a certain amount of mass actually disappeared, a certain amount of energy would be created in its place. This was a radical assumption at the time, but it has turned out to be correct. The reason uranium 235 liberates a tremendous amount of energy is that the products of its breaking apart weigh less than the uranium that disappears, and the energy created relative to the mass lost is enormous. When only one gram of mass is lost, it is converted into 2.14×10^{13} calories of energy.

Another example of a nuclear reaction is the hydrogen bomb. A small percentage of hydrogen atoms have a mass number of two instead of one. If those heavy hydrogen, or deuterium, atoms are separated from hydrogen 1 atoms, they can be used to create a hydrogen bomb. The heavy hydrogen atoms are converted to helium 4 atoms with a loss in mass that is converted into energy. So far, it has not been possible to control this reaction and use it for the peaceful production of electrical power.

Summary

In ordinary chemical reactions, the weight of the products formed is exactly the same as the weight of the reactants that disappear. This is the law of the conservation of mass. Likewise, if a reaction or a change of state (gas to liquid, etc.) evolves a certain amount of energy, then the same amount must be employed to reverse the process. This is the law of the conservation of energy.

Substances consist of elements or compounds. A compound consists of two or more elements combined in a fixed proportion by weight.

Elements consist of atoms. Atoms, in turn, consist of a nucleus containing protons and neutrons, with enough extranuclear electrons to balance the positive charge of the protons. The atomic number of an element is the number of protons in the nucleus. This is what makes the atoms of one element different from the atoms of another element.

The number of electrons in the outermost energy level (valence electrons) determines the chemical nature of an element. Most metallic elements have one to three valence electrons, while some nonmetals have six or seven. The noble gases have the outermost energy level filled with as many electrons as that level can hold.

In chemical reactions, atoms of one element lose valence electrons to atoms of another element, thus forming positive and negative ions. In other cases, the atoms of a compound are held together by the sharing of two electrons, called a covalent bond.

Isotopes of an element consist of atoms that have the same number of protons in the nucleus but a different number of uncharged neutrons and a different atomic weight.

Atomic weights are the average relative weights of atoms of any element when compared with the average weight of oxygen atoms taken as 16.00.

When atoms of different elements combine chemically, molecules of a compound are formed. In some cases the compound consists of positive and negative ions instead of molecules. In many chemical reactions, one element is oxidized and another is reduced at the same time.

Acids are compounds that release hydrogen ions, H^+, when dissolved in water. Some acids are strong and some are weak, depending on the percentage of the acid molecules that ionize.

A base is a substance that reacts with the hydrogen ions of an acid or produces hydroxide ions, OH^-, when dissolved in water. Acids react chemically with bases. If the proper weights are mixed, the base neutralizes the acid, and vice versa.

By using a balanced chemical equation and by calculating the weight of a mole of each reactant and product, it is possible to calculate what weight of one substance will react with a given weight of another substance. It is also possible to calculate the weights of the products of the reaction.

Many chemical reactions do not proceed to completion. Instead, they reach an equilibrium and go no farther. Compounds that hydrolyze in water are examples of reactions that proceed only a little way before reaching an equilibrium. However, the amount is enough to make water solutions of these compounds either alkaline or acid, depending on the compound.

Compounds vary widely in their solubility in water. When

two solutions containing two different soluble compounds are mixed, a precipitate (solid) will form if another compound can be formed that has low solubility.

If a compound ionizes when dissolved in water, the solution will carry an electric current. The positive ions move toward the negative electrode; the negative ions move toward the positive electrode. Reactions occur at each electrode; and oxidation reaction occurs at the one electrode, and a reduction reaction occurs at the other.

Metals vary in their activity, including their tendency to react with the oxygen of the air, or to react with acids. It is possible to list metals in the order of their decreasing activity. Such a list is helpful in determining which of two metals will corrode if the two metals are fastened together.

Most of the material in this chapter is concerned with inorganic chemistry. The chemistry of carbon is called organic chemistry. Organic chemistry is covered in a later chapter.

2   What pH Is and How to Measure It

The term pH, indicating a measure of acidity or alkalinity, is a familiar one. Pressmen operating lithographic presses often make pH measurements of the water fountain solution. Such measurements are helpful particularly when the pH of the local water supply varies. Coating can be scraped from a coated paper and suspended in water to obtain the pH of the coating. Effluents from a plant can be measured to see if they satisfy safety and health requirements in this respect. These examples are only some of the applications of pH measurement in the graphic arts.

If the pH of a solution is 7, the solution is neutral; it is neither acid nor alkaline. A solution with a pH of 5 is slightly acid, while one with a pH of 3 is considerably more acid. The lower the pH reading, the more acid a solution is. The opposite is true as the pH of a solution rises above 7. Thus a solution with a pH of 8 is slightly alkaline, while one with a pH of 10 is considerably more alkaline.

It is possible to make pH determinations in a plant and interpret them correctly without knowing more than is covered in the preceding paragraph. But effective use of such information is improved by deeper understanding. The following material explains what pH means and explains the relationship between pH values and the hydrogen ion concentration of a solution.

Ionization of Water

Even the purest water conducts electricity to a very small extent. It does so because a very small percentage of water molecules ionize to give hydrogen ions, H^+, and hydroxide ions, OH^-. The electrical charges in any solution must balance, so there must be as many H^+ ions as there are OH^- ions. A mole of hydrogen ions is one gram. A mole of OH^- ions is 17 grams. The *concentration* of these ions is measured in moles per liter. In pure water, the molar concentration of hydrogen ions is the same as the concentration of OH^- ions, but on a weight basis the OH^- ions weigh 17 times as much as the H^+ ions. In pure water, the concentration of H^+ ions and the concentration of OH^- ions are each 10^{-7} mole per liter. This is a very low concentration: since 10^{-6} is one millionth, 10^{-7} is a tenth of a millionth.

Notice that the exponent of 10 in the number representing the hydrogen ion or hydroxide ion concentration in pure water (a neutral solution) is -7. Also remember that the pH of a neutral solution has been given the value 7. Now you have a clue about the relationship of these concentrations and pH numbers.

The degree of acidity or alkalinity of a solution depends on the comparative concentration of hydrogen ions and hydroxide ions. When these concentrations are equal, the solution is neutral. When the hydrogen ion concentration is greater, the solution is acid. When the hydroxide ion concentration is greater, the solution is alkaline. And the greater the difference between them, the greater is the degree of acidity or alkalinity.

There is a definite relationship between these two concentrations, as explained in a later paragraph. So if you know one of the concentrations, the other can be determined. When the system for expressing acidity/alkalinity by a number was being developed, the H^+ ion concentration was used as the basis. Since this is a kind of electrical potential, the abbreviation pH (for "potential of Hydrogen") was adopted.

It was desired to have a scale of numbers that would indicate H^+ concentration in a simple, convenient way. The system of expressing concentration (in moles per liter) by using 10 with an exponent, as illustrated above, provides the basis for assigning a simple number to indicate pH: only the exponent is used, and without the minus sign. Thus, if the H^+ concentration is 1/1,000, or 10^{-3}, the pH value is 3; if the concentration is 1/1,000,000,000,000, or 10^{-12}, the pH is 12. You can see that this system permits expressing wide ranges of H^+ concentration simply.

Relationship of hydrogen ion concentration to pH.

Hydrogen Ion Concentration (moles/liter)	pH
1/1 or 10^{0}	
1/10 or 10^{-1}	1
1/100 or 10^{-2}	2
1/1,000 or 10^{-3}	3
1/10,000 or 10^{-4}	4
1/100,000 or 10^{-5}	5
1/1,000,000 or 10^{-6}	6
1/10,000,000 or 10^{-7}	7
1/100,000,000 or 10^{-8}	8
1/1,000,000,000 or 10^{-9}	9
1/10,000,000,000 or 10^{-10}	10
1/100,000,000,000 or 10^{-11}	11
1/1,000,000,000,000 or 10^{-12}	12
1/10,000,000,000,000 or 10^{-13}	13
1/100,000,000,000,000 or 10^{-14}	14

The exponent of 10 that will give a certain number is called the *logarithm* (log) of that number. Therefore, pH can be defined precisely by means of a simple formula:

$$pH \;\; = \;\; -\log (H^+)$$

where (H^+) represents the concentration of hydrogen ions in moles per liter. (The minus sign in front of "log" indicates that the sign of the logarithm is changed.) Use of logarithms makes it possible to express values of pH between even-integer values (for example: pH = 8.3) and to convert such values into concentrations if desired.

An illustration making use of this defining formula explains why the pH of pure water or any neutral solution (which, remember, has a hydrogen ion concentration of 10^{-7} mole per liter) is 7:

$$pH \;\; = \;\; -\log 10^{-7} \;\; = \;\; -(-7) \;\; = \;\; 7$$

The pH of Acid Solutions

If any acid material is added to pure water, there will be an increase in the hydrogen ion concentration. Instead of 10^{-7} mole/liter the H^+ concentration may increase to 10^{-6}, 10^{-5}, or even higher. Keep in mind that 10^{-6} is a higher concentration than 10^{-7}. In fact, it is 10 times as high. A concentration of 10^{-5} mole per liter is a concentration 10 times as high as 10^{-6} and 100 times as high as 10^{-7}.

Now it is easy to establish a pH figure for these acid solutions. You merely use the correct power of ten without its minus sign. Thus, if the hydrogen ion concentration is 10^{-6} mole per liter, the pH is 6. If it is 10^{-5}, the pH is 5. These examples illustrate that a change of 1 pH unit represents a 10-fold change in the concentration of acid.

The pH of Alkaline Solutions

If any alkaline material is added to pure water, there will be an increase in the hydroxide ion concentration of the solution. The greater the amount of alkaline material added, the higher will be the OH^- concentration. Instead of an OH^- concentration of 10^{-7} mole per liter, the concentration may increase to 10^{-6}, 10^{-4}, or an even higher level.

These exponents of 10 cannot be used with hydroxide concentrations to give a pH of the alkaline solutions, since pH is defined as the negative log of the *hydrogen* ion concentration. But it is possible to give a pH value to such alkaline solutions if we understand what happens to the H^+ concentration as the OH^- concentration increases.

At this point, it is necessary to understand that either an acid solution or an alkaline solution contains *both* H^+ and OH^- ions. As a solution becomes more acid, the H^+ concentration increases. At the same time, the OH^- concentration decreases, but it never becomes zero. Similarly, as a solution becomes more alkaline, the OH^- concentration increases, and at the same time, the H^+ concentration decreases but never becomes zero.

What happens is that the *product* of the concentration of H^+ and OH^- ions remains constant. We can determine the value of this product, since we know that the concentration of each ion is 10^{-7} mole per liter in pure water, as follows:

$$(H^+) \ \cdot \ (OH^-) \ = \ (10^{-7}) \ \cdot \ (10^{-7}) \ = \ 10^{-14}$$

This product, 10^{-14}, remains constant, even though the concentration of the two ions is not the same. For example, if the OH^- concentration increases to 10^{-5}, then the H^+ concentration must decrease to 10^{-9}, because the product of the two concentrations must still equal 10^{-14}.

Now we have established that in an *alkaline* solution where the OH^- concentration is 10^{-5}, there is a H^+ concentration of 10^{-9}. So, from what has been presented previously, we know the pH of this alkaline solution is 9.

Let's analyze one more alkaline solution to see the trend of alkaline pH. Let's consider a solution that is more alkaline than the one just calculated. Assume that the OH^- concentration is 10^{-4} mole per liter. Then the H^+ concentration must be 10^{-10} mole per liter for the product of the two concentrations to remain 10^{-14}. Therefore the pH of this alkaline solution is 10.

The trend, then, is for the pH of an alkaline solution to *increase* as the solution becomes more strongly alkaline.

Approximate pH of Some Common Solutions

Below are listed the approximate pH values of some common solutions:

Hydrochloric acid, HCl (1 fl. oz./gal.)	pH = 1.2
Acetic acid, CH_3COOH (3 fl. oz./gal.)	pH = 3.0
Acetic acid (6 fl. oz./gal.)	pH = 2.8
Gum arabic solution (not acidified)	pH = 4.2–4.3
Ammonium hydroxide, NH_4OH (ammonia) (1 fl. oz./gal.)	pH = 11.2
Trisodium phosphate, Na_3PO_4 (TSP)	pH = 12
Sodium hydroxide, NaOH (lye)	pH = 13–14

In Chapter 1, the difference between a strong and a weak acid is explained. A strong acid is almost completely ionized when dissolved in water, while only a small percentage of the molecules of a weak acid are ionized.

The pH of a water solution of HC1 (a strong acid) is lower (more acid) than a solution of acetic acid (a weak acid). If the acetic acid solution is made with six fluid ounces per gallon, instead of three, the pH drops slightly—from 3.0 to 2.8—but is still considerably higher than the pH of a solution of HC1 made with 1 fluid ounce per gallon.

Alkaline materials, too, can be strong or weak. Ammonium hydroxide is a weak base with a pH of about 11.2 in a water solution. A water solution of the strong base sodium hydroxide is much more alkaline, with a pH of 13–14.

The pH values given above will vary somewhat, depending on how much of the material is dissolved in a certain quantity of water. However, they will not change appreciably from the values listed.

How to Measure the pH of a Solution

Two general methods are used for the measurement of the pH of a solution. One method is *colorimetric*. This method depends on the color change of materials called *indicators*, which are added to the solution. The other method is *electrical*, which depends on the change of the voltage of a little electrical cell.

Determination of pH with Colored Indicators

Indicators useful for the determination of pH are complicated organic compounds with names like bromcresol green, bromphenol blue, and thymol blue. Each of these indicators changes color over a range of about two pH units. Thus bromcresol green is yellow at a pH of 4.0 and changes through various shades of green until it is blue at a pH of 5.6. Such an indicator is useful only in this narrow range of pH. At any pH below 4.0, it remains yellow, and at any pH above 5.6 it remains blue. To measure a solution whose pH is outside of this range, you must use another indicator. Thymol blue, which is sensitive to a pH range from 8.0 to 9.6, can be used for these values.

A few drops of an indicator can be added to a solution in a test tube. The color is compared with a series of control test tubes that contain the same indicator in solutions of different pH values. Such series of control test tubes can be purchased for each indicator. You match the color of the solution of unknown pH with the color of one of the solutions in the series of test tubes, and read the pH as printed below the matching test tube.

Paper strips for the colorimetric measurement of pH are also available. These paper strips are impregnated with a solution of one of the indicators previously mentioned, and they are then dried. To use these papers, you merely tear off a one-inch or two-inch strip of the paper and immerse it for two or three seconds in the solution to be tested. The color developed in the paper is then compared with a pH color chart that comes with the paper strips. The pH is given under each of the colors on the chart.

Determination of fountain solution pH using pH papers.

Short-range pH papers of this kind are useful for approximate pH measurements, such as the pH of a lithographic press water fountain solution. The accuracy is usually not closer than 0.3 to 0.5 pH to the actual pH value. If the color developed in the test strip is the same as the color at either end of the color chart, then the solution must be retested with another short-range pH paper containing a different indicator. Several of these papers are available; they cover a considerable part of the pH scale when used together.

Determination of pH with a pH Meter

Electrically operated pH meters are offered by several manufacturers. Models are available that operate on 110- to 120-volt, 50- to 60-cycle alternating current. There are also portable, battery-operated pH meters. Most modern pH meters include solid-state electronics and are much more stable than older meters. Some show pH with a dial; others have a digital readout. Depending on the instrument, pH readings can be obtained with an accuracy of 0.01–0.05 pH.

Digital pH meter.
Courtesy of Western Litho Plate

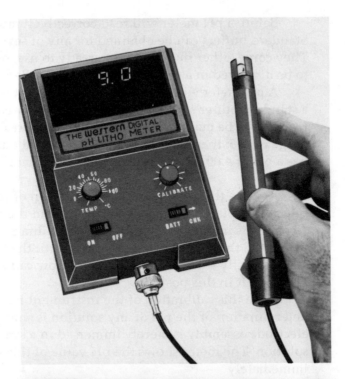

Laboratory pH meter.
Courtesy of Sargent-Welch Scientific Co.

Before a pH meter will read correctly, it must be calibrated. Standard buffers can be obtained for any of several pH values. They come either in liquid form, ready to use, or in tablet form, to be dissolved in a certain quantity of distilled water.

A pH meter will read very accurately if it is calibrated with a standard buffer solution that has a pH fairly close to the pH readings to be made. For example, if the pH readings are in the range of 3–5, then one should use a standard buffer solution that has a pH of 4.00, or whatever is available that is close to this value.

Assume that a standard buffer solution of pH 4.00 is selected, is placed in a small container, and the pH electrode assembly is immersed in it. Using the calibration knob on the pH meter, the pH reading is adjusted until the meter reading shows exactly 4.00. The instrument is now calibrated, and the knob is left in this position.

Once this calibration of the instrument has been made, the determination of the pH of any solution is simple. The pH electrode assembly is merely immersed in a sample of the solution. The meter shows the pH value of this solution almost immediately.

The meter is now calibrated to measure changes in voltage of the pH cell. The meter reading changes approximately 1.00 in pH for each 0.059 volt change of the solutions being measured. This enables the manufacturers to produce scales that read in pH, even though the meter is actually recording differences in the voltage of a particular electrical cell.

The term "volts per unit change in pH" is called the slope of the response curve. It is 0.059 volt/pH at 25°C. Some pH meters allow the operator to calibrate the slope of the response curve. Two standard buffer solutions are used for this calibration. One may have a pH of perhaps 3.00, and the other may have a pH of perhaps 8.00. By a proper adjustment of the meter, it is possible to get the meter to read *both* pH values correctly. This result means that a slight adjustment has been made in the slope of the response curve. Now a certain change in the voltage of the pH cell corresponds exactly to a change of 1 unit in the pH of a solution in which the pH cell is immersed.

Why an Electrical Cell Can Measure pH

Every electrical cell has two electrodes. It is assumed that the voltage of any cell is the sum of the voltages produced at each electrode. For example, a cell can be made using a piece of zinc immersed in a solution containing zinc ions for one electrode. The other electrode can be a piece of copper immersed in a solution containing copper ions. A voltage is produced at both the zinc electrode and the copper electrode. The voltage of the cell is the sum of these voltages.

A cell for the measurement of pH also has two electrodes. One is the glass electrode; the other is the reference electrode. The accompanying figure shows a typical cell. In practice, the glass electrode and the reference electrode are assembled into one unit that can be easily immersed into any solution whose pH is to be measured.

Electrodes of pH meter.

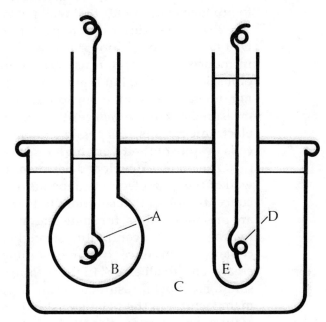

The glass electrode is made of a special glass, as described later. Inside of the glass is electrode A, which is immersed in solution B. Similarly, the reference electrode consists of electrode D, immersed in solution E. There is a small opening at the bottom of the reference electrode that allows a small electric current to pass from the reference electrode into solution C, whose pH is being measured.

The total voltage of such a cell is assumed to consist of the algebraic sum of several partial voltages as follows:

1. Voltage between electrode A and solution B
2. Voltage between solution B and the inside wall of the glass electrode
3. Voltage between solution C and the outside wall of the glass electrode
4. Voltage between electrode D and solution E

Since solutions B and E always remain the same, it means that the partial voltages 1, 2, and 4 never change. But, due to the special glass used for the glass electrode, the partial voltage 3 *does* change, and it changes 0.059 volts for every 1.00 change in the pH of solution C.

The total voltage of a pH cell is immaterial. Only its property of changing voltage with a change in the pH of solution C is important. By incorporating the proper electrical circuits and meter dials, the manufacturers of pH meters are able to produce instruments that read pH values directly.

For an electric current to pass from electrode A to electrode D, it must first pass through the wall of the glass electrode. This introduces a very high resistance, approximately 100 million ohms, into the cell. But it must be kept in mind that such a cell is not intended to produce an appreciable current. Instead, measurement of the *voltage* of the cell is desired. With modern electronic circuits, it is possible to measure the voltage of pH cells in spite of their very high internal resistance.

The voltage developed between solution C and the outer wall of the glass electrode depends only on the hydrogen ion concentration of that solution. It does not change if other ions are present—unless, for some reason, those ions affect the hydrogen ion concentration. Strongly alkaline solutions usually contain a high concentration of sodium or potassium ions. This creates an "alkali error" in the measurement of pH of such solutions. If pH measurements are to be made in this region, the manufacturer of the pH meter should be consulted as to how to make a correction for the alkali error.

Materials Used in Reference and Glass Electrodes

The metal used for electrode A and the solution B, in which electrode A is immersed, can vary from manufacturer to manufacturer. Even the electrodes offered by one manufacturer can vary. The same is true of the reference electrode, electrode D, and solution E. Here are some of the common combinations:

● **Calomel electrode.** The electrode metal is mercury. It is immersed in a saturated solution of potassium chloride, KCl. The solution is also saturated with slightly soluble mercurous chloride, Hg_2Cl_2, which is commonly called "calomel." This combination is often used for the reference electrode in a pH cell.

● **Silver-silver chloride electrode.** The electrode metal is silver that is coated with a thin layer of silver chloride, AgCl. The solution is usually saturated with KCl and with the very slightly soluble compound AgCl. This combination is often used inside the glass electrode.

● **Thalamid electrode.** One manufacturer uses this electrode inside both the glass electrode and the reference electrode in some of its electrode assemblies. The electrode metal is mainly mercury that contains 40% of thallium, Tl, by weight. The solution is saturated with KCl and with slightly soluble thallium chloride, TlCl.

Different combinations of electrodes give different total voltages when immersed in a solution (C) of a particular pH. As mentioned before, this total voltage is not important since the meter reading can be calibrated to read the correct pH value.

Summary

The hydrogen ion concentration of a solution can be expressed as a certain pH value. If the hydrogen ion concentration is 10^{-7} mole per liter, the pH is 7; the solution is neutral. As the pH decreases, the hydrogen ion concentration increases considerably (10 times for a change of 1 pH unit, 100 times for 2, etc.). As the pH increases above 7, the solution becomes more and more alkaline in the same ratio.

The pH of a solution can be obtained colorimetrically by the use of special colored indicators that change color over a pH range of about 2. Short-range pH papers contain such indicators. At best, colored indicators are accurate to 0.5 pH unit.

Modern pH meters give pH values rapidly and very accurately. They make use of the voltage generated between a glass electrode and a reference electrode. All partial voltages in such an electrical cell are constant with the exception of the voltage generated between the solution being measured and the outside wall of the glass electrode. This voltage changes 0.059 volt for a change of one pH unit in the solution being measured. The scales of the meters are so calibrated that changes in voltages are read directly as pH values.

3 Water — An Important Chemical

Water is a very important "chemical," necessary for the survival of all plants and animals, including humans. It is also important in many industrial operations. In the graphic arts, water is used for the making of photographic developers and fixing baths, light-sensitive coatings for lithographic and relief plates, and plate developing solutions and for the dampening of lithographic plates on the press. Heatset inks for web presses often contain a considerable amount of water to replace part of the organic solvents and thus help to reduce air pollution. And water-based flexographic inks have been in use for many years.

Minerals Present in Natural Waters

As water flows from melting snow fields or glaciers in the mountains, it is quite pure. But as it flows down miles of rivers, it gradually dissolves minerals, or inorganic compounds.

Since these dissolved compounds are almost completely ionized, it is customary to refer to the positive and negative ions in the water. The principal ones are:

Positive Ions (Cations)	Negative Ions (Anions)
Calcium, Ca^{++}	Carbonate, CO_3^{--}
Magnesium, Mg^{++}	Bicarbonate, HCO_3^-
Sodium, Na^+	Chloride, Cl^-
Iron, Fe^{++}	Sulfate, SO_4^{--}
Manganese, Mn^{++}	Nitrate, NO_3^-

In some water, there are trace amounts of a few other ions, but those listed above are the ones usually present. Positively charged ions are called cations (pronounced cat-ions) because they migrate to the cathode, or negative electrode, when a current of electricity is passed through the solution. Negatively charged ions are called anions (pronounced an-ions) because they migrate to the anode, or positive electrode.

Why Water Is Hard

A particular water may contain a considerable amount of dissolved compounds, called "totally dissolved solids" (TDS), and yet not be particularly hard. The characteristic that makes a water hard is the amount of calcium and magnesium ions dissolved in it.

When soap is dissolved in hard water, a reaction such as the following takes place:

$$2RCOONa + Ca^{++} \text{ (in the water)} \longrightarrow (RCOO)_2Ca + 2Na^+$$

soap   calcium soap

Soap usually is a sodium salt of a high-molecular-weight fatty acid. The soap reacts with the calcium and magnesium ions in the water to form calcium and magnesium soaps. These soaps are sticky materials insoluble in water. They are responsible for the bathtub ring which forms when soap is added to hard water. In fact, soap will not form lasting suds with hard water until enough soap has been consumed to react with all the calcium and magnesium ions in the water.

One way to record the hardness of water is the number of "parts per million." Calcium carbonate is used as the standard in this method. If a water has a hardness of 200 parts per million (ppm), it is as hard as if it contained 200 parts of calcium carbonate in a million parts of water. The metric units of milligrams per liter, which are almost identical with ppm, can also be used. A water with a hardness of 200 ppm has a hardness of 200 mg/L. Hardness can also be expressed as so many grains per gallon. One grain/gal is equal to 17.118 ppm or 17.118 mg/L.

In different parts of the country, water varies greatly in hardness, from very low amounts up to as much as 1,000 ppm. It is possible to obtain the hardness figure for the water in your area by contacting the local water officials.

How Pure Should Water Be for Industrial Use?

There is no easy answer to the question of how high the quality of water should be from the standpoint of dissolved mineral solids. It depends on the use that is to be made of the water. In many cases, no treatment is required. In others, however, filtration may be necessary for the removal of suspended matter. In one lithographic plant, it was almost impossible to get a good light-sensitive coating applied with a whirler, because there was so much suspended matter in the city water. Here a good water filter was the solution. It must be kept in mind that filtration alone will not remove any of the compounds that are *dissolved* in water.

In many other uses of water, a reduction or almost elimination of dissolved compounds is desirable. Again, it depends on what you want the water to accomplish. If you merely want to soften the water for washing clothes or to prevent buildup of scale in a boiler, then a water softener unit is needed. But, if you want quite pure water (low in TDS), with almost complete removal of all positive and negative ions, then distillation, deionization, or reverse osmosis must be employed. All of these methods will be discussed and compared.

Softening of Water

When water is softened, it is treated to remove only the calcium, magnesium, and iron ions from the water and to replace those ions with sodium ions. Even though the total amount of dissolved solids remains almost the same, the water has been softened, since the ions that make water hard have been replaced by others that don't.

Softening of water is accomplished by passing the water through a tank filled with tiny beads of a cation exchange resin. These beads are initially charged with replaceable sodium ions. For simplification, a cation exchange resin can be expressed by the general formula Na_2R.

As the hard water passes through the bed of resin particles, the calcium and magnesium ions have a greater affinity for the ion exchange resin than the sodium ions do. When the calcium and magnesium ions become attached to the resin, a chemically equivalent number of sodium ions are released into the water. A typical exchange reaction is:

$$Mg^{++} \ + \ Na_2R \ \longrightarrow \ 2Na^+ \ + \ MgR$$

| (in the water) | (cation exchange resin) | (go into the water) | (exhausted resin) |

A similar reaction occurs with calcium and iron ions. As a result, the ions responsible for making water hard are removed; the water is softened. Stain-forming iron ions are also mostly removed, along with much of any suspended matter.

This process continues automatically until the supply of sodium ions in the exchange resin is almost depleted. When this happens, the cation exchange resin has lost most of its power to soften any more water and is said to be exhausted. To restore the resin to its original condition, a strong solution of common salt, sodium chloride (NaCl), is passed through the bed. The high concentration of sodium ions in the sodium chloride solution causes a reversal of the ion exchange reaction. A typical reaction is:

$$MgR \ + \ 2Na^+ \ \longrightarrow \ Na_2R \ + \ Mg^{++}$$

| (exhausted resin) | (strong NaCl solution) | (regenerated resin) | (in the NaCl solution—goes to sewer) |

The calcium, magnesium, and iron ions in the original water finally go to the sewer. The regeneration process can be described as one in which common salt is used to soften water. This cannot be accomplished by adding salt directly to the water to be softened. But it can be done indirectly by the process just described. Several million water softeners of this type are in use in homes and industries. The energy cost for this process is very low.

Removal of Dissolved Solids from Water

For some industrial uses, it is desirable to have nearly pure water, with most of the dissolved solids removed. Three ways to accomplish this removal are: distillation, demineralization, or deionization, and reverse osmosis.

Distillation of Water

Distilled water is produced by boiling ordinary tap water in a water still. The steam that rises from the boiling water is almost free of the mineral matter that was present in the tap water. This steam is fed through condenser coils, where it is converted back into liquid water, called distilled water.

Apparatus for distilling water in the laboratory.

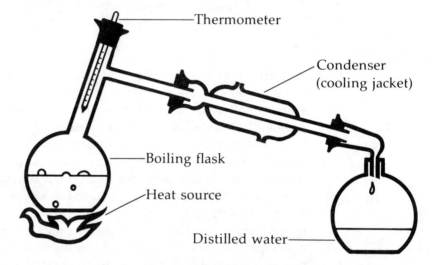

One might assume that distilled water would be free of all mineral matter because the mineral matter is not volatile. However, a small amount of mineral matter is carried over with the steam. If the water initially contained about 200 ppm of dissolved solids, the distilled water will often contain 10 to 20 ppm. Since this is a considerable reduction, such water will be suitable for some applications. If still purer water is required, the distilled water can be distilled again and sometimes a third time. Energy costs are high for this process.

**Demineraliza-
tion, or
Deionization**

The demineralization, or deionization, process has been in use
for many years. It requires two ion exchange resins. The cation
exchange resin is initially charged with hydrogen ions; the
anion exchange resin is initially charged with hydroxide ions.
The water is passed first through a bed of cation exchange resin.
Here almost all of the positive ions (cations) in the water become
attached to the resin, and an equivalent amount of hydrogen
ions leave the resin and enter the water. A typical reaction is:

$$\text{Na}^+ \;+\; (\text{CR})-\text{H} \;\longrightarrow\; (\text{CR})\text{Na} \;+\; \text{H}^+$$

(in the water)	(cation exchange resin)	(exhausted resin)	(goes into the water)

A similar ion exchange takes place with all of the other positive
ions in the water.

As the water leaves the bed of cation exchange resin, it still
contains all of the negative ions (anions) and hydrogen ions. In
other words, it is a dilute solution of acids, such as HCl, HNO_3,
H_2CO_3, and H_2SO_4. This water solution now passes through a
bed of anion exchange resin. Here almost all of the negative ions
become attached to the resin, and an equivalent amount of
hydroxide ions leave the resin and enter the water. In the water,
these hydroxide ions combine with the hydrogen ions to form
molecules of water. Here is a typical set of reactions:

$$\text{SO}_4^{--} \;+\; (\text{AR})-\text{OH} \;\longrightarrow\; (\text{AR})\text{SO}_4 \;+\; 2\text{OH}^-$$

(in the water)	(anion exchange resin)	(exhausted resin)	(go into the water)

$$2\text{OH}^- \;+\; 2\text{H}^+ \;\longrightarrow\; 2\text{H}_2\text{O}$$

As the water issues from the second bed, it is quite pure;
most of the positive and negative ions have been removed. But
note that this process will not remove un-ionized dissolved
solids.

Both ion exchange resins finally become exhausted and
must be regenerated. The cation exchange resin is regenerated
with a solution of a strong acid, such as hydrochloric acid or
sulfuric acid. Regeneration removes the calcium, magnesium,
and other positive ions, and replaces them with hydrogen ions,
H^+, thus returning the resin to its initial condition. The acid
solution containing these positive ions then goes into the sewer.

Demineralization, or deionization, process.

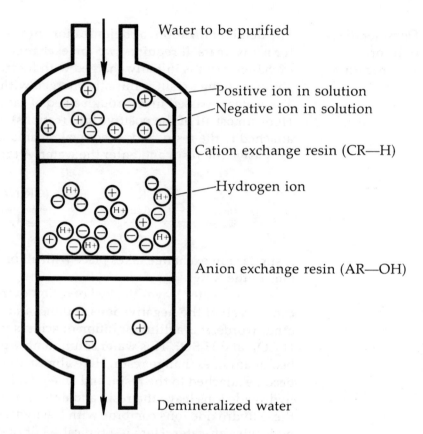

Water to be purified

Positive ion in solution
Negative ion in solution

Cation exchange resin (CR—H)

Hydrogen ion

Anion exchange resin (AR—OH)

Demineralized water

Commercial demineralization unit.

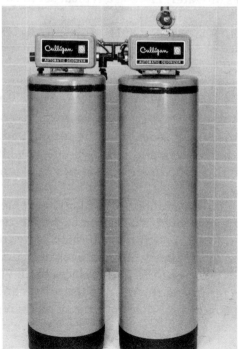

The anion exchange resin is regenerated with a solution of sodium hydroxide, NaOH (also called caustic soda). This solution removes all of the negative ions that are attached to the resin and replaces them with hydroxide ions, OH^-, thus returning the resin to the initial condition. The solution of sodium hydroxide containing these negative ions then goes into the sewer.

It is important to mix the regeneration wastes from the cation and anion exchange resins, so that the acid from the one will be neutralized by the base from the other before the mixture goes to the sewer.

The purest water is produced by mixing the beads of cation and anion exchange resins in a single tank. Water issuing from such a tank is superior to triple-distilled water and energy costs for the single-tank system are moderate: considerably less than the cost of producing triple-distilled water. The two resins must be separated before they can be regenerated, since one requires an acid for regeneration and the other requires a base. This separation can be accomplished easily because of a difference in the density of the two resins.

Reverse Osmosis A large percentage of dissolved solids can be removed, at a cost less than that of producing distilled water, by a newer method for water purification called reverse osmosis. Some commercial units employing this method have been in use since the middle 1960s.

To understand this process, it is necessary first to understand what is meant by osmosis. When two aqueous solutions of different concentrations are separated by a semipermeable membrane, water passes through the membrane from the weaker solution to the stronger solution, as shown in the accompanying figure.

Osmosis.

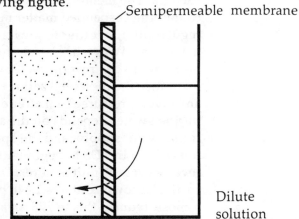

Semipermeable membrane

Concentrated
solution

Dilute
solution

Reverse osmosis is the opposite of osmosis. Applying pressure to the more concentrated solution forces water through the semipermeable membrane into the more dilute solution. The membrane allows water to pass through, but only a small amount of materials dissolved in the water pass through. See the accompanying figure.

Reverse osmosis.

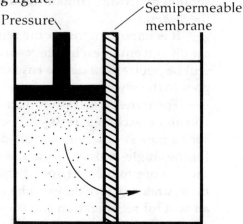

For water purification, the "more concentrated solution" is the initial tap water. On the other side of the membrane you get quite pure water, with only a small amount of dissolved solids remaining. Some positive or negative ions are held back better than others. Approximately 90% to 95% of dissolved solids are held back with an applied pressure of 50 pounds per square inch (35 grams per square millimeter). As the pressure is increased above 50 pounds/square inch, the purity of the water increases, since more dissolved solids are rejected by the membrane.

Reverse osmosis not only removes most of the positive and negative ions in the initial water, but also removes un-ionized dissolved solids (such as sugar), suspended matter, and even bacteria. The membrane is such a good filter that water containing suspended matter must first be passed through a regular filter, in order to prevent clogging the semipermeable membrane. With a hard-scale-forming water supply, it may be necessary to pretreat the water with an ion exchange softner.

Since the dissolved solids removed by reverse osmosis at any given pressure is a matter of percentage, the quality of the purified water depends on the amount of dissolved solids in the initial water supply (and the applied pressure). If the water is not as high in TDS to begin with, then the effluent from a reverse osmosis unit is purer. For example, a water supply in one particular town contains 1,440 ppm of dissolved solids. Reverse osmosis reduces this to 228. In another town, water with 1,150 ppm is reduced to 71.

The only energy required is for the production of the necessary pressure. Unlike the case with demineralization, no regenerating chemicals are needed with reverse osmosis. But because it is a continuous process, storage capacity is required for the treated water, and another pump is frequently needed to pump the stored water to its place of use. The semipermeable membranes must be replaced about every two years.

In order to obtain a reasonable amount of purified water, it is necessary to have a fairly large semipermeable membrane area. One company uses special cellulose acetate tubing for the membrane, wrapping it into a spiral. Several tubes of this kind can be hooked together in parallel to give the desired rate of flow. (See accompanying figure.) Another method makes use of long membranes in the form of tiny hollow fibers of a special nylon. These fibers are about the diameter of a human hair. The water to be treated enters a housing and surrounds the outside of these fibers. Under pressure, the water penetrates through the fibers into the hollow centers, from which it flows to the product outlet. In both the spiral-wound module and the hollow fiber system, it is necessary to have an outlet for the wastewater stream.

(Left) Commercial reverse osmosis unit, using spiral-wound semipermeable membrane to purify water.

(Right) Reverse osmosis process, using spiral-wound semipermeable membrane.

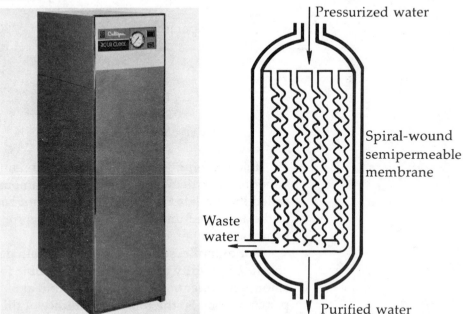

Pressurized water

Spiral-wound semipermeable membrane

Waste water

Purified water

These various methods for the treatment of water vary in principle. Processes such as softening and demineralization involve the removing of impurities from water. In contrast, distillation and reverse osmosis involve the removing of water from its impurities.

Absolute Humidity and Relative Humidity

Pressmen are often interested in the relative humidity of the air in the pressroom, as this will determine whether paper will pick up moisture from the air or lose moisture to the air. If the relative humidity is too low, as it often is in winter, the pressmen will have problems with static electricity and tight-edged sheets. High relative humidity can cause wavy-edged sheets, and it can retard the drying of ink. So it is important to know what is meant by relative humidity and how it is related to absolute humidity.

The amount of water vapor present in the air is measured in grains of water vapor per cubic foot of air. (There are 437.5 grains in one avoirdupois ounce.) Using metric units, water vapor can be measured as the number of grams of water vapor per cubic meter of air. (One grain per cubic foot equals 2.29 grams per cubic meter.)

The maximum amount of water vapor that air can hold depends on the temperature of the air. It increases rapidly as the temperature increases. A table in the back of this book gives the maximum amount for a number of temperatures. Here are a few:

Maximum Water Vapor in Air

Temperature		Grains/	Grams/
°F	°C	Cubic foot	Cubic meter
50	10	4.108	9.401
60	15.6	5.798	13.27
80	26.7	11.06	25.31
100	37.8	19.99	45.74

Usually, air does not contain the maximum amount of water vapor for a particular temperature. The amount it does contain is called the *absolute humidity*. Then the *relative humidity* is the ratio of the absolute humidity to the maximum for that temperature, expressed as a percentage.

For example, suppose that on a certain day air at 60°F has an absolute humidity of 4.100 grains per cubic foot. The maximum amount of water vapor that air can hold at 60°F is 5.798 grains per cubic foot. So the relative humidity of this air is:

$$\frac{4.100}{5.798} \times 100 = 70.7\%$$

In printing plants, various methods are available to obtain the relative humidity. One method uses a device with two thermometers. One thermometer is the "dry bulb," which merely records the room temperature. The other, the "wet bulb," has a cotton sleeve that is saturated with water over the bulb. The device is swung around rapidly for a couple of minutes. Some of the water on the wet bulb evaporates, causing the temperature of this thermometer to drop. The less water vapor in the air (the lower the relative humidity), the more water evaporates from the wet bulb, and the more this temperature drops. By reading the dry-bulb and wet-bulb temperatures, you can determine the relative humidity from a table based on these two readings.

Wet-and-dry-bulb hygrometer.

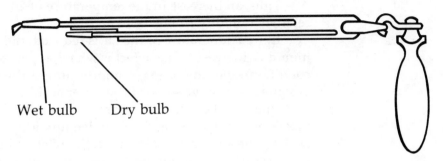

Wet bulb   Dry bulb

How Temperature Changes Affect Relative Humidity

One reason for measuring the relative humidity of the air is that ways are available for changing it to some extent. One of these is to change the temperature of the room.

The general rule is: if the room temperature is increased, the relative humidity goes down; if the room temperature is lowered, the relative humidity goes up. So if it is possible to change the room temperature, the relative humidity can very likely be brought into the range desired.

The figures already given can be used to calculate how much the relative humidity will change with a certain change in temperature. The calculation is based on the fact that the absolute humidity does not change when the temperature changes; there is no change in the number of grains of water vapor per cubic foot of air.

Let's assume that the air on a particular day is 60°F (16°C) and the relative humidity is 90%. We want to reduce this relative humidity, so we raise the temperature to 80°F (27°C). The calculation of the new relative humidity is made as follows:

Maximum amount of water vapor at 60°F is 5.798 grains per cubic foot. If relative humidity is 90%, then the absolute humidity is (5.798)(0.90), or 5.218 grains per cu. ft.

Maximum amount of water vapor at 80°F is 11.06 grains per cu. ft. So the relative humidity at 80°F is:

$$\frac{5.218}{11.06} \times 100 = 47.18\%$$

Thus, an increase in the temperature of 20°F lowers the relative humidity from 90% to 47.18%.

If the temperature of the air is reduced, the relative humidity increases. This effect is what happens with air conditioning in the summer months, unless the equipment is designed to remove some of the water at the same time that it cools the air. The calculations are similar to those given above. If incoming air at 96°F has 50% relative humidity and is cooled to 76°F by the air-conditioning unit, the relative humidity increases to 91.3% if no moisture is removed from the air. It is easy to see why some air-conditioned areas feel damp and "sticky."

The effect of temperature on relative humidity explains some of the things that you have probably observed. For instance, the relative humidity in a plant area, such as a pressroom, is not 100% even though rain outside indicates that the outside air is at 100% relative humidity. The reason is that the temperature inside is usually higher than it is outside. The same thing happens in cold weather. Cold air that may itself be at rather low relative humidity is brought into a plant and heated, perhaps 50 degrees or more. The result is that the heated air has a very low relative humidity, which can cause severe problems with static electricity and with paper behavior on the press.

Summary

One way to soften water is by use of a cation exchange resin. A common water softener of this kind does not remove the dissolved solids in the water. To achieve such removal, several methods are used, including distillation, demineralization, and reverse osmosis. With these methods, it is possible to produce water that has only a very small amount of dissolved solids in it.

There is always some water vapor in the air. The amount that air can hold increases rapidly with an increase in temperature. The relative humidity is the ratio between the amount of water vapor actually present in the air and the maximum amount of water vapor that the air could hold, depending on the temperature. The relative humidity of a particular quantity of air can be lowered by increasing the temperature or raised by decreasing the temperature.

4 Chemistry of the Compounds of Carbon

Up to this point, the subject matter treated has been *inorganic chemistry*. It includes the chemistry of the metals and nonmetals, acids, bases, and the many compounds that are formed from various positive and negative ions. The other major branch of chemistry is *organic chemistry*, which includes most of the compounds of the element carbon.

Carbon is a great "joiner." Carbon atoms will link with other carbon atoms to form a long-chain type of molecule. They will also combine with atoms of other elements such as hydrogen, oxygen, nitrogen, chlorine, and bromine. Many of these compounds are solvents used in the graphic arts.

Forms of Elementary Carbon

Carbon exists alone in several forms. Diamonds, graphite, lampblack, wood charcoal, and coke consist mostly of elementary carbon. A diamond is pure carbon in a crystalline form. The other materials are largely carbon but contain a small percentage of impurities; for example:

● **Coke.** When soft coal is heated out of contact with air, it changes chemically. This process is called *destructive distillation*. Some of the complicated molecules break down into simpler molecules with fewer atoms. Some of these products are gases—called coal gas—that can be burned to produce heat energy. Others change to a thick liquid called coal tar. About eight gallons of coal tar are obtained from a ton of coal. Another coal product is ammonia, NH_3. When this gas is purified and dissolved in water, it makes "ammonia water," a weak base with the formula NH_4OH.

Most of the coal remains as a solid consisting mainly of elementary carbon and the mineral matter that was present in the soft coal. This remaining solid is called *coke*. It can be burned as a fuel; it is also used in the reduction of iron ore (iron oxide) to metallic iron.

● **Charcoal.** When wood is heated in the absence of air, it decomposes as soft coal does, but the products are different. The recovered liquid is a mixture of wood tar, wood alcohol (methyl alcohol), acetone (a common solvent), and acetic acid. The solid that remains is *charcoal*, which is principally elementary carbon.

● **Activated Charcoal.** Activated charcoal (also called activated carbon) is obtained by heating granulated charcoal to remove adsorbed gaseous materials. Activated charcoal is used to adsorb other gaseous materials from a stream of air. In the graphic arts, air containing solvents from gravure inks is passed through tanks containing activated charcoal; the solvents are adsorbed onto the charcoal and removed from the air stream. Later, the bed of charcoal is regenerated by passing steam through it. Hydrocarbon solvents from heatset lithographic inks can also be adsorbed onto activated charcoal. To regenerate the charcoal, the hydrocarbon solvents are removed by the use of heat and vacuum distillation.

● **Graphite.** Graphite, like diamond, is a crystalline form of carbon. It is found in nature in certain parts of the world. It is also made artificially by heating coke in an electric furnace to about 5,000°F (2,760°C).

Graphite is the only nonmetal that is a fair conductor of electricity. It is used for electrodes in certain electrochemical processes. It is also used in some lubricants. If graphite is mixed with clay, the mixture forms the "lead" in lead pencils.

Reaction of Carbon with Oxygen

All forms of elementary carbon react with oxygen in the same way. Under the proper conditions, they burn in an atmosphere of oxygen gas to form carbon dioxide gas. The reaction is:

$$C \; + \; O_2 \; \longrightarrow \; CO_2$$

It is much harder to get a diamond to burn than it is to get coke or charcoal to burn. When it does burn, it forms carbon dioxide as coke and charcoal do.

If carbon is burned with an insufficient supply of oxygen, some carbon dioxide and some carbon monoxide are formed. The reaction for producing carbon monoxide gas is:

$$2C \; + \; O_2 \; \longrightarrow \; 2CO$$

Carbon monoxide is very poisonous. If a person breathes air containing only one part of CO in about 750 parts of air, he will die in a short time. It is the CO content in the exhaust fumes of an automobile that kills people if an automobile engine is allowed to operate in a closed area.

While neither carbon dioxide nor carbon monoxide are included among the organic compounds, carbon dioxide plays an important role in life processes in what is called the "carbon dioxide cycle" in nature. People and animals eat food and breathe air containing oxygen. Inside the body, a reaction between the food and the oxygen occurs, supplying the energy that keeps the body active. The principal products of the reaction are water and carbon dioxide gas. The carbon dioxide gas and some water vapor are exhaled through the nose and mouth and thus go out into the air.

The "carbon dioxide cycle."

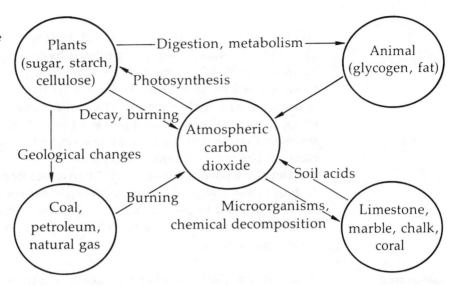

The air contains about 0.04% CO_2. Even this small amount of carbon dioxide in the air is very important. Plants take it through their leaves and convert it, together with water and other materials taken from the soil, into organic compounds such as starches, sugars, proteins, fats, and cellulose. This completes the "carbon dioxide cycle"—CO_2 in the air goes to organic compounds in plants, which are eaten by people and other animals, producing CO_2 that goes back into the air again.

Raw Materials for Organic Compounds

Organic compounds are produced from a wide variety of raw materials. A large number of compounds are produced from petroleum and natural gas. Others are made from coal, plants, fish, animals, and birds. For example, trees supply cellulose fibers that are used to make the paper for printing and other uses. The flax plant supplies flaxseed, which is pressed to produce linseed oil. Toluene, xylene, and many other organic chemicals are produced from petroleum.

There are now over one million known compounds of carbon. They are organized into classes. Those classes and compounds having graphic arts uses are given main attention here.

Hydrocarbons

Organic compounds which contain only carbon and hydrogen atoms are called *hydrocarbons*. There are three main classes of hydrocarbons. They are:
● **Aliphatic hydrocarbons.** Commonly called paraffins, aliphatic hydrocarbons are often referred to as "straight-chain" or "branched-chain" hydrocarbons, depending on the chainlike structure of the carbon skeleton. Gasoline, kerosene, fuel oil, and

oils for heatset inks consist largely of hydrocarbons of this type. There are two subdivisions of aliphatic hydrocarbons: saturated hydrocarbons and unsaturated hydrocarbons.

● **Aromatic hydrocarbons.** Aromatics are frequently referred to as benzene ring hydrocarbons. The carbon atoms are arranged in rings. In general, the solvent power of liquid aromatics is much stronger than that of the aliphatics. Common compounds in this class are benzene, toluene, and xylene.

● **Alicyclic hydrocarbons.** Alicyclic hydrocarbons also have carbon atoms arranged in rings. Alicyclic hydrocarbons include naphthenes and terpenes. Turpentine is the best known of the terpenes. Alicyclic hydrocarbons have at least one carbon ring in their structure.

Saturated Hydrocarbons

A *saturated* hydrocarbon is a hydrocarbon (either aliphatic or alicyclic) having only single bonds between carbon atoms. Any carbon-to-carbon bond in a saturated hydrocarbon consists of the sharing of a single pair of valence electrons.

The simplest saturated hydrocarbon is *methane* (also called "marsh gas"). Its formula is CH_4. Natural gas consists largely of methane.

The element carbon has an atomic number of 6. This means that the atoms of carbon have two electrons in the first energy level and four valence electrons in the second energy level. Carbon atoms never gain or lose the valence electrons to form ions. Instead, they share a pair of electrons with an atom of another element to form a covalent bond. Because of the number of valence electrons, carbon can form four covalent bonds. In methane, for example, each hydrogen atom furnishes one valence electron to form a covalent bond, and four hydrogen atoms combine with one carbon atom to form a molecule of CH_4. This molecule can be pictured as follows:

$$H : \overset{\displaystyle H}{\underset{\displaystyle H}{C}} : H$$

There are thus four covalent bonds in a CH_4 molecule. It is simpler to write the structural formula of methane as:

$$
\begin{array}{ccc}
\quad H & & \\
\quad | & & H \\
H-C-H & \text{or as} & HCH \\
\quad | & & H \\
\quad H & &
\end{array}
$$

One of the reasons that there are so many compounds of carbon is that one carbon atom can share a pair of electrons with another carbon atom, the second carbon atom with a third, etc. This characteristic can lead to a long chain of carbon atoms.

The first example of such sharing is *ethane*, C_2H_6. Its structural formula is:

$$
\begin{array}{ccc}
\text{H} & \text{H} \\
| & | \\
\text{H---C---C---H} \\
| & | \\
\text{H} & \text{H}
\end{array}
$$

Ethane, like methane, is a gas and occurs to a small degree in natural gas.

The next saturated hydrocarbon is *propane*, C_3H_8. Its structural formula is:

$$
\begin{array}{ccc}
\text{H} & \text{H} & \text{H} \\
| & | & | \\
\text{H---C---C---C---H} \\
| & | & | \\
\text{H} & \text{H} & \text{H}
\end{array}
$$

Then comes butane, C_4H_{10}. Both propane and butane are gases. Bottled gas is largely compressed propane.

The next twelve members of this series are liquids; those with more than 16 carbon atoms are solids. The general formula for any saturated aliphatic hydrocarbon is:

$$C_nH_{2n+2}$$

where "n" is the number of carbon atoms. For example, *hexane* is a liquid with six carbon atoms in each molecule, so its formula must be C_6H_{14}. It is used as a solvent in some flexographic and screen printing inks. Next in the series is *heptane*. It is a liquid with seven carbon atoms in each molecule; its formula is C_7H_{16}. Heptane is also used in some flexographic, screen printing, and gravure inks.

Chemicals from Petroleum and Natural Gas

The gaseous saturated hydrocarbons occur in natural gas, but petroleum is the source for most of the remainder of the series. That is, petroleum is a mixture of many of the longer-chain saturated hydrocarbons. It even contains some propane and butane, because gases are soluble in liquids that are chemically similar. Also some solid hydrocarbons are present in liquid petroleum; solids as well as gases dissolve in solvents that are chemically similar.

At an oil refinery, petroleum is boiled and separated (distilled) into different fractions. The part which changes into vapor first contains more of the lower-molecular-weight hydrocarbons. Later fractions contain more and more of the heavier hydrocarbons. The separation obtained by this distillation process is not complete; each fraction which is obtained is a mixture of several of the saturated hydrocarbons. The fraction called gasoline contains mostly the hydrocarbons from C_5H_{12} to C_9H_{20}.

Single-stage crude distillation process.

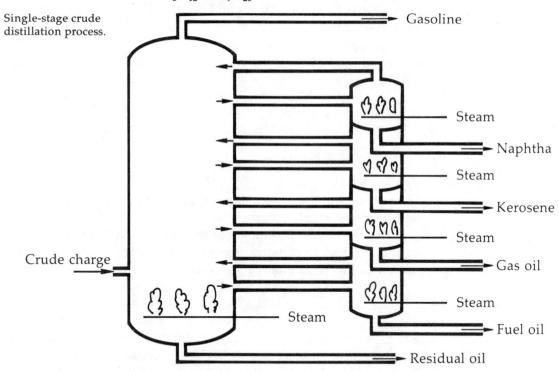

Mixtures such as this do not have a single, fixed boiling point. When gasoline is heated in such a way that it does not catch on fire, it starts to boil at about 140°F (60°C). The boiling point keeps increasing, and the last material boils at about 375°F (190°C).

Solvents and fuels produced by the fractional distillation of petroleum include petroleum ether, gasoline, naphtha, mineral spirits, kerosene, fuel oil, and heatset-ink oils. Some of the physical properties of these and other liquids are presented later in this chapter.

Unsaturated Hydrocarbons

In the saturated hydrocarbons, each carbon atom holds as many hydrogen atoms as possible. In the unsaturated hydrocarbons, fewer than the maximum number of hydrogen atoms are attached to the carbon atoms; there are multiple bonds between carbons. For example, the formula for the saturated hydrocargon ethane is C_2H_6, with the structure:

$$
\begin{array}{ccc}
& H & H \\
& | & | \\
H- & C-C & -H \\
& | & | \\
& H & H
\end{array}
$$

A two-carbon unsaturated hydrocarbon, called ethylene (ethene), has the formula C_2H_4, with the structure:

$$
\begin{array}{ccc}
H & & H \\
\diagdown & & \diagup \\
& C=C & \\
\diagup & & \diagdown \\
H & & H
\end{array}
$$

In this compound, the two carbon atoms are held together with a *double bond*. This means that two pairs of electrons are shared between the two carbon atoms.

Ethylene (ethene).

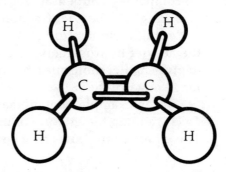

Double bonds are weaker than single bonds and so are more reactive. Unsaturated hydrocarbons are more reactive than saturated ones. Under proper conditions, ethylene will react chemically with substances such as hydrogen, bromine, hydrochloric acid, and water. Ethylene molecules will also link with each other, forming a long chain. This action is called *polymerization*, and the result is the plastic called polyethylene. A lot of printing, particularly by flexography, is done on films of polyethylene.

The polymerization of ethylene to make polyethylene.

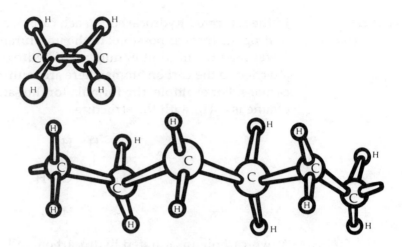

In oxyacetylene welding, one of the materials used is acetylene gas. It is a highly unsaturated hydrocarbon, with formula C_2H_2 and structure $H-C{\equiv}C-H$. As the structural formula indicates, there is a *triple bond* between the carbon atoms in this compound. This means that three pairs of electrons are shared between the two carbon atoms.

When petroleum is separated by fractional distillation, the amount of each fraction does not necessarily correspond to the market demand. There is less of the gasoline fraction than is needed, and too much of the kerosene and fuel oil fractions. The oil companies compensate for this undesirable proportion by "cracking" the heavier fractions, such as kerosene and fuel oil, under high temperature and pressure. Under these conditions, the heavier hydrocarbon molecules break into two or more parts to give smaller molecules, many of which are in the boiling range of gasoline.

As an example, fuel oil may contain tetradecane molecules, $C_{14}H_{30}$, among the mixture of molecules that make up fuel oil. These heavy molecules may be cracked as follows:

$$C_{14}H_{30} \longrightarrow C_7H_{16} + C_7H_{14}$$

The second product molecule, C_7H_{14}, is unsaturated. Gasoline obtained by this cracking process is thus a mixture of saturated and unsaturated hydrocarbons. The unsaturated hydrocarbons impart a considerable degree of "antiknock" properties to the automobile gasoline.

The heatset oils used in web letterpress and web offset inks contain about 3% to 5% of unsaturated hydrocarbons, called *olefins*. Special ink oils, treated to remove the olefins and other impurities that cause much of the odor and smoke in the effluent from press dryers, are being employed with increasing frequency.

Alkyl Halides   Organic compounds in which a halide—fluorine, chlorine, bromine, or iodine—has replaced one or more of the hydrogen atoms in a saturated hydrocarbon are called alkyl halides. One of the halides is chloroform, $CHCl_3$, with structure:

$$\begin{array}{c} Cl \\ | \\ H-C-Cl \\ | \\ Cl \end{array}$$

Trichloro-methane is the generic name for chloroform.

If all of the hydrogen atoms in methane are replaced with chlorine atoms, the result is the compound carbon tetrachloride, CCl_4. Methane burns in air, but carbon tetrachloride does not. The vapor of carbon tetrachloride is highly toxic. CCl_4 is a common solvent, but it should never be used except in a well ventilated place. If it is used in a closed room it can cause the death of those in the room.

An alkyl halide that is not nearly as toxic as carbon tetrachloride is bromotrifluoro-methane, CF_3Br. It has been used in hand-held fire extinguishers for several years. More recently, it is being used to extinguish fires in entire rooms. If any quantity of air contains only 5% of this compound, a fire will be extinguished rapidly. It is claimed that people can breathe in such an atmosphere without toxic effects for up to five minutes.

The formula for ethane is C_2H_6. If the three hydrogen atoms on the first carbon atom are replaced with chlorine atoms, the compound is called 1,1,1-trichloro-ethane and has the structure:

$$\begin{array}{c} Cl \quad H \\ | \quad \; | \\ Cl-C-C-H \\ | \quad \; | \\ Cl \quad H \end{array}$$

It is nonflammable, much less toxic than carbon tetrachloride, and a good substitute for it in liquid cleaners.

Methyl chloride, an
alkyl halide.

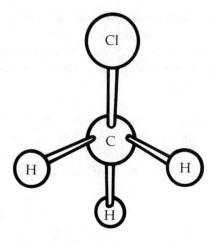

**Alkyl Groups,
or Organic
Groups**

If one hydrogen atom could be removed from a methane molecule, the group $-CH_3$ would remain. Such a group is called an *alkyl group*, or *organic group*. Groups like this cannot exist alone, since one carbon atom has only three of its four bonding forces satisfied. But they do occur in many organic compounds in combination with something else. Their names, which usually end in "yl," are derived from the names of the corresponding hydrocarbons. The ones encountered most often in the graphic arts are:

Hydrocarbon		Organic Group	
CH_4	methane	$-CH_3$	methyl
C_2H_6	ethane	$-C_2H_5$	ethyl
C_3H_8	propane	$-C_3H_7$	propyl
C_4H_{10}	butane	$-C_4H_9$	butyl
		$-C_nH_{2n+1}$	(general formula)
		$-R$	(general symbol)

The names of the organic groups are often used in the naming of an organic compound. Thus the compound:

$$CH_3-\overset{\displaystyle O}{\overset{\displaystyle \|}{C}}-C_2H_5$$

is called methyl ethyl ketone, or MEK.

The letter R is often used as a shorthand notation to represent any organic group.

Alcohols: ROH   If an organic group is combined with an –OH group, the compound is called an *alcohol*. The names and formulas of the three lowest-molecular-weight alcohols are:

CH$_3$OH   Methyl alcohol, also called methanol or wood alcohol

C$_2$H$_5$OH   Ethyl alcohol, also called ethanol or grain alcohol. (This is drinking alcohol.)

C$_3$H$_7$OH   Propyl alcohol, also called propanol.

Methyl alcohol is obtained from the destructive distillation of hardwood. Today, most of it is produced synthetically, from either coal or natural gas. Methyl alcohol is used in some printing inks for food wraps and in some screen printing inks. Very toxic, this kind of alcohol causes blindness if enough is taken internally.

Methyl alcohol, or methanol.

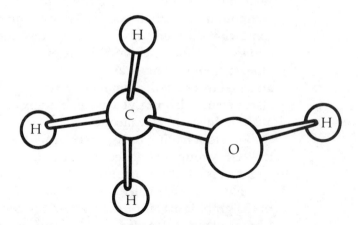

Ethyl alcohol is the drinking kind. Various alcoholic beverages are made by fermentation of grapes, grain, or potatoes. Ethyl alcohol produced in this way is too expensive for industrial uses. Most industrial ethyl alcohol is made synthetically from petroleum gases. Ethyl alcohol is used in both flexographic and gravure inks. Its structural formula is:

$$
\begin{array}{ccc}
\text{H} & \text{H} & \\
| & | & \\
\text{H}-\text{C}-\text{C}-\text{OH} \\
| & | & \\
\text{H} & \text{H} &
\end{array}
$$

The molecular formula of propyl alcohol is C_3H_7OH. Since there are three carbons atoms in each molecule, it is possible to have the –OH group attached to a carbon atom at either end or to the one in the middle. Both compounds are produced commercially. The names and structures of the two compounds are:

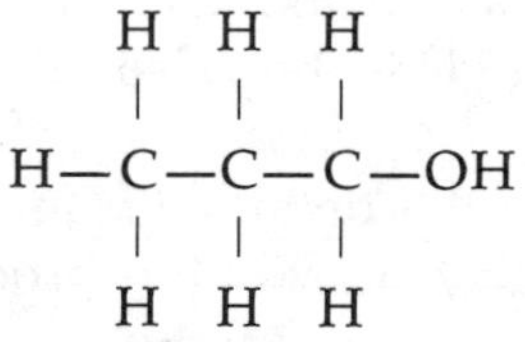

$$
\begin{array}{ccc}
\text{H} & \text{H} & \text{H} \\
| & | & | \\
\text{H—C—C—C—OH} \\
| & | & | \\
\text{H} & \text{H} & \text{H}
\end{array}
\qquad
\begin{array}{ccc}
\text{H} & \text{H} & \text{H} \\
| & | & | \\
\text{H—C—C—C—H} \\
| & | & | \\
\text{H} & \text{OH} & \text{H}
\end{array}
$$

Normal propyl alcohol 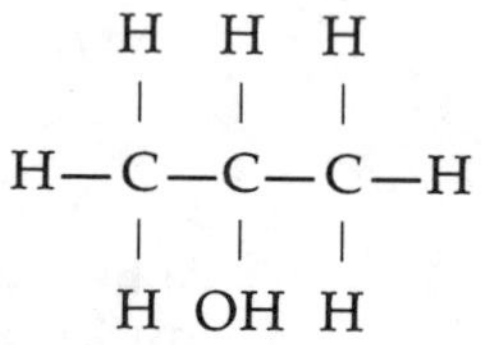   Isopropyl alcohol

Each of these two compounds has molecules with exactly the same number of carbon and hydrogen atoms as the other. Such compounds are called *isomers*. They are quite similar, but have somewhat different physical properties, such as boiling point and evaporation rate. Normal propyl alcohol is an example of a *primary* alcohol. This is an alcohol that has the –OH group attached to a carbon atom having two or three hydrogen atoms also attached. Isopropyl alcohol is an example of a *secondary* alcohol. In secondary alcohols, the –OH group is attached to a carbon atom having only one hydrogen atom also attached. If the –OH group is attached to a carbon atom with no hydrogen atoms, it is a tertiary alcohol.

Normal propyl alcohol and isopropyl alcohol are both used in the graphic arts for flexographic and screen printing inks. Isopropyl alcohol is also used in considerable amounts for lithographic fountain solutions and for washing lithographic deep-etch plates.

Other Alcohols   Alcohols can contain more than one –OH group. A common one is ethylene glycol, with the structure:

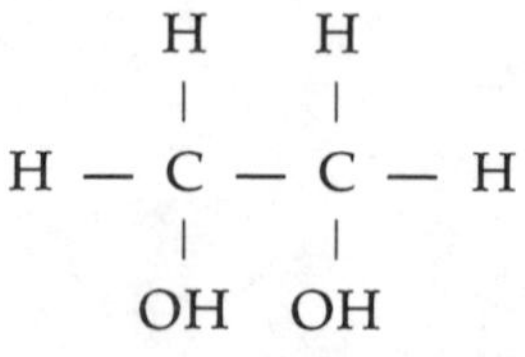

$$
\begin{array}{cc}
\text{H} & \text{H} \\
| & | \\
\text{H — C — C — H} \\
| & | \\
\text{OH} & \text{OH}
\end{array}
$$

This compound is produced synthetically from petroleum gases. It is used as a permanent type of antifreeze. It is also employed in some screen printing inks and in the manufacture of polyester film base.

Glycerine (or more correctly "glycerol") has the formula $C_3H_5(OH)_3$, with the structure:

$$
\begin{array}{ccccc}
H & & H & & H \\
| & & | & & | \\
H - C & - & C & - & C - H \\
| & & | & & | \\
OH & & OH & & OH \\
\end{array}
$$

Glycerol is often used as one of the ingredients in the water fountain solution for lithographic duplicator machines.

Aldehydes: R-CHO

If a primary alcohol is oxidized carefully, an *aldehyde* can be produced. An aldehyde has the general structural formula:

$$
\begin{array}{c}
O \\
\parallel \\
R-C-H \\
\end{array}
$$

where an oxygen atom is double-bonded to a carbon atom. An aldehyde of interest in the graphic arts is formaldehyde, HCHO. With formaldehyde, the "R" is simply a hydrogen atom. Formaldehyde is a preservative and also a hardening or tanning agent.

Formaldehyde.

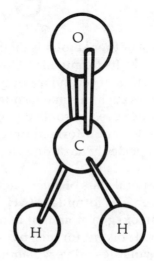

Ketones:
R-CO-R^1

If a secondary alcohol is oxidized, a *ketone* is produced. It has the general structural formula:

$$\overset{\displaystyle O}{\overset{\displaystyle \|}{R-C-R^1}}$$

where an oxygen atom is double-bonded to a carbon atom and where R and R^1 are organic groups that may be either alike or different. One common ketone is acetone, CH_3–CO–CH_3. This solvent is obtained as one of the products of the destructive distillation of wood. Most acetone is now made synthetically from propylene. It is a good solvent for certain resins and is used in some screen printing inks.

Acetone, a common ketone.

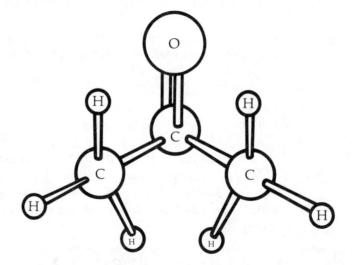

Another ketone is methyl ethyl ketone, usually referred to as MEK. Its formula is CH_3–CO–C_2H_5. It is produced by the oxidation of secondary butyl alcohol. It is a good solvent and is used as such in some lacquers for lithographic deep-etch plates. It is also used in some flexographic, gravure, and screen printing inks. Recent information suggests that these ketones are unexpectedly hazardous to the health.

Ethers: R-O-R^1

A general class of *ethers* includes diethyl ether, or common "ether." Its formula is C_2H_5-O-C_2H_5. The ethers are characterized by an oxygen atom that is single-bonded to two carbons. Ether is a good solvent for oils, but it must be used very carefully because it is volatile and very flammable. Diethyl ether is made commercially from ethyl alcohol.

Diethyl ether.

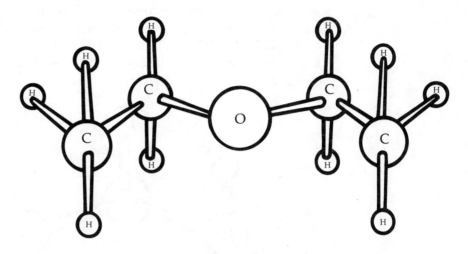

The glycol ethers have both alcoholic and ether groups, and this combination gives them unusual solvent properties. A common one is called ethylene glycol monoethyl ether. Long names like this are often encountered in organic chemistry; they accurately tell how the molecules are constituted. In this case, the "R" of the general formula represents ethylene glycol, and the "R^1" represents an ethyl group. The structure is:

$$
\begin{array}{c}
\quad\;\; \text{H}\;\; \text{H}\qquad \text{H}\;\; \text{H} \\
\quad\;\; | \quad | \qquad\; | \quad | \\
\text{H}-\text{C}-\text{C}-\text{O}-\text{C}-\text{C}-\text{H} \\
\quad\;\; | \quad | \qquad\; | \quad | \\
\quad\;\; \text{OH}\; \text{H}\qquad \text{H}\;\; \text{H}
\end{array}
$$

$$\text{R}-\text{O}-\text{R}^1$$

This glycol ether is used as a solvent in lacquers and is used in certain gravure, flexographic, and screen printing inks. It is sometimes used in the processing of lithographic deep-etch plates.

Organic Acids: R-COOH

If an organic "R" group is combined with a *carboxyl* group, –COOH, a simple organic acid results. A carboxyl group has the structure:

$$
\begin{array}{c}
\text{O} \\
\parallel \\
-\text{COH}
\end{array}
$$

with one oxygen atom double-bonded to a carbon atom and a hydroxyl group, –OH, bonded to the same carbon atom. Acetic acid is CH_3–COOH; that is, it consists of a methyl group attached to a carboxyl group. Acetic acid is the weak acid present in vinegar.

Acetic acid.

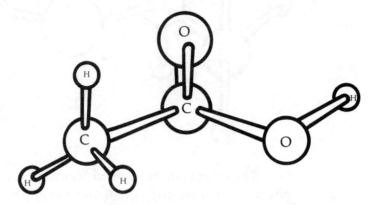

When an organic acid is dissolved in water, the hydrogen ion that dissociates from the acid is the hydrogen atom of the –COOH group. Most organic acids are weak acids: only a small percentage of the molecules ionize to give a H^+ ion and an organic negative ion.

Some organic acids consist of molecules with two or three carboxyl groups; some have hydroxyl groups, –OH, instead of hydrogen atoms attached to certain carbon atoms. Here are the formulas and structures of three common organic acids of these kinds:

Oxalic acid, $H_2C_2O_4$, with structure:

COOH
|
COOH

Tartaric acid, $H_2C_4H_4O_6$ with structure:

COOH
|
H—C—OH
|
HO—C—H
|
COOH

Citric acid, $H_3C_6H_5O_7$, with structure:

$$
\begin{array}{c}
H \\
| \\
H-C-COOH \\
| \\
HO-C-COOH \\
| \\
H-C-COOH \\
| \\
H
\end{array}
$$

Only the hydrogen atoms that form part of a carboxyl group can ionize to furnish H^+ ions in solution. Thus tartaric acid has two ionizable hydrogen atoms, and citric acid has three.

Esters:
R–CO–OR[1]

Esters are formed by the reaction between an organic acid and an alcohol. The organic group of the alcohol replaces the hydrogen atoms of the –COOH. Most of the esters used in the graphic arts are formed from acetic acid and some alcohol, and they are called acetates. A typical reaction for the formation of an ester is:

$$CH_3COOH \quad + \quad CH_3OH \quad \longrightarrow \quad CH_3COOCH_3 \quad + \quad H_2O$$

acetic acid   methyl   methyl acetate   water
                 alcohol   (an ester)

Methyl acetate is a solvent used to some extent in screen printing.

Other esters used as solvents in the graphic arts are:

Ethyl acetate, $CH_3COOC_2H_5$ (gravure, flexographic, and screen printing inks)

Normal-propyl acetate, $CH_3COOC_3H_7$ (gravure and flexographic printing inks)

Isopropyl acetate, $CH_3COOC_3H_7$ (gravure and screen printing inks)

Normal-butyl acetate, $CH_3COOC_4H_9$ (screen printing inks)

Methyl acetate.

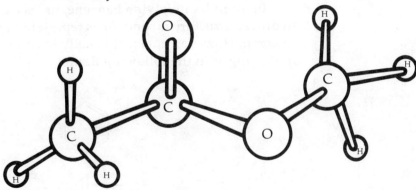

Benzene

Benzene is a volatile solvent with the formula C_6H_6. Benzene is an example of an aromatic hydrocarbon, and it is one of the materials obtained when soft coal is heated in the absence of air. Benzene has a ring structure, as shown in the following figure:

Benzene Derivatives

Benzene can be considered to be the "parent" of thousands of other compounds, called *benzene derivatives*, that are made from benzene. These include dyes, pigments, medicines, photographic developers, and insecticides.

Many of the benzene derivatives are obtained by the reaction of benzene with certain other chemicals, in which one or more of the hydrogen atoms in benzene are replaced with other atoms or groups of atoms. Some of these atoms and groups are:

–OH	hydroxyl
–NH₂	amino (the compound formed is an amine, an organic base)
–COOH	carboxyl (the compound formed is an acid)
–F	fluoro
–Cl	chloro
–Br	bromo
–I	iodo
–R	alkyl groups such as methyl, $-CH_3$, and ethyl, $-C_2H_5$
–SO₃H	sulfonic acid group

In formulas involving benzene, its "six-sided" carbon and hydrogen structure is sometimes represented by a simple hexagon. However, chemists usually indicate the double bonds in the ring as in the following figure:

Following are some common benzene derivatives:
● **Carbolic acid.** The chemical name of carbolic acid is phenol. It is a simple derivative of benzene in which one of the hydrogen atoms has been replaced with a hydroxyl group, –OH. The formula of phenol is C_6H_5OH and the structure is:

OH

Phenol is a good preservative and is often added to gum arabic solutions to prevent souring.

Phenol, or carbolic acid.

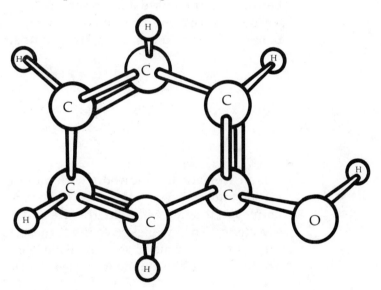

● **Aniline.** Aniline, also called amino-benzene, has the formula $C_6H_5NH_2$ and the structure:

NH_2

Aniline is the starting chemical for the production of aniline dyes.

● **Benzoic acid.** The formula for benzoic acid is C_6H_5COOH, and the structure is:

$$COOH$$

One hydrogen atom of benzene has been replaced with a –COOH group. When this acid reacts with the base NaOH, the main product is a compound called sodium benzoate. Sodium benzoate is often used as a preservative.

● **Toluene.** Toluene, or toluol, has the generic name of methyl benzene. Its formula is $C_6H_5CH_3$, and its structure is:

$$CH_3$$

It is an aromatic hydrocarbon, with molecules containing only carbon and hydrogen atoms. An important organic solvent, it is employed to some extent in gravure and screen printing inks.

● **Xylenes.** The xylenes have the formula $C_6H_4(CH_3)_2$. Two of the hydrogen atoms of benzene have been replaced with methyl groups, –CH_3. The xylenes are used in some gravure and screen printing inks.

Three compounds have the xylene formula, differing in regard to which hydrogen atoms of the benzene molecule have been replaced with methyl groups. These three compounds are examples of aromatic *isomers*—compounds with the same molecular formula but with a different molecular structure.

To distinguish one isomer from another, it is convenient to number the carbon atoms around the benzene ring, as illustrated:

If the hydrogen atoms in "1, 2" position are replaced, the result is an *ortho* compound. If the substitution occurs in the "1, 3" position, the result is a *meta* compound. And if it occurs in the "1,4" position, the result is a *para* compound.

The structures of the three xylenes are as follows:

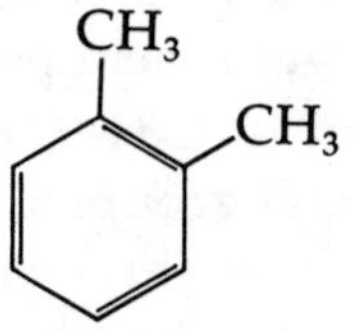

| ortho-xylene | meta-xylene | para-xylene |
| 1,2-dimethyl benzene | 1,3-dimethyl benzene | 1,4-dimethyl benzene |

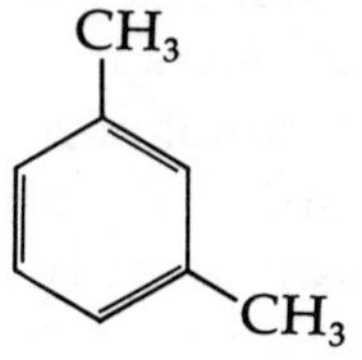

Commercial xylene consists of a mixture of these three isomers. It is a good solvent that is used in some gravure and screen printing inks.

Proteins

The three principal classes of foods are proteins, fats, and carbohydrates; all of these consist of rather complicated organic compounds. A few of the compounds are used in the graphic arts.

Proteins are complicated compounds of carbon, hydrogen, oxygen, nitrogen, and sulfur. Many foods are high in protein. Some common commercial protein products are casein, soybean protein, gelatin, and glue.

Protein molecules are very large. For example, the molecular weight of egg albumin, a protein material, is about 34,000. A chemist can differentiate between different proteins by decomposing them in water. They split apart and form what are called *amino acids*. Various proteins form from four to fifteen different amino acids of the more than twenty known. Proteins differ from fats and carbohydrates in having nitrogen atoms in their molecules. All amino acids contain the $-NH_2$ group, called the amino group. (An amino group is an organic base.) One of the simple amino acids is glycine or amino acetic acid.

$$
\begin{array}{c}
\text{H} \\
| \\
\text{H---C---COOH} \\
| \\
\text{NH}_2
\end{array}
$$

Fats and Oils

From the chemical viewpoint, fats and oils are the same. If the material is a solid, it is a *fat*. If it is a liquid, it is called an *oil*. Of course it is easy to convert one into the other merely by changing the temperature. The term "oil" as used here refers to vegetable and animal oils and not to lubricating oil.

Fats and oils are esters, which we know are formed by the combination of an organic acid and an alcohol. Fats and oils are particular esters in which the organic acid portion is a fatty acid and the alcohol portion is glycerine, $C_3H_5(OH)_3$. A fatty acid is an aliphatic acid with one carboxyl group. Since there are three –OH groups in a glycerine molecule, three molecules of a fatty acid are required to react with one molecule of glycerine. The principal fatty acids and the corresponding esters, or fat molecules, are:

Fatty Acid	Fat molecule
Stearic acid, $C_{17}H_{35}COOH$	$(C_{17}H_{33}COO)_3C_3H_5$
Oleic acid, $C_{17}H_{33}COOH$	$(C_{17}H_{33}COO)_3C_3H_5$
Linoleic acid, $C_{17}H_{31}COOH$	$(C_{17}H_{31}COO)_3C_3H_5$
Linolenic acid, $C_{17}H_{29}COOH$	$(C_{17}H_{29}COO)_3C_3H_5$
Palmitic acid, $C_{15}H_{31}COOH$	$(C_{15}H_{31}COO)_3C_3H_5$

Stearic and palmitic acids are saturated acids, since they have only single carbon-to-carbon bonds. Oleic acid is an unsaturated acid, with one double bond between two of the carbon atoms. Linoleic acid is a more highly unsaturated acid, with two double bonds in a molecule. And linolenic acid is a very highly unsaturated acid, with three double bonds in a molecule.

Fats and oils are produced by plants and animals. Common fats and oils are lard, butter, beef tallow, soybean oil, linseed oil, and cottonseed oil. Each of these is a mixture of different fat molecules. The only thing that makes one fat or oil different from another is the type and amount of particular fat molecules in that fat or oil.

A drying oil is one that contains a large percentage of fat molecules of unsaturated fatty acids. Linseed oil and chinawood oil (tung oil) are good examples. Oil varnishes for printing inks are made from this kind of oil.

Carbohydrates

Carbohydrates are compounds of carbon, hydrogen, and oxygen in which there are twice as many hydrogen atoms as oxygen atoms. There are four kinds of carbohydrates, as follows:

● **Sugars.** Sucrose (common cane or beet sugar), lactose (milk sugar), and maltose all have the formula $C_{12}H_{22}O_{11}$. Dextrose (glucose) and fructose (fruit sugar) are simpler sugars; both have the formula $C_6H_{12}O_6$.

● **Starches.** Starches have much higher molecular weights than sugars. They have the general formula $(C_6H_{10}O_5)n$, where n is about 250 to several thousand. Antisetoff spray powders consist of special grades of starches.

● **Dextrins.** When starch is heated in the presence of a small amount of HCl, a catalyst, the big starch molecules are broken down into shorter molecules, *dextrins*. Dextrins are more soluble in water than starches; they are used as adhesives on postage stamps and envelopes.

● **Cellulose.** Cellulose has the same formula as starch, $(C_6H_{10}O_5)n$. However, the atoms are arranged differently, and the molecular weight is higher. Cellulose is not soluble in water, even though cellulose fibers swell in the presence of water. Cellulose is of great interest to all branches of the graphic arts because it is the basis of printing paper. Most cellulose fibers for making paper come from wood pulp, but cellulose fibers can also be obtained from cotton, linen, jute, hemp, cornstalks, and straw.

Organic Solvents   Many of the compounds discussed in this chapter are organic solvents. A solvent is a liquid that can dissolve another substance. Thus, methyl alcohol is a solvent for shellac; ethyl acetate is a solvent for nitrocellulose. A solvent that dissolves one material may have no solvent power for another. Millions of gallons of solvents are used annually in the graphic arts for inks, type washes, roller and blanket washes, plate developers, and lithographic fountain solution additives.

It is often important to know the physical and chemical properties of individual solvents. These properties include specific gravity, refractive index, K. B. number, aniline point, vapor pressure at different temperatures, and heat of vaporization. If needed, this information can be obtained from the manufacturer or distributor of the solvent in question.

For many people in the graphic arts, the two most important properties are the solvent's flammability and its relative toxicity. Both of these are directly related to the safety of its use.

Flash Point   The *flash point* of a liquid is the lowest temperature at which its vapor will ignite when a small flame is passed over the liquid's surface. At this temperature and within a range of several degrees above it, the vapor will ignite but will not continue to burn. The *fire point* is defined as the lowest temperature at which a mixture of air and the vapor from the liquid will continue to burn in an open container once it has been ignited.

There are two methods for the determination of the flash point of a liquid: the closed cup method and the open cup method. In general, the closed cup method is used for liquids with low flash points; the open cup method is used for liquids with higher flash points. Flash point readings of the same solvent with the open cup method are about 5°F to 10°F (3°C to 6°C) higher than readings made using the closed cup.

A flammable substance is one that ignites easily—has a low flash point. (Note the use of "flammable" instead of "inflammable.") Care should be exercised when using such materials. They should be stored in special containers.

The terms "flammable" and "combustible" do not mean the same thing. According to a definition that is standard in some U.S. government agencies, a flammable substance has a flash point below 100°F (38°C), closed cup method, and a combustible liquid has a flash point between 100°F and 200°F (38°C and 93°C).

Toxicity

All manufacturers and users of chemicals have become more aware of the relative toxicity of different materials. Some solvents are relatively safe, while others are highly toxic. It is not a simple matter to list solvents in their order of relative toxicity. Some solvents will cause only temporary body dysfunction; continued exposure to others will cause some permanent damage. And while it is mainly the amount of vapor in the air that determines how toxic some chemicals are, others also give trouble if absorbed through the skin or ingested into the body.

The American Conference of Governmental Industrial Hygienists (ACGIH) has been concerned for many years with the relative toxicity of a wide variety of chemicals. The organization has established "Threshold Limit Values" (TLVs) for these chemicals.

The TLV is the concentration level to which it is believed most people can be exposed for 8 hours without adverse effects. The averages are time-weighted, permitting higher concentrations when exposures are only for short intervals. A few substances are assigned ceiling concentrations: the concentration of vapor in the air should not exceed the ceiling concentration even for a short length of time.

Most TLV values are expressed in "parts per million" (ppm) based on volumes—the parts by volume of the vapor of the chemical that is present in one million parts by volume of air. They can also be expressed by the number of milligrams of the vapor (or mist) of the substance that is present in one cubic meter of air.

What must be kept in mind is that a material is more toxic the lower its TLV. Carbon tetrachloride, with a TLV of only 10 ppm, is very toxic. Benzene, C_6H_6, is also very toxic, with a TLV of 25 ppm. On the other hand, any material with a TLV of 400 or higher is much less toxic. Those with TLVs of 100 to 200 can be used if proper precautions are taken not to let their vapor concentration in the air get too high.

It is important to note that any material can become toxic under some circumstances: pure water and air are both toxic under special conditions. Similarly, highly hazardous materials such as bromine and sulfuric acid are handled safely in tank-car quantities. It becomes the chemist's responsibility to learn how to handle each chemical.

The proper choice of a solvent or a mixture of solvents to accomplish a particular task is one that requires considerable attention to the properties of the materials. For instance, if a cleaner is needed, solvents must be chosen that will do the job as well as possible without having TLVs or flash points that are too low. In addition, the solvents usually must evaporate neither too slowly nor too rapidly. The accompanying table lists a number of solvents that are used, one way or another, in the graphic arts.

Threshold Limit Values (TLVs) and Flash Points of Selected Graphic Arts Solvents

Name	TLV (parts per million)	Flash Point (closed cup)	
		°F	°C
Saturated Hydrocarbons			
Hexane	500	Below 0	Below −18
Heptane	500	Below 20	Below −7
Lactol spirits	300	Below 20	Below −7
Petroleum ether		0	−18
Gasoline		−60	−51
Naphtha		52–53	11–12
High-flash naphtha		58–65	14–18
Stoddard solvent (mineral spirits)	100	100–110	38–43
Kerosene		130	54

(Continued on following page)

Threshold Limit Values (TLVs) and Flash Points of Selected Graphic Arts Solvents (continued)

Name	TLV (parts per million)		Flash Point (closed cup)
Alcohols			
Methanol (wood alcohol)	200	54	12
Ethanol	1,000	54–58	12–14
Normal propanol	200	71	22
Isopropanol, anhydrous	400	53	12
Isopropanol, 91%	400	61	16
Ethylene glycol	100	240	116
Aromatics			
Benzene	25 (ceiling)	10	−12
Toluene	100	45	7
Xylene	100	81	27
Esters			
Methyl acetate	200	15	−9
Ethyl acetate (99%)	400	24	−4
Normal propyl acetate	200	55	13
Isopropyl acetate	250	35	2
Normal butyl acetate	150	76	24
Ketones			
Acetone	1,000	−4	−20
Methyl ethyl ketone (MEK)	200	16	−9
Miscellaneous			
Carbon tetrachloride	10 (ceiling)	none	none
1, 1, 1-trichloroethane (chlorothene)	350	none	none
Ethylene glycol monoethyl ether	200 (skin)	115 (open cup)	46
Turpentine, gum	100	93	34
Turpentine, steam distilled	100	91	33

NOTE: These are typical specifications, and may vary somewhat from one supplier to another. Also, the TLVs are in a state of flux and some of the values may change from one year to the next.

Heatset Oils

High-boiling-point hydrocarbon solvents are used in the manufacture of heatset (and "quickset") inks for web letterpress and web offset. Heatset varnishes are made by cooking a solid synthetic resin with a heatset oil. The oil dissolves the resin; the result is a varnish suitable for making heatset inks. Varnishes of different viscosities (thicknesses) are made by using different resins and different proportions of resin and oil. In addition to varnish, heatset inks contain a considerable percentage of "free" heatset oil, to give them the correct body for good printing.

Quickset inks for sheetfed printing also contain resin-solvent varnishes with some free oil. Such inks set rapidly by the absorption of some of the oil into the paper.

Heatset inks are dried very rapidly by passing the printed paper web through a dryer. Here a considerable proportion of the heatset oils in the inks are changed into vapor and pass out of the dryer into the air (unless a device such as an incinerator is used to eliminate them). As a result, the inks on the web become dry as soon as the paper web is cooled sufficiently.

Although the heatset oils that have been used for many years consist mainly of aliphatic hydrocarbons, mostly branched and alicyclic compounds, they also contain about 10% to 17% of aromatic materials and about 3% to 5% of unsaturated hydrocarbons, or olefins. It is these materials that cause a considerable amount of the odor and smoke in the effluent from web press dryers.

Some years ago one company began treating heatset oils with hydrogen gas, at high temperature and pressure, in the presence of a catalyst. It is believed that this process converts the aromatic compounds into naphthenes, and the olefins into saturated hydrocarbons. The resulting oils contain only negligible amounts of aromatics and olefins. Inks made with these are the "low odor" and "low smoke" type of heatset inks that are being offered by many of the ink manufacturers.

There has been a considerable increase in the use of the hydrogen-treated oils. One problem is that some resins that will dissolve when heated in the regular oils will not dissolve in the hydrogen-treated oils. So it is necessary for the varnish makers to choose resins that will dissolve in these purer oils.

5   Chemistry of Photography

Photography is involved in image conversion and platemaking in all of the major printing processes. Therefore it is desirable to understand enough of the chemistry of photography to explain the principal reactions that are of interest to graphic arts photographers.

Photographic Materials

Most photography is accomplished with films or papers coated with an emulsion that contains compounds of silver. These materials are exposed to light that has been either reflected from copy or passed through imaged film, positive or negative. Following exposure, the film or paper is developed, then fixed, washed, and dried.

Bases

It is necessary to have a base on which to apply the light-sensitive emulsion. The base of photographic paper is a special grade of paper. Most graphic arts films today employ a polyester base, although cellulose acetate was used for a long time and is still used to some extent.

The raw materials for making the polyester film base are dimethyl terephthalate and ethylene glycol. The polyester film has exceptional properties compared with cellulose acetate. The property of particular interest in graphic arts photography is the dimensional stability of the film with changes in the relative humidity of the air. Cellulose acetate changes in size about four times as much as does polyester film.

Silver Halide Film Emulsions

A photographic emulsion consists of tiny particles of a silver halide dispersed in gelatin. The silver halide is sensitive to light. The gelatin serves to hold and protect the silver halide, and acts as an adhesive to hold the emulsion to the film, glass, or paper.

Silver Halides

The term "silver halide" refers to silver chloride, silver bromide, or silver iodide. Since the valence of silver is $+1$ and the valence of the halide ions is -1, the silver halide formulas are $AgCl$, $AgBr$, and AgI respectively. Of these, $AgCl$ is the least light-sensitive and is used in the emulsions of certain photographic papers, particularly papers used to make contact prints. In making enlargements, a given amount of light passing through the negative spreads out over a greater area on the enlarging paper. Therefore the emulsion for enlarging papers must be faster, or more light-sensitive, if a very long exposure time is to be avoided. Such emulsions usually contain $AgBr$ or a mixture of $AgBr$ and $AgCl$. When a negative is to be made from the original copy, a fast emulsion is needed. Negative emulsions contain AgBr or a mixture of AgBr and AgI.

Preparation of a Silver Halide Emulsion

Film manufacturers use complicated procedures to produce silver halide emulsions. The following is a simplified description of these procedures.

Silver halides are almost insoluble in water. So they are formed chemically in a solution of gelatin. A solution containing from 1% to 5% gelatin is made, and enough potassium bromide, KBr, is dissolved in it to give a 10% KBr solution. In a separate container silver nitrate, $AgNO_3$, is dissolved in water. Then the solutions are heated to a temperature of from 160° to 195°F (70° to 90°C), and the silver nitrate solution is poured slowly into the potassium bromide–gelatin solution. The following reaction occurs:

$$AgNO_3 \ + \ KBr \ \longrightarrow \ AgBr \ + \ KNO_3.$$

In this discussion, KBr is used as an example. If a chloride emulsion is desired, then KCl is used. If a mixture of bromide and iodide is desired, then the gelatin solution contains a mixture of KBr and KI. In any case, the chemical reaction is similar to the one given above.

AgI is more light-sensitive than AgBr, and AgBr is more light-sensitive than AgCl. But the size of the particles of solid silver halide formed is also a factor determining the sensitivity of the emulsion to light. If the silver nitrate is added rapidly, the particles, or "grains," are very tiny, and the sensitivity of the emulsion is low. If the temperature of the solutions is raised before they are mixed, and the silver nitrate solution is added slowly, then the particles are somewhat larger; the sensitivity to light is greater. Even if the initial size of the grains is very small, they increase in size as the solution is allowed to "ripen." In the ripening process, the solution is allowed to stand, in a swollen gel form, for a considerable length of time. During this time, the very tiny particles dissolve, and the somewhat larger particles become still larger.

Another method is also used to obtain larger grains. In this method, precipitation of the silver halide is made in the presence of ammonia at lowered temperatures.

High-speed emulsions used for negatives are prepared by slow addition of the silver nitrate and by long ripening at high temperatures. Lower-speed emulsions used for process work or for positive film are made with a more rapid addition of the silver nitrate at a lower temperature. These lower-speed emulsions have a grain finer and more uniform than high-speed emulsions.

After the emulsion has been ripened, more gelatin is added to bring the total gelatin concentration up to about 10%. Then the mixture is cooled rapidly, whereupon it sets to form a gel. The gel is cut into small shreds and washed with cold water to remove the excess KBr and also the KNO_3 formed in the chemical reaction given previously. It is not desirable to leave these soluble salts in the emulsion (except for paper emulsions, which are usually not washed to remove soluble salts).

Then the emulsion is melted, and sometimes more gelatin is added. At this point the emulsion is still low in sensitivity to light. The temperature is held at about 120°F (50°C) for 10 minutes or more. In this second ripening process, the sensitivity continues to increase. How much it increases depends in part on the nature of the gelatin used.

The final liquid emulsion is adjusted to contain about 6% gelatin and 4% silver halide. It is then coated on the paper or film. The final dried emulsion contains about 0.05 grains per square inch (0.5 milligram per square centimeter) on paper or 0.15 gr./sq.in. (1.5 mg/cm^2) on film.

One role of gelatin in an emulsion is that of a "protective colloid." If silver nitrate is added to potassium bromide, each of them being in water solution with no gelatin present, the solid silver bromide clumps and soon settles to the bottom of the container. But if one of the solutions contains gelatin, the silver bromide is precipitated in such a finely divided state that it is more or less uniformly distributed and suspended in the gelatin solution.

Ionic Structure of a Silver Halide Grain

The grains of silver halide in an emulsion do not consist of individual molecules of the silver halide used. Instead, an "ionic lattice" is built up. For AgBr, this lattice consists of a Ag^+ ion positioned next to a Br^- ion, and another Ag^+ ion next to this Br^- ion, and so on in three dimensions, forming an octahedral crystal. A very small two-dimensional part of such a crystal is illustrated here.

$$Ag^+$$
$$Ag^+Br^-\ Ag^+$$
$$Ag^+Br^-\ Ag^+Br^-$$
$$Ag^+Br^-\ Ag^+Br^-$$
$$Br^-\ Ag^+Br^-$$
$$Br^-$$

Similar layers of Ag^+ and Br^- ions lie in front of and behind the ones shown. In such an ionic lattice, one Ag^+ ion does not "belong" to one Br^- any more than to any other Br^- that is next to it. Instead, every silver ion "belongs" partly to six bromide ions, and each bromide ion in turn "belongs" partly to six silver ions.

Bromide Body

Any silver or bromide ion in the center of such a crystal of AgBr has its electrical forces satisfied. There are oppositely charged ions all around it—left and right, below and above, in front and behind. But at the surface of the crystal, a different situation exists. Here there are no ions on one side of a particular surface ion. Such surface ions still have an electrical force remaining which could hold something else. If the solution contains an excess of KBr over the amount required to form the AgBr, then the Br^- ions of the KBr are attracted to the surface silver ions and are held there by the attraction of the opposite electrical charges. Of course, for every Br^- ion thus held, a K^+ ion is left in the solution. These potassium ions wander around in the neighborhood of the Br^- ion. Thus the final picture of part of a AgBr grain formed in the presence of an excess of KBr is as shown in the accompanying illustration. A silver bromide grain formed in this way is called a *bromide body*.

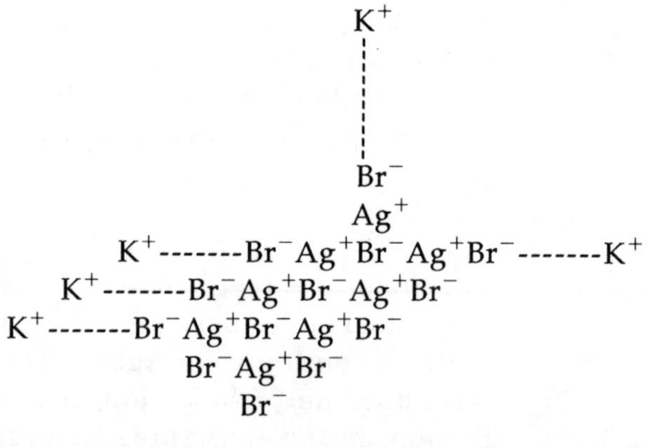

$$K^+$$
$$\vdots$$
$$Br^-$$
$$Ag^+$$
$$K^+ \text{------} Br^- Ag^+ Br^- Ag^+ Br^- \text{------} K^+$$
$$K^+ \text{------} Br^- Ag^+ Br^- Ag^+ Br^-$$
$$K^+ \text{------} Br^- Ag^+ Br^- Ag^+ Br^-$$
$$Br^- Ag^+ Br^-$$
$$Br^-$$

Varying Properties of Emulsions

Emulsions can vary in several properties, such as grain, speed, contrast, maximum density after development, and sensitivity to the different wavelengths of light. The effect of grain size on the speed of the emulsion is discussed at a previous point. An emulsion with small, uniform-size grains is required for lith-type (high-contrast) films. Continuous-tone films have a range of grain sizes. This range makes it possible to change contrast with development time. The contrast of lith film is very high, while that of contact film is lower, and that of continuous-tone film, the lowest.

The maximum density that can be produced, D_{max}, also varies with the type of film. With lith film, it is above 4.0; with contact film, usually more than 3.0; and with continuous-tone film, about 2.0–2.5.

Films also vary in their sensitivity to the different wavelengths of light. All silver halide films are sensitive to ultraviolet light, but it is possible to add certain dyes (sensitizers) that broaden the sensitivity to other wavelengths. Some emulsions are only sensitive to ultraviolet and blue light; orthchromatic emulsions are sensitive to ultraviolet, blue and green light; panchromatic emulsions are sensitive to ultraviolet and all colors of the visible spectrum.

Wedge spectrums showing the approximate color sensitivities of the human eye and blue-sensitive, orthochromatic, and panchromatic emulsions.

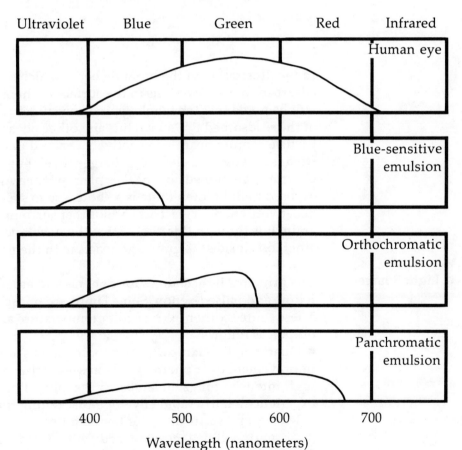

Exposure

The Reaction of the Emulsion to Light

If parts of an emulsion are exposed to light, the exposed portion (called the latent image) is acted upon by the developer much more readily than is the nonexposed portion. But no *visible* reaction occurs when an emulsion is exposed to light. The typical black-and-white portions of a negative do not appear until the emulsion has been placed in the developer bath for a certain length of time.

Exactly what happens when a AgBr grain is exposed to light is not known for certain, but a widely accepted theory holds that the action of light causes an electron to shift from an adsorbed Br^- on the surface of a AgBr grain to one of the Ag^+ ions in the interior of the grain. Since electrons are negatively charged, if a Br^- ion loses an electron, it becomes a bromine atom, $Br°$, and a Ag^+ ion, which gains the electron, becomes a silver atom, $Ag°$.

$$Br^- \longrightarrow Br° + 1e^-$$
$$Ag^+ + 1e^- \longrightarrow Ag°$$

In the illustration of the bromide body, which shows Br^- adsorbed to the silver ions in the surface of the AgBr grain, it will be noted that the whole grain is negatively charged because of these adsorbed Br^- ions. Thus any other negatively charged particle coming near this negatively charged grain is repelled from it because like electrical charges repel. But if the shift of electrons mentioned above takes place when a AgBr grain is exposed to light, then there is a "hole," so to speak, in the negatively charged electrical armor that surrounds the AgBr grain. It is through this "hole" that the developer gets to the other ions inside the grain and reacts with them.

Light Sources

The principal light sources for cameras and enlargers are quartz-iodine and pulsed-xenon. Some lamps are phosphor-coated. These sources differ in their color temperature and spectral output, as follows:

● **Quartz-iodine lamps.** Quartz-iodine lamps are an improvement over photoflood lamps—short-lived, high-intensity tungsten lamps. In use, photoflood lamps experience a fairly rapid envelope-blackening that reduces lamp efficiency and shifts the color temperature.

Quartz-iodine lamps are made with a clear or frosted fused-quartz envelope. The light is produced by a tungsten filament, but iodine compounds are added to retard the evaporation of the filament. As a result, the blackening of the envelope and color temperature change are eliminated, and lamp life is greatly extended.

General spectral data for various light sources.

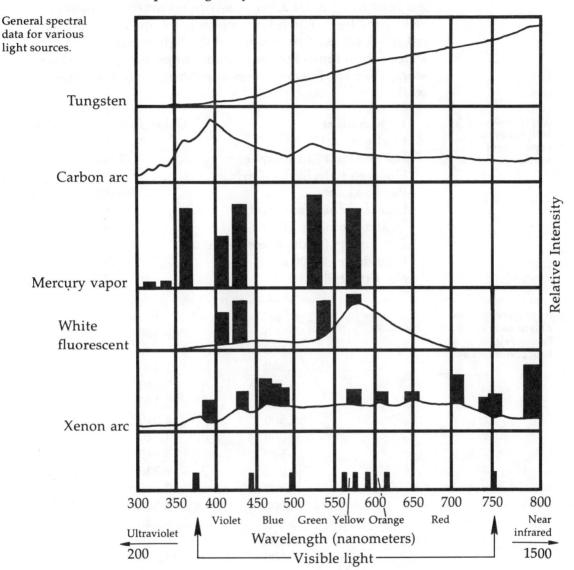

Different light sources vary as to their *color temperature*, which is commonly measured in "degrees Kelvin" (°K). (Degrees on the Kelvin scale are the same size as those on the Celsius scale, but the Kelvin scale starts at *absolute zero*, −273°C. See accompanying chart for comparison with Fahrenheit.) The color temperature refers to the spectral distribution emitted by a "perfect radiator" heated to the specified temperature. Black iron is an almost-perfect radiator. The higher the temperature, the bluer the light. At low temperatures red predominates.

The color temperature of daylight varies, but averages 6,500°K. In contrast, ordinary tungsten bulbs have a color temperature of about 2,300°K, which means their output is yellow-red light. The color temperature of quartz-iodine lamps is 3,200–3,400°K. This means that the light produced is quite warm, which limits the use of these lamps in color separation work. They are, however, very suitable for line and halftone work.

Approximate color temperature of various light sources.

Light Source	Color Temperature (°K)
Daylight	6,500
Fluorescent lights (daylight)	6,500
Fluorescent lights (cool white)	4,200
Pulsed xenon	6,000
Quartz-iodine (low level)	2,950
Quartz-iodine (high level)	3,400
Carbon arcs (white flame cored)	5,000
Incandescent (100 watt)	3,000
No. 1 photoflood	3,400

A comparison of the Kelvin and Fahrenheit temperature scales.

°K	°F
0	−460
500	440
1,000	1,340
1,500	2,240
2,000	3,140
2,500	4,040
3,000	4,940
3,500	5,840
4,000	6,740
4,500	7,640
5,000	8,540
5,500	9,440
6,000	10,340
6,500	11,240

● **Pulsed-xenon lamps.** Pulsed-xenon lamps are made of quartz tubing filled with xenon gas under low pressure. Xenon is one of the rare gases, which are found in air in a very small percentage. The light from pulsed-xenon lamps covers the entire spectral range of visible light, with a color temperature of about

5,600°K. In addition, these lamps have the advantage of instant start, constant color temperature, and a life of 300–1,000 hours. For these reasons, they are by far the best lamps for color separation work, either in cameras or enlargers.

- **Phosphor-coated lamps.** Green phosphors are used to coat one type of lamp; therefore the peak light output of the lamp is in the green region. For this reason, the lamp is suitable only for the illumination of line work and halftone prints. It produces only a small amount of heat, has low power consumption, and has a life of about 5,000 hours. The exposure time is approximately 15% longer than is required with four 12-inch (0.35-meter) pulsed-xenon lamps.

Processing

Development of the Image

The reaction that occurs when an exposed emulsion is placed in the developer bath is one of oxidation and reduction. The photographic developing agent, such as hydroquinone, is oxidized, and the silver ions that were exposed to light are reduced to metallic silver. The metallic silver is black and forms the black part of the negative or the positive. Remember, when a substance is oxidized it loses electrons, and when a substance is reduced it gains electrons. Thus we can write:

$$\text{Developing agent} \longrightarrow$$
$$\text{oxidized developing agent} \quad + \quad \text{electrons}$$

That is, when the developing agent is oxidized, it loses electrons. These electrons are available to reduce the silver ions which were exposed to light.

$$\text{Ag}^+ \text{ (exposed to light)} \quad + \quad 1e^- \longrightarrow \text{Ag}° \text{ (black)}$$

In order for silver ions to be reduced to black metallic silver, they must react with, or take on, electrons. But electrons are negatively charged and would be repelled from a negatively charged AgBr grain. Here is where the reaction, which occurs when light hits the AgBr grain, comes in. If the negative "armor" has been broken by the conversion of some of the Br^- ions to $Br°$, then the electrons from the developing agent can enter the AgBr grain at this point and proceed to reduce the silver ions to black metallic silver.

Thus the grains that were exposed to light react with the developer and are changed to black metallic silver. But the grains that were not exposed to light still have their negative armor and consequently resist reaction with the developer, at least for a time. Even such grains are eventually attacked by the developer, causing an overall graying, called *fogging*, of the negative.

Developing Agents

A photographic developing agent must be strong enough to reduce the silver halide grains that have been exposed to light, but not so strong that it will also reduce the unexposed grains. Most of the materials that meet these requirements are organic compounds that are derivatives of benzene. These derivatives include pyrogallol, hydroquinone, catechol, p-phenylene diamine, p-aminophenol, metol (or elon), amidol, and pyramidol. In general, these compounds contain two —OH groups, two —NH$_2$ (amino) groups, or one of each. These groups are attached to the benzene ring in either the ortho or para position. Some have other groups attached to the benzene ring in addition to the basic —OH or —NH$_2$ groups.

The two most common developing agents are hydroquinone and metol. The structure of hydroquinone is:

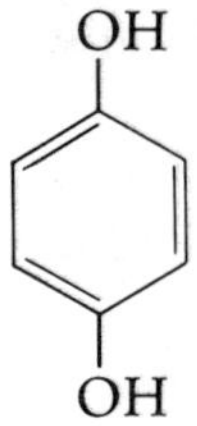

OH

OH

If one of the —OH groups is replaced with an —NH$_2$ group, the result is para-aminophenol, with the structure:

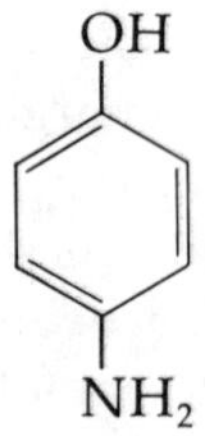

OH

NH$_2$

Para-aminophenol is a photographic developing agent. If one of the hydrogen atoms in the –NH$_2$ group is replaced with a methyl group, –CH$_3$, the result is the developer metol, with the structure:

$$OH$$

$$
\begin{array}{c}
\text{OH} \\
\hline
\\
\\
\text{N} \\
\text{H} \quad \text{CH}_3
\end{array}
$$

Ingredients in Common Developer Solutions

In general, a photographic developer solution contains the following ingredients:

- **One or more developing agents.** These are the basis of the developer solution. The other materials are added to aid the developing agent in some way.

- **Accelerator.** The developing agent is much more active in alkaline solution than in one that is neutral or acid. So the accelerator is an alkaline material. The bases commonly used are sodium hydroxide, $NaOH$; sodium carbonate, Na_2CO_3; and sodium tetraborate, $Na_2B_4O_7$ (borax). These accelerators also neutralize the acid that is formed during development, and thus they prevent the solution from becoming acid.

  Developers with sodium hydroxide have a pH of about 12.0 and are very active. Those with sodium carbonate have a pH of about 10.2 and are quite active. Those with borax have a pH of about 8.5 to 9.0 and have rather low activity and a long development time.

- **Preservative.** Sodium sulfite, Na_2SO_3, is usually used as the preservative. It reduces the effect of oxidation of the developing agent by the oxygen of the air and helps to keep the solution colorless during mixing and storing. It also enters into the chemical reactions of development.

- **Restrainer.** A small amount of potassium bromide, KBr, is often added to restrain the formation of fog. The bromide ions of the KBr attach themselves to the unexposed silver halide grains. These grains are so completely surrounded by bromide ions that it is very difficult for the developer to reach the silver ions and reduce them to metallic silver.

  A common all-purpose developer contains metol and hydroquinone (two developing agents), sodium carbonate (accelerator), sodium sulfite (preservative), and potassium bromide (restrainer). A low-contrast developer often uses borax as the alkali, instead of sodium carbonate, and contains no potassium bromide.

Infectious Developers

Two general types of developer are used in graphic arts photography. They are the infectious type and the noninfectious (continuous-tone) type.

Infectious developers are used for high-contrast halftones and line work exposed in the camera. They are also used to obtain the hardest dots in halftones produced by screening continuous-tone originals. With this type of developer, only hydroquinone is used for the developing agent.

The induction period is the time interval between immersion of the film in the developer and the time at which the image begins to appear. With infectious developers, there is a long induction period (perhaps half a minute); but when the image begins to appear, its density builds up rapidly. The final result is an image with very high contrast.

The various chemicals in infectious developers are divided into two parts (usually called A and B). How the chemicals are separated varies with the manufacturer. One method is to include the hydroquinone and the preservative in part A, and the alkali and potassium bromide in part B. When solutions A and B are mixed, they begin to react slowly with each other. With infectious developers, operators must be careful about the development time, the temperature of the solution, and the amount and kind of replenishment.

It is believed that hydroquinone molecules lose the two hydrogen atoms attached to the oxygen atoms and form ions with a -2 charge. These negatively charged ions are responsible for image development, but are strongly repelled by the bromide ions that are adsorbed to the silver halide grains. This condition makes the bromide ion concentration in the developer critical.

When the hydroquinone ions react with exposed AgBr, the AgBr is reduced to $Ag°$ (metallic black silver), and the hydroquinone is oxidized to semiquinone. The reaction is:

hydroquinone ion   semiquinone ion

Semiquinone is an even more active developing species than hydroquinone. As a result, reduction of silver halide continues, and in fact accelerates, as semiquinone is oxidized to quinone. The reaction is:

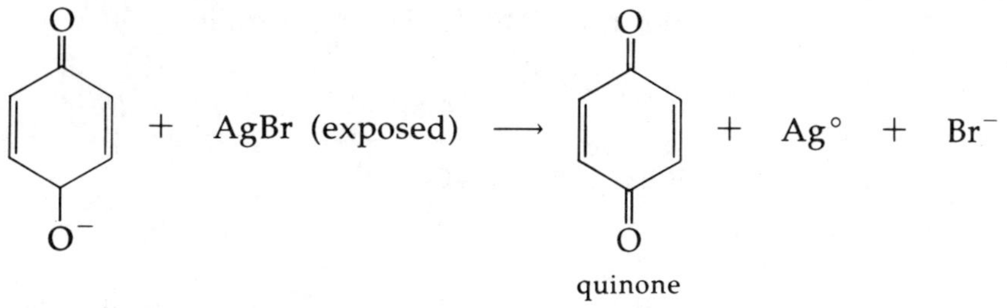

+   AgBr (exposed) $\longrightarrow$ + Ag° + Br⁻

quinone

The quinone can then react with more hydroquinone ions to form more semiquinone. This reaction is:

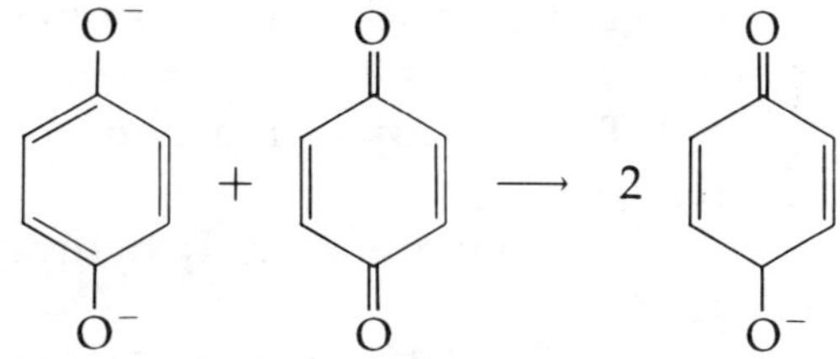

This is a chain reaction, which can be repeated many times. The extent of this reaction is limited only by the quantity of hydroquinone and reducible silver halide in a given location. The result is a rapid development rate, once past the induction period, and the production of images with high contrast.

Sodium sulfite reacts with quinone to form hydroquinone monosulfonate. Here is the reaction:

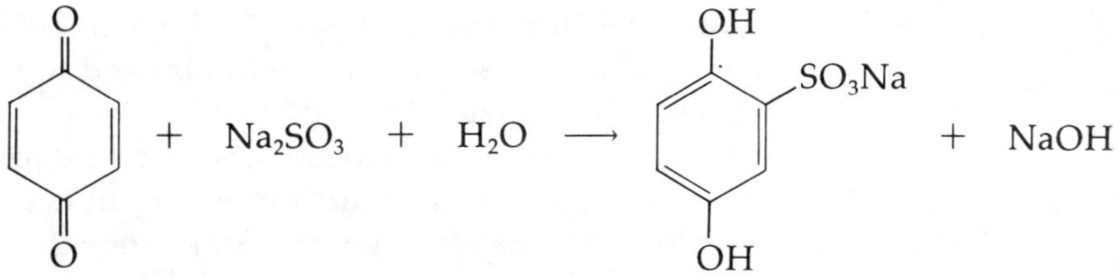

+ Na_2SO_3 + H_2O $\longrightarrow$ +   NaOH

To the extent that this reaction takes place, the chain reaction just described is partially stopped. The result is that the images have somewhat lower contrast. However, sulfite ions are needed in a developer to protect it from aerial oxidation.

Although a developer must contain some sulfite ions, it

should not contain too many. This requirement is often fulfilled by the use of a sulfite buffer to replace part or all of the sodium sulfite. The buffer most commonly used contains sodium formaldehyde bisulfite, SFB. In an alkaline solution, a small percentage of this compound dissociates to form sodium sulfite and formaldehyde. The reaction is:

$$
\text{NaOH} \;+\; \underset{\text{SFB}}{\text{H}-\overset{\displaystyle \text{OH}}{\underset{\displaystyle \text{H}}{\text{C}}}-\text{SO}_3^{\ -}\text{Na}^+} \;\longrightarrow\; \underset{\text{formaldehyde}}{\overset{\displaystyle \text{O}}{\underset{\text{H}\quad\text{H}}{\text{C}}}} \;+\; \text{Na}_2\text{SO}_3 \;+\; \text{H}_2\text{O}
$$

As the sodium sulfite is used up in the reactions given above, more of the SFB dissociates to provide more sodium sulfite. This dissociation characteristic is typical of materials that are used as buffers.

To summarize, infectious developers can be characterized as follows:

1. They contain only hydroquinone for the developing agent.

2. The developer has a low sulfite ion concentration.

3. A sulfite buffer is used to control the concentration of sulfite ions.

4. The developer is sensitive to bromide ion concentration and to pH.

Automatic Film Processing

Despite some problems, lith developers have functioned very satisfactorily for tray processing for many years. Their use in automatic film processors has been another matter and has led to problems of uneven development ("drag lines") and to difficulties in restoring the original developer concentration with a replenisher. Various methods for diminishing these problems have been devised.

As mentioned previously, the usual infectious-type developer has a long induction period. In machine processing, development begins when the film enters the developer and ends when it enters the fixer. During the last portion of this period, the film is out of the developer tank and is crossing over into the fix tank. While the film is making its crossover, exhausted developer has no chance to be replenished by fresh developer. The result is that development may be terminated prematurely, at a time when the rate of development is building to its maximum. If premature termination occurs, halftone images will have reduced contrast.

One system designed to improve this situation has a much shorter induction period, followed by a faster increase in development rate during the early part of the cycle and a much lower rate near the end of the cycle. Nearly full development is obtained while the film is passing through the developer solution, with less development occurring during the crossover. In addition, the film emulsions have been designed to hold more developer to aid in the completion of development during crossover.

It is reported that these changes have helped to minimize drag lines. Drag lines appear where areas of a high-development level are next to areas of a low-development level. With this system, the combination of characteristics of the film emulsion and the developer tend to minimize local developer exhaustion. As a consequence, drag lines are reduced. Furthermore, there is a higher development rate as the film moves down the processor rack and a slower development rate as it moves up—where drag lines are more apt to occur.

The four types of film usable with this system—lith, contact, duplicating, and phototypesetting—can all be intermixed without upsetting the balance of the developer.

A different approach in the handling of lith films with automatic film processors has resulted in a blending system.

The "blending" system for developer replenishment. *Courtesy of E.I. du Pont de Nemours & Company*

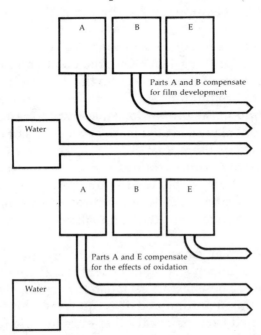

Parts A and B compensate for film development

Parts A and E compensate for the effects of oxidation

When films are processed, hydroquinone and sodium sulfite are consumed and bromides are produced, as the previously expressed equations indicate. The replenisher should contain sufficient hydroquinone and sodium sulfite to replace this loss, but should contain a lower percentage of a bromide compound than was in the initial developer in order to maintain the developer solution at its original composition.

When the processor is running but no films are being processed, the hydroquinone is being oxidized by exposure of the solution to the air. This reaction is similar to the reactions of image development in that quinone is produced but different in that no bromides are formed. Therefore, replenishment to take care of hydroquinone oxidation should be different. It should contain enough hydroquinone and sodium sulfite to replace the loss due to oxidation by the air, but should contain more of the bromide compound than when films are being processed. (You might think at first that it should contain no bromide, since none is involved in the oxidation reaction. But keep in mind that some of the developer solution leaves the tank when replenisher is added, so the replenisher must contain sufficient bromide to maintain a constant bromide concentration.)

There is always some loss of developer strength during shutdowns and over weekends. Loss of strength is nearly eliminated in the blending system by the addition of a special stabilizer.

Blender equipment has three containers, A, B, and E, attached. Each of these contains a concentrated solution with a special balance of developer ingredients. To replenish the developer for films developed, the blender pumps concentrate A, concentrate B, and water into the developing solution. These supply hydroquinone, sodium sulfite, and the bromide compound in the proportions necessary to restore the developer for the unbalance created by the processing of the films.

To compensate for oxidation by the air, the blender pumps concentrate A, concentrate E, and water into the developing solution. These supply hydroquinone, sodium sulfite, and the bromide compound in different proportions than before to restore the developer for the unbalance created by atmospheric oxidation.

As with any system, the amount of replenishment must vary with the number, size, and percent image coverage of the films processed. These factors establish the replenishment rate. Besides this, a minimum daily requirement of replenishment is determined from practical experience in a plant.

The blender is equipped with a timer. If, at the end of a 2-hour period, the amount of replenisher required for film processing is equal to, or exceeds, the established minimum, the timer merely resets for another 2-hour period. But if usage has been slow, or nonexistent, the blender automatically calculates and delivers the correct amount of the replenisher to compensate for oxidation. This compensation is made in such a way that the sum of the developer activity of the two replenishers remains the same for every 2-hour period.

The object of the blending system is to keep the concentration of all of the reacting chemicals as nearly as possible to the initial developer composition.

Noninfectious Developers

Noninfectious developers produce densities in proportion to exposure. They usually contain both metol and hydroquinone for developing agents, and they have a high concentration of sodium sulfite. Such developers are often referred to as "MQ" developers. They are quite stable and have a considerable latitude in development time and in the amount of replenishment required. Another advantage is longer life, since the rate of oxidation is lower with noninfectious than with infectious developers.

Noninfectious developers are used for the development of continuous-tone, contact, and duplicating films. If a scanner produces halftones directly with a laser beam, it is possible to develop the film with noninfectious developers, since the laser gives a "go–no go" type of exposure. It should be understood that a particular film can produce a different-shape curve when different chemistry is used for development, as illustrated in the accompanying diagram.

Relative density-producing characteristics of infectious and noninfectious developers as a function of time.

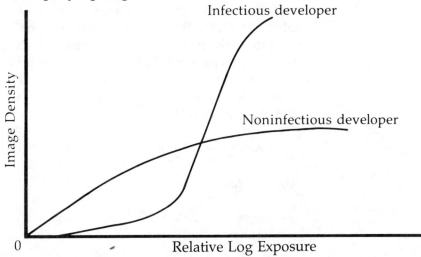

Rapid-Access Processing

The advent of automatic film processors has led to the development of variations in the formulas of developers designed for tray development. One of these variations is rapid-access processing. With a modification in developer formulation, it is possible to develop films in about 60–90 seconds by using a developer temperature of over 100°F (38°C).

The developer is a low-contrast continuous-tone type, containing hydroquinone and metol (MQ) for the developing agents, and using a special restrainer to hold down fogging of films at the high developer temperature.

The developer also has a high concentration of sodium sulfite. Because of the formulation of the developer solution and the high temperature, the induction period is very short, and a visible image begins to appear almost as soon as the film enters the developer solution.

Rapid-access processing works best if used with films that have a low fogging tendency. Even lith-type films can be developed by this process if they have a low fogging tendency. The process is used mostly for the development of contact films. It can be used for developing camera line work and also for developing halftones produced by the laser scanning of color separations.

Fixing of the Emulsion

The parts of the negative or positive that have not been reduced to black metallic silver during development still contain AgCl or AgBr. These compounds will gradually be reduced to metallic silver if the negative or positive is exposed to strong light. So it is necessary to remove them from the emulsion. This process is called *fixing*.

A chemical that will dissolve AgCl or AgBr is needed in the fixing bath, since these compounds are only very slightly soluble in water. Sodium thiosulfate ("hypo"), $Na_2S_2O_3$, is used to dissolve them. Ammonium thiosulfate, $(NH_4)_2S_2O_3$, is also used for this purpose. Either of these compounds forms a complex ion with silver ions, and the sodium or ammonium compound of this complex ion is soluble in water. The reaction of AgCl and $Na_2S_2O_3$ is:

$$AgCl + Na_2S_2O_3 \longrightarrow Na(AgS_2O_3)_2 + NaCl$$

Another reaction is:

$$AgBr + 2Na_2S_2O_3 \longrightarrow Na_3[Ag(S_2O_3)_2] + NaBr$$

Compounds like this are also soluble in water in accordance with the previously stated rule that practically all compounds with sodium or ammonium ions are soluble in water.

Purpose of Other Ingredients in a Fixing Bath

While sodium thiosulfate is the main ingredient in a fixing bath, the bath usually contains other chemicals such as acetic acid, sodium sulfite, potassium alum, and boric acid. Potassium alum has the formula $K_2SO_4 \cdot Al_2(SO_4)_3 \cdot 24H_2O$. It is the hardener in the fixing bath and prevents undue swelling of the gelatin of the emulsion. Potassium alum is not stable in neutral or alkaline solutions because of the precipitation of aluminum hydroxide. So the bath is kept acid with acetic acid. Since the fixing bath is acid, it neutralizes the alkalinity of the developer solution and stops development immediately.

When a solution of sodium thiosulfate is made acid, as with acetic acid, it begins to decompose, forming elementary sulfur as a finely divided white precipitate. The white precipitate forms when the hardener solution is added too rapidly to the sodium thiosulfate solution in the preparation of a fixing bath. If the fixing solution contains sodium sulfite, this chemical combines with the sulfur to form more sodium thiosulfate, as follows:

$$Na_2SO_3 \quad + \quad S \quad \longrightarrow \quad Na_2S_2O_3$$

Thus the sodium sulfite in the fixing bath stabilizes the solution and prevents formation of cloudy, milky sulfur.

The boric acid acts as a buffer to limit the change of pH of the fixing bath solution. It helps to prevent the precipitation of aluminum compounds that occurs when the pH changes too much.

Thus it is seen that each ingredient of a fixing bath serves a useful purpose. Of course it is possible to add more chemicals or to replace certain of the above-mentioned chemicals. For example, for processing in tropical regions or at elevated temperatures, the potassium alum may be replaced with potassium chromium sulfate, $K_2SO_4 \cdot Cr_2(SO_4)_3 \cdot 24H_2O$ (called chrome alum). Chrome alum is a more effective hardener than potassium alum. But chrome alum solutions lose their hardening action faster than do potassium alum solutions when the fixing bath is allowed to stand. Also, chrome alum has a greater tendency to form sludge than potassium alum has. Because of these difficulties, chrome alum is sometimes used in a separate hardening bath, preceding the fixing bath. Aluminum chloride, $AlCl_3$, is also used as a hardener.

Useful Life of a Fixing Bath

As more and more film or paper is fixed in a bath, more silver is added to the bath in the form of complex silver compounds. When the concentration of silver reaches a critical amount, some relatively insoluble compounds are formed that cannot be removed from the emulsion during the washing process. When prints are being fixed, the maximum concentration of silver is about 0.27 ounces per gallon (2 grams per liter) of fixing bath. In the case of films, this maximum is about 0.8 oz./gal. (6 g/L)— although the maximum concentration can be twice this amount when ammonium thiosulfate is used instead of sodium thiosulfate.

A typical fresh fixing bath has a pH of about 4.1. As films or prints are transferred to it from the developer solution, they carry some of the alkaline developer with them. This transfer of developer gradually raises the pH of the fixing bath. When the pH rises to about 5.5, the hardener in the bath is less effective. The bath should then be discarded or the pH lowered by the addition of more acetic acid. The rise in the pH of the fixing bath is largely prevented if an acid stop bath is used before the films or prints reach the fixing bath.

Reclaiming of Silver from Fixing Baths

There are several reasons for reclaiming the silver from fixing baths. Some profit can be obtained by selling the recovered silver. Since silver is in short supply, its conservation is important. Furthermore, a silver recovery process reduces the amount of effluents going into the sewer.

Today, the electrolytic method of silver recovery is the one most widely used. With this method the fixing bath is transferred to the silver recovery unit. The unit contains two electrodes: a carbon anode and a stainless steel cathode. A low-voltage direct current is passed between them. The result is a deposit of metallic silver on the cathode. The equation for the reaction is:

$$Ag^+ \; + \; e^- \; \longrightarrow \; Ag^\circ$$

The external source of current pumps electrons (e^-) to the cathode, and these electrons reduce silver ions to metallic silver. With this method, the treated fixer can continue to be used.

A recommended maximum level of silver in a fixing bath is 0.6 troy ounce per gallon (5 grams per liter). The amount present can be checked with silver-estimating test papers that are available from most graphic arts suppliers.

Typical electrolytic
silver recovery unit.
*Courtesy of The
X-Rite Company*

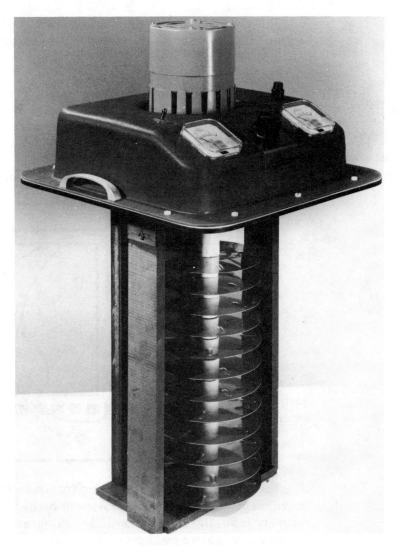

One ampere-hour of plating current will deposit 0.125 troy ounce (4 grams) of silver, which can usually be sold by a plant at 80% of its market value. If a recirculation system is employed, the makeup for the fixing bath can consist of 50% desilvered solution and 50% fresh solution.

Metallic replacement is another method used for silver recovery. Cartridges are supplied that usually are filled with steel wool. The spent fixing bath is pumped into the cartridge, where it must remain long enough for the chemical reaction to take place. The ionic equation for this reaction is:

$$2Ag^+ + Fe^\circ \longrightarrow 2Ag^\circ + Fe^{++}$$

This is an oxidation-reduction reaction. Two silver ions each pick up one electron from one metallic iron atom Fe°. This reaction reduces the silver ions to metallic silver, and oxidizes the iron to ferrous ion.

Cutaway of a metallic-replacement silver recovery unit. *Courtesy of Eastman Kodak Company*

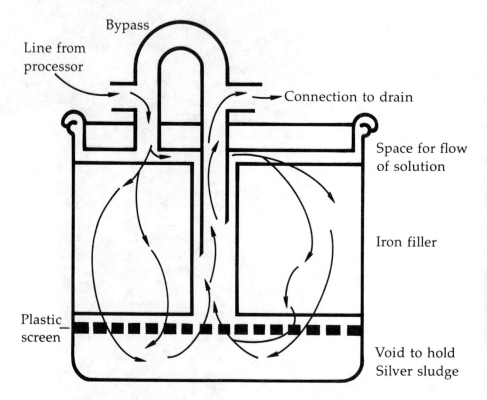

Bypass

Line from processor

Connection to drain

Space for flow of solution

Iron filler

Plastic screen

Void to hold Silver sludge

The amount of silver recovered from a cartridge depends on the concentration of silver in the spent bath. The average recovery is 80–100 troy ounces (2.5–3 kilograms). The effluent from a cartridge can be checked with silver-estimating test papers. When the amount of silver in the effluent begins to increase, it is time to replace the cartridge. The cartridge is then shipped to the supplier, who separates the silver and pays the company for the amount recovered.

Washing of Negatives and Positives

After the negative or positive is fixed, the gelatin emulsion layer contains the fixing bath chemicals in solution dispersed throughout the gelatin. If the sodium thiosulfate (hypo) present in this solution is not removed completely from the gelatin emulsion layer, it can later react with the silver in the emulsion to form yellowish-brown silver sulfide. The reaction is:

$$Na_2S_2O_3 \ + \ 2Ag° \ \longrightarrow \ Ag_2S \ + \ Na_2SO_3$$

If complex silver salts are left in the emulsion layer along with sodium thiosulfate, a reaction can occur which will also form silver sulfide. This causes a discoloration of the film over the entire surface and not in the image areas only.

Because of these possibilities, these materials must be removed from the emulsion layer as completely as possible. This removal is accomplished by washing the films in water. If the films are placed in a tray of water, the water dissolves some of the hypo from the emulsion. But soon an equilibrium is reached between the hypo in the water and the hypo that remains in the emulsion. When this occurs, no more hypo will come out of the gelatin. The films must then be transferred to a tray of fresh water. This process must be repeated a number of times in order to get most of the hypo out of the emulsion layer.

The process is much more efficient if the films are washed in running water. The flow of water should be adjusted to give a complete change of the water in the tray once every 5 minutes. In this way, the emulsion layer is always in contact with a very weak hypo solution, and the hypo in the emulsion moves out of it continuously into the water.

The method by which the water enters and leaves the washing tank also affects the efficiency of the washing process. Best results are obtained when the water enters at the bottom of the tray and leaves over the top of the tray.

Water entering at bottom of wash tray.

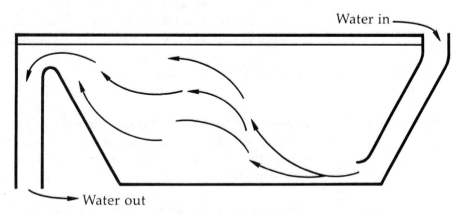

Water in

Water out

The effect of the temperature of the water on the rate of hypo removal was controversial for some time. Recent carefully controlled tests have proved that a moderately warm wash water helps the removal of the hypo. With film material, the total time required to remove all of the hypo is decreased about 30% by raising the temperature of the wash water from 40 to 80°F (5 to 27°C).

The pH of the water used to wash film material also has some bearing on the rate of removal of hypo from the emulsion. The gelatin in the emulsion adsorbs thiosulfate ions, $S_2O_3^{--}$ from the fixing bath if its pH is below 4.9. Therefore, a considerably longer time in the wash water is required to remove the hypo from the emulsion than when the pH of the fixing bath is higher than 4.9, under which condition thiosulfate ions would not be adsorbed onto the gelatin. A fixing bath of the acid hardening type usually has a pH below 4.9. But adding a little ammonia to the wash water makes it sufficiently alkaline to bring the pH of the film emulsion quickly to a value above 4.9.

During World War II, it was found that both films and prints could be washed free of hypo more rapidly in sea water than in ordinary tap water. In fact, films can be washed hypo-free in sea water in about one-third of the time required with tap water. The exact reason for this fact is not known, but it is certainly connected with the salts dissolved in sea water. Other salts have been found to be nearly as effective as sea water, and these are called "washing aids."

Photographic Reducers

Reducers are solutions that reduce the density of the black silver deposit by oxidizing some of the metallic silver to form a soluble silver salt. In some cases the silver salt is insoluble in water, and the solution must contain another chemical that converts the silver salt into a soluble silver compound.

A mixture of ferric ammonium sulfate and sulfuric acid is an example of a reducer. The reaction is as follows:

$$2FeNH_4(SO_4)_2 \quad + \quad 2Ag° \longrightarrow$$
$$Ag_2SO_4 \quad + \quad 2FeSO_4 \quad + \quad (NH_4)_2SO_4$$

The silver sulfate formed is soluble enough to be washed away.

Farmer's reducer is a common one. It is a mixture of potassium ferricyanide and sodium thiosulfate. First the potassium ferricyanide reacts with the metallic silver as follows:

$$4K_3Fe(CN)_6 \quad + \quad 4Ag \longrightarrow Ag_4Fe(CN)_6 \quad + \quad 3K_4Fe(CN)_6$$

Thus, some of the silver on the plate or film is oxidized to form silver ferrocyanide. At the same time, the iron in the ferricyanide ion (iron with a charge of $+3$) is reduced to form ferrocyanide ions (iron with a charge of $+2$). Then the sodium thiosulfate reacts with the insoluble silver ferrocyanide, converting it into soluble complex ions, such as $AgS_2O_3^{-}$ and

$Ag(S_2O_3)_2^{---}$. Farmer's reducer is used to dot-etch positives or negatives and to clear foggy negatives.

Another reducer consists of a mixture of sulfuric acid with ceric sulfate or ceric bisulfate. In the presence of acid, the ceric ions of the ceric sulfate can react with black, metallic silver. The silver is oxidized to silver ions, and the ceric ions are reduced to cerous ions. The ionic equation for the reaction is:

$$Ce^{+++} + Ag^\circ \longrightarrow Ag^+ + Ce^{++}$$

Photographic Intensifiers

The purpose of a photographic *intensifier* is to increase the blackness of the silver deposit. Intensifiers may be classified as physical or chemical. A *physical intensifier* deposits an additional amount of silver or mercury on the developed silver grains of the emulsion. One such intensifier contains silver nitrate, pyrogallol, and citric acid. Another contains a mercury salt, metol, and citric acid. Intensification produced in this way is usually permanent.

In chemical intensification the image is first bleached and then redarkened to give an intensified image. There are a number of ways of doing this: a couple of examples are given here. A common bleach is a mixture of mercuric chloride, $HgCl_2$, and potassium bromide, KBr. The mercuric chloride bleaches the black metallic silver by oxidizing it to white, insoluble AgCl. At the same time the mercuric chloride is reduced to white, insoluble mercurous chloride, Hg_2Cl_2. The reaction is:

$$2HgCl_2 + 2Ag \longrightarrow 2AgCl + Hg_2Cl_2$$

The image areas are now covered with an insoluble silver salt chemically equivalent to the amount of black silver in the image areas before the bleach was applied. In addition, these areas now contain an insoluble mercury salt. It is easy to see that, if both salts can be reduced to the metallic state, the areas will be blacker than they were before. There will be black, finely divided mercury in addition to the black silver.

The reduction of the insoluble chlorides to the metallic state can be accomplished with a photographic developer solution, a sodium sulfite solution, or an ammonium hydroxide solution. The developer acts the same as it does in the development of an emulsion that has been exposed to light. The reaction of sodium sulfite with silver chloride is as follows:

$$2AgCl + Na_2SO_3 + HOH \longrightarrow$$
$$2Ag + 2NaCl + H_2SO_4$$

A similar reaction occurs which reduces the mercurous chloride to black, metallic mercury. If an ammonium hydroxide (ammonia) solution is used, only the mercury is converted to the metallic state, while the insoluble AgCl is converted into a soluble salt, which washes off the plate. The reactions are:

$$Hg_2Cl_2 \ + \ 2NH_3 \ \longrightarrow \ HgNH_2Cl \ + \ Hg \ + \ NH_4Cl$$
$$\text{(black)}$$

$$AgCl \ + \ 2NH_3 \ \longrightarrow \ Ag(NH_3)_2Cl \ \ \text{(a soluble salt)}$$

This produces intensification only because the metallic mercury is blacker than the original silver deposit on the plate.

Disposal of Photographic-Processing Solutions

The improvement in the quality of effluents to sewer systems is receiving increased attention from regulatory agencies. It is easy to remove one ingredient, namely dissolved silver, by the use of a silver recovery system. However, this still leaves a considerable number of chemicals, such as those in developers, hardeners, and fixing baths.

None of these substances is toxic, but most are *biodegradable:* they are gradually consumed by bacteria present in water. In this process, oxygen dissolved in the water is involved in the chemical reactions that take place. If too many biodegradable materials enter a stream or lake, so much oxygen may be consumed that not enough remains to support the life of fish.

The amount of biodegradable material in an effluent can be measured by the biochemical oxygen demand (BOD). Regulatory agencies make such BOD readings.

Industrial plants that have a small amount of photographic-processing wastes can combine them in a holding tank and then trickle them into the sewer system. A small or medium-size plant can eliminate up to 95% of the BOD value of photographic waste solutions by installing a waste treatment unit based on the *activated sludge* principle. Packaged units can be purchased, or a plant can make its own. Such a system employs a large steel drum with intake and exit pipes and a perforated pipe leading to the bottom of the drum. Compressed air is forced through the perforations and bubbles through the solution. In this way, the oxygen of the air reduces the BOD value of the solution. In the process, a sludge forms on the surface, giving the name "activated sludge system" to this treatment.

Special Silver Halide Films

Duplicating Films

With conventional films and papers, a negative is produced from a positive, or vice versa. With contact and slow-projection-speed duplicating films, a positive is produced from a positive, or a negative from a negative, by exposure with white light.

These duplicating films are chemically "fogged" during manufacture. After exposure, they are developed with an infectious-type developer. The *unexposed* areas develop to D_{max}; that is, they become black. But the exposing light defogs the emulsion, so the *exposed* areas develop out clear (without metallic silver). The result is a duplicate of the film through which the exposure is made.

The original duplicating films were very slow and required exposure with quartz-iodine lamps or other powerful light sources. Newer duplicating films have a much faster emulsion speed and can be exposed with a point light source or even in a process camera.

Diffusion Transfer Film for Direct-Screen Color Separations

The mechanism involved in the preparation of diffusion transfer lithographic plates is explained in Chapter 8, "Lithographic Plates—Positive-Working." A diffusion transfer system has also been developed for panchromatic film.

Two different films are needed. The light from a colored original passes through a contact screen and exposes the panchromatic negative film. This film has a considerably faster speed than regular pan films, making possible reduction in the amount of exposure.

In the processing step, the exposed negative film and a sheet of special positive film are passed simultaneously through a diffusion transfer processor. The positive film has a nucleated coating on both sides, applied to a polyester base. This film is not light-sensitive.

The developer reduces the light-exposed areas of the negative film to metallic silver. Then the two films are tightly mated, and the hypo in the developer causes the unexposed silver compound in the nonexposed areas of the negative film to diffuse to the surface of the positive film. On this surface, the nucleated coating reduces the silver to metallic silver, creating a high-contrast positive halftone on the film. Because of the developing method, there is no problem with adjacency effects. The processing time is about two minutes.

Silverless Films

With the cost of silver steadily increasing, many attempts have been made to replace silver-based photography with other imaging systems. Diazo films have been in use for many years. There are also vesicular films and, more recently, photopolymer and electrostatic films.

Vesicular Films

A type of vesicular (honeycomb-like) film used in graphic arts consists of a polyester base coated with a thermoplastic resin that is a copolymer of vinylidene chloride, $CH_2\!\!=\!\!CCl_2$, and acrylonitrile, $CH_2\!\!=\!\!CH\!\!-\!\!C\!\!\equiv\!\!N$. This resin is mostly amorphous (noncrystalline), but also contains minute crystals. Other coating constituents include a light-sensitive diazonium salt, $R\!\!-\!\!N\!\!=\!\!N$, and a polymer with a catalyst to facilitate cross-linking in the later heating step.

Upon exposure to ultraviolet light, the diazonium salt decomposes and liberates nitrogen gas and other materials, creating an internal pressure in the thermoplastic resin. Thus a latent image is formed.

To develop the latent image, the film is heated to about 250°F (120°C) for a second or less. The pressure of the nitrogen gas causes the amorphous resin strands to be pushed together to form a vesicular structure. At the same time, the minute crystals melt and then recrystallize on the walls of the vesicles (cells). The polymer, aided by the catalyst and heat, cross-links to give additional mechanical support.

The image, produced in this way on a vesicular film, depends mostly on the scattering of the incident light, rather than its being absorbed as with silver emulsions. Strong light-scattering is obtained because the crystalline walls of the vesicles have a different index of refraction than that of the amorphous parts of the resin.

The unexposed areas of a vesicular film remain light-sensitive, even after heat processing. Therefore it is possible to expose another image or several other images on the film. Each additional exposure is followed by heat treatment.

After the final imaging exposure and heat development, the film is fixed by giving it an overall exposure to ultraviolet light—not followed with a heat treatment. The ultraviolet exposure causes the remaining diazonium salt to be decomposed; the resulting nitrogen gas diffuses out of the coating over a period of several hours. (Nitrogen also diffuses out slowly after image-forming exposures, but this is no problem if the heat treatment follows soon after the exposure.)

It is also possible to produce a positive image from a positive with a vesicular film. Exposure through a positive causes nitrogen gas to be liberated in the non-image areas. The film is left long enough for all of this gas to diffuse out and is then given an overall exposure to ultraviolet light, which is followed by heat treatment. The result is a positive image on the vesicular film.

Photopolymer Film for Contact Printing

Another nonsilver film consists of a dimensionally stable base coated with a photopolymer containing carbon black as the opaque replacement for silver. Exposure time with a 1,000-watt, high-pressure mercury-vapor lamp is about 10 seconds. Such an exposure causes the photopolymer to harden in the light-exposed areas. The film is then processed dry-to-dry in 20 seconds in an automatic processor using a weak alkaline solution. This processing removes the coating from the unexposed areas.

The contact films produced in this way are characterized by sharp rendition of halftone dots and fine lines. The system is nonpolluting, since neither the films, the processing solution, nor the processing effluent contain any harmful ingredients. The weak alkaline solution is neutralized before disposal.

Electrostatic Film

The speed of most silverless films is much lower than that of silver emulsions. But some electrostatic films have speeds comparable with silver films, and have high resolution as well. One such film consists of a 0.004-inch (0.025-mm) polyester base on which millions of tiny hexagonal crystals of cadmium sulfide, CdS, forming a very thin layer, are grown in a vacuum. These crystals are semiconductors.

The film is not light-sensitive until it is given an electrostatic charge. Exposure can be made by contact or projection. The charge is removed by the light on the exposed areas, but remains on the rest of the film. These areas are then toned with a liquid toner, and the toner is fixed onto the film.

Since the cadmium sulfide layer is not removed, it is possible to recharge the film, expose it to a second image, and apply and fix the toner again. If an error is made in an exposure, the toner can be removed before fixing, making the film reusable.

6 Lithographic Plates — Introduction

The basic principles of chemistry, which are dealt with in previous portions of this book, are here directed to the first in a series of specific graphic arts areas of application. Chemistry is central to the subject of lithographic plates. Applications to other graphic arts areas are treated in subsequent chapters.

A lithographic plate is planographic: the image areas are neither above nor below the non-image areas. In making a lithographic plate, the object is to make the image areas ink-receptive and the non-image areas water-receptive. This condition is brought about by chemical changes on the surface of the plate. When a properly made plate is run on the press, the water rollers keep the non-image areas of the plate moist so that these areas do not accept ink. The ink rollers then transfer ink only to the image areas.

Comparison of printing surfaces.

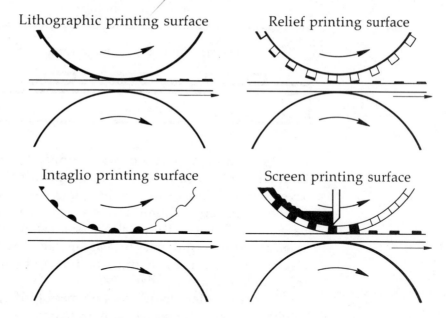

Lithographic printing surface

Relief printing surface

Intaglio printing surface

Screen printing surface

Lithographic plates can be exposed either through a negative or a positive, depending on the type of plate. In the early days of lithography, grained metal plates were coated with a bichromated albumin solution, dried, and exposed through a negative. This process is now obsolete.

The deep-etch platemaking process uses a coating of dichromated gum arabic that is exposed through a positive. This method is still in use. It is explained in a later chapter.

Cross sections of various lithographic printing plates.

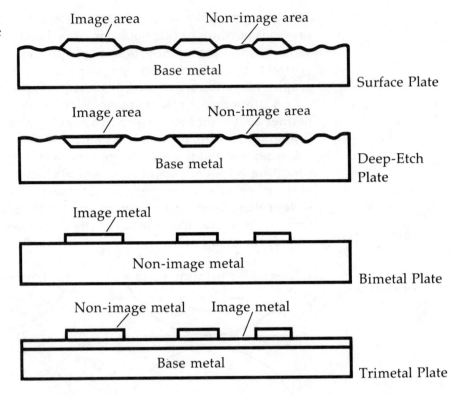

Image area   Non-image area

Base metal

Surface Plate

Image area   Non-image area

Base metal

Deep-Etch Plate

Image metal

Non-image metal

Bimetal Plate

Non-image metal   Image metal

Base metal

Trimetal Plate

As the lithographic process continued to gain popularity, both for commercial work and for the printing of newspapers, several other methods for making plates were developed. These methods use paper, aluminum, or anodized aluminum for the base material. The multimetal plates use stainless steel, mild steel, aluminum, and brass for base metals. The base metal is electroplated with copper or chromium, or both, depending on the type of multimetal plate.

It is convenient to divide the types of lithographic plates into those that are exposed through negatives (negative-working) and those exposed through positives (positive-working). The negative-working plates include:

1. Additive diazo presensitized
2. Subtractive diazo presensitized
3. Photopolymer presensitized
4. Wipe-on
5. Dry
6. Multimetal
7. Projection speed

The positive-working plates include:

1. Copperized-aluminum deep-etch
2. Presensitized
3. Diffusion transfer
4. Multimetal
5. Electrostatic
6. Projection speed
7. Laser-exposed

Many of these plates have certain considerations in common: choice of base materials, sensitivity of light-sensitive coatings to various wavelengths of light, exposure to light, light sources for exposure, use of a sensitivity guide to check exposures, dark reaction of coatings, and making non-image areas water-receptive. These topics are discussed in this chapter.

The Plate Base

A tremendous number of small lithographic plates use paper as a base. For larger plates, aluminum or anodized aluminum is now used almost exclusively except with some of the multimetal plates.

There are several reasons why aluminum is a good lithographic plate material. It is reasonable in cost, available in fairly uniform thicknesses, and strong enough for the purpose. Since it does not stretch when mounted on the press, maintaining good register is easy. Aluminum is lightweight, weighing only about 38% as much as zinc. Chemically, it does not corrode easily, and the nonprinting areas are easily made water-receptive.

The two types of aluminum used most commonly for lithographic plates are No. 1100, which is 99% aluminum, and No. 3003, which contains 1% to 1.5% manganese and about 1.8% of a combination of other metals. Generally, No. 1100 aluminum is used when plates are to be grained mechanically, and No. 3003 aluminum is used when chemical or electrochemical means are employed to create the desired texture.

Anodized Aluminum

Many of the presensitized and wipe-on aluminum plates are now anodized. Anodized aluminum has an excellent surface for litho plates, providing ceramic qualities that make it behave much like the old lithographic stone. It is hard and scratch-resistant, characteristics that add greatly to the plate's press life. On the original Mohs' scale for relative hardness, with numbers varying from 1 (soft talc) to 10 (diamond), anodized aluminum rates between 8 and 9.

Anodizing does not change the "hills and valleys" of a plate surface significantly, so plates must be chemically or mechanically grained before they are anodized.

To anodize an aluminum plate, it is made the anode (positive pole) of a cell that commonly contains sulfuric acid, although other chemicals can be used. Usually a direct current is passed through this cell, coating the surface of the plate with aluminum oxide. The thickness of the oxide coating formed depends on the amount of current used and the length of time it is applied. The anodized film thickness can vary from 0.0001 to 0.0012 inch (0.0025 to 0.030 millimeter). It is claimed that plates with a heavier film will run longer on the press, even in the case of the long-run photopolymer plates.

The anodized coating of litho plates is porous, consisting of millions of very tiny hexagonal-shaped cells. In the center of each is a star-shaped "pore" or "well." These cells are so small that they can be seen only with an electron microscope.

These tiny cells differ in size, depending upon the voltage used in anodizing. As the voltage increases (in a range from 5.5 volts to 18 volts), the cell sizes increase. And the larger the cell size, the harder and more wear-resistant is the film.

After anodizing, plates are treated to close the cell pores a certain amount depending on the end-use of the plate. This process is often called "sealing." One method is to immerse the plate in boiling water. A solution of a silicate compound is used for plates that are later to be coated with a light-sensitive diazo material.

Anodized aluminum is not of itself water-receptive. However, it is easy to make it so where desired (in the nonprinting areas) by treatment with an acidified solution of gum arabic. The aluminum oxide which forms the anodized film is quite acid-resistant, but it can be attacked by alkalies.

Graining of Plates

The term "graining" means the altering of the surface of a plate so that it has a matte finish, which consists of many thousands of tiny "hills" and "valleys." This process adds to the plate's total surface area. The area after graining is probably somewhere between two and four times the area of a smooth plate. Graining can be done chemically, or it can be done mechanically with either ball- or brush-graining techniques.

Some Reasons for Graining

Many presensitized litho plates and certain multimetal plates are being run satisfactorily with practically no grain on them. Nevertheless, there are some reasons for the graining of plates.

Corase-grained
aluminum.

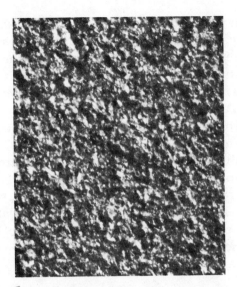

Grained plates are said to "hold water" better on the press.
Water collects in all of the little valleys of the grain, allowing
the plate to hold more water without being flooded. Unless an
ungrained plate is thoroughly cleaned, water will collect on it in
drops instead of as a complete film. A grained plate, on the other
hand, is wet quite easily with water over its entire surface.

The grain acts as a reservoir for water, preventing the plate
from drying as quickly or flooding as easily as an ungrained
plate. The grain also helps to hold the image on a plate and to
hold the developing ink on the image areas.

**Mechanical
Graining**

Litho plates are either ball-grained or brush–grained.
Ball-graining involves the rotation of steel balls over the surface
of plates that are laid on the bed of the graining machine. Water
and then silica sand, SiO_2, are added. The sand, acting as an
abrasive, is responsible for the graining. But to accomplish it
requires some pressure, which the steel balls contribute.

Various chemicals, such as sodium metasilicate (Na_2SiO_3),
and wetting agents are also added to the water used in ball-
graining. These materials emulsify any grease on the plates and
help to keep the graining "mud" suspended in the water.

The type of grain produced by ball-graining depends on the
size and therefore the weight of the steel balls, the rotational
speed of the grainer, the size and amount of sand particles, and
the total time of graining.

The brush-graining of litho plates has advanced rapidly
since it was introduced by GATF (then LTF) in 1956. Smooth
aluminum plates are fed into a brush-graining machine. They

are wet with water, then sprinkled with silica sand. Next, they move slowly under rotating, oscillating brushes. In this method, the sand is responsible for the graining, and the rotating brushes act as a substitute for steel balls. As plates continue to move through the machine, they are rinsed to remove the sand, treated with a water solution of a silicate compound, and dried with heat. The process is automatic; plates come out ready to be packed for shipment.

Generally, plates are ball-grained if they are to be used to make copperized-aluminum deep-etch plates. The percentage of plates that are ball-grained has been dropping, because fewer copperized-aluminum plates are being used. Plates for the wipe-on process are usually brush-grained. If plates are to be anodized, they are either brush-grained or chemically grained before they are anodized.

Light-Sensitive Coatings

For a lithographic plate to be made photographically, the base material must be coated with something that is sensitive to light. What these coatings are depends on the type of plate; the variety of plates available makes it difficult to generalize. With the diffusion transfer and electrostatic processes, there is no light-sensitive coating on the base material, even though light is involved otherwise in the creation of images.

Sensitivity of Coatings to Light of Different Wavelengths

There are several forms of energy that travel through space in the form of electromagnetic waves. They differ in their wavelengths.

Most light sources used in the graphic arts consist of visible and ultraviolet light of many wavelengths.

The various coatings used on lithographic plates have a peak sensitivity over a narrow range of wavelengths; the sensitivity drops off more or less rapidly at higher and lower wavelengths. The peak sensitivity varies somewhat from one coating to another, but in general is in the region between 365 and 436 nanometers. This region extends from the ultraviolet area into the deep blue area of visible light.

Most lithographic plates are insensitive to yellow, green, and red light. In other words, a considerable amount of the light employed to expose plates is wasted. Coatings are sensitive to lower wavelengths in the ultraviolet region, but these wavelengths are absorbed by the film base and the glass of the vacuum frame. A polyester film base and the plate glass of the vacuum frame absorb most of the ultraviolet radiation below 330 nanometers.

For an effect to occur when a plate is exposed to light, the light must be absorbed into the coating. While light consists of waves of different wavelengths, it can also be considered to consist of bundles of energy, called *photons*. In the case of litho plates, the amount of change in the coating is related to the number of photons that are absorbed.

The effect of exposure to light on plate coatings follows an S-shaped curve, similar to that for photographic films. For the first few seconds of exposure (the "threshold" time, representing inertia), there is no measurable effect. Then the effect increases slowly in the portion of the curve called the "toe." Next, there is a rapid increase in almost a straight line. On this portion of the curve, the effect produced in the coating is proportional to the number of photons of light absorbed. The proportionality is represented by the slope—the steepness—of the straight line. Finally, the effect levels off; very little further change occurs with increasing exposure. This part is called the "shoulder" of the curve. (See diagram.)

Effect of light exposure on a plate coating.

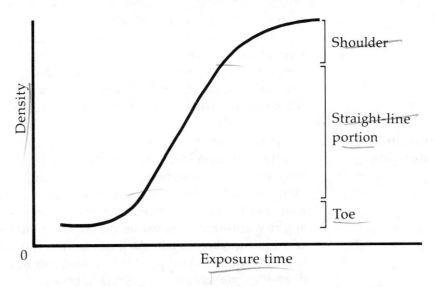

Dark Reaction   The effect produced on light-sensitive plate coatings by light will also occur to a much less extent when plates are stored in the dark. This effect is called *dark reaction*. It has the effect of an overall pre-exposure. For this reason, plate coatings that have undergone some dark reaction can be exposed in a somewhat shorter length of time. Referring to the diagram, if the effect due to dark reaction has nearly passed the toe of the curve, then exposure to light will begin on the straight-line portion. As a result, the plate speed will be faster.

It must be kept in mind that dark reaction occurs over the entire area of a plate coating. If this fogging effect proceeds far enough, a negative-working plate will not develop completely and will scum on the press, while a positive-working presensitized plate will show a loss of highlight dots.

Litho coatings vary widely in their resistance to dark reaction. With modern plates, the dichromated-gum arabic coating on copperized-aluminum deep-etch plates is most subject to dark reaction. Plates must be processed within a period of a few hours to a few days, depending on the temperature and relative humidity of the air. Presensitized plates are much better. If proper precautions are taken, they can be stored for at least a year. With storage of several months, a small amount of dark reaction may occur, but not enough to prevent making good plates.

It must be kept in mind that, with some coatings, dark reactions increase at high relative humidity. It increases with all coatings, including those on presensitized plates, as the temperature goes up. Platemakers should store presensitized plates in a place as cool and dry as possible.

The opposite is true as the temperature goes down. It was found years ago in the GATF research laboratory that plates with deep-etch coatings could be stored in a refrigerator for at least eight weeks and still make good plates. Apparently a temperature of about 41°F (5°C) greatly retards dark reaction.

Continuing Reaction

It was discovered in research work at GATF that the effect produced in deep-etch plate coatings by light continues for some time after the exposure has ended. It gradually drops to zero in about one hour. This has been termed *continuing reaction*. The first, middle, and last shots on a photocomposed plate may have slightly different tone values due to the combined effect of continuing reaction and dark reaction. It has been suggested that this tone variation on photocomposed copperized-aluminum deep-etch plates can be minimized by allowing a coating to age for one hour before making the first shot, then allowing it to stand in the dark for an hour after the final shot, before starting to develop the plate.

There is a distinct difference between continuing reaction and dark reaction. Continuing reaction occurs only in the areas exposed to light, and it becomes slower and slower after the exposure ends. Dark reaction occurs on all areas of a plate and continues indefinitely, with a speed that depends partly on the temperature and relative humidity of the air.

Safe Lights   It has been mentioned that most lithographic plate coatings are insensitive to yellow, green, and red wavelengths of light. This insensitivity makes it safe to use a red, orange, or yellow light in the platemaking room. Yellow fluorescent lamps are satisfactory.

For best results, daylight should be avoided in the platemaking room. Daylight has a considerable content of the ultraviolet and near-ultraviolet wavelengths to which plate coatings are sensitive.

Reciprocity Law   The intensity of a light source is measured in *lumens*. The reciprocity law states that:

$$E = I \times T$$

where E is the amount of exposure effect on a coating, I is the intensity of light, in lumens, at the surface of the coating, and T is the exposure time. As long as the reciprocity law holds, the effect on a coating will be the same if the product of light intensity and time remains the same. For example, if a good exposure is obtained in 2 minutes with a light intensity of 100 lumens at the surface of the plate, then exactly the same exposure should be obtained in 4 minutes with a light intensity of 50 lumens.

This law is valid as long as the light intensity is not varied too much. But if the intensity is cut to 5 lumens, for instance, and an exposure made for 40 minutes, the exposure effect is not quite as great. This is termed *reciprocity failure*. At low intensities of light, the effect produced on a coating is not as great even though exposure time is increased proportionately.

Sensitivity Guide   The best practical way to find out how great a particular exposure has been is to expose, along with other copy on a plate, a stepped continuous-tone gray scale, each step of which acts as a filter to decrease the amount of light than can reach the coating. The GATF Sensitivity Guide is such a scale.

In general, the transmission of light is cut in half as you moved up two steps on a guide; step 5 lets through only half as much light as step 3, and step 7 lets through only half as much light as step 5.

Usually, lithography is considered to be a "go–no go" process. That is, any area on a plate either takes ink or does not take ink. This is true even in the reproduction of pictures with many tone values. Since halftones are used, each small halftone dot takes ink while the spaces between dots do not take ink.

Since the light-sensitive coatings on most lithographic plates are high-contrast, a continuous-tone gray scale does not produce a continuous-tone image when a plate is developed. If the gray scale is exposed onto a negative-working plate, the first few steps (perhaps five or six) will hold ink completely. The next step will appear as a dark gray, and the next step or two as lighter grays. These last few steps are referred to as the "gray steps." Beyond these, the coating is exposed so little that the remaining steps will not hold ink at all. The highest numbered step on a negative-working plate that still holds a solid film of ink is called the critical step.

On a positive-working plate, a sensitivity guide works in reverse. The higher numbered steps will hold ink. Then there are usually two or three gray steps, and the steps lower than the gray steps will not hold any ink. With such a plate, the critical step is the lowest numbered step that will still hold a solid film of ink.

The use of a sensitivity guide enables a platemaker to know how much the coating has been affected. The critical step is the result of all the factors that affect a coating—dark reaction, exposure, coating thickness, coating sensitivity, temperature, and relative humidity. With this information, the platemaker can make some intelligent judgments about how he should handle succeeding plates on the same day.

A good plate of a particular type usually shows a certain number of gray steps on a sensitivity guide. A platemaker becomes familiar with this amount. If, for some reason, a plate coating has suffered considerable dark reaction, there will be an increase in the number of gray steps. Plates that produce about six or seven gray steps may be more sensitive to filling in or sharpening when the plates are run on the press.

With the diazo-type presensitized plates, studies indicate, a sensitivity guide's critical step can be varied as much as three steps with no perceptible change in the tone values of halftones. The reason is partly due to the fact that the thinness of the coating allows practically no undercutting of halftone dots.

Negative-working photopolymer plates have a heavier coating. Such plates are subject to some undercutting of shadow dots. Tone values can vary slightly, depending on the intensity and length of exposure. For this reason, it is important to expose these plates to a constant step on a sensitivity guide. A common recommendation is to expose to give a solid step 7.

Light Sources for Platemaking

The efficiency of a light source is defined as the ratio between total lumen output and total power input. A considerable portion of the light output of most lamps is not in the deep blue and ultraviolet wavelengths to which litho plate coatings are most sensitive. The deep blue and ultraviolet wavelengths are called *actinic* light. For plate exposure, the efficiency of a light source can be defined as the ratio between actinic light output and total power input.

General spectral data for various light sources.

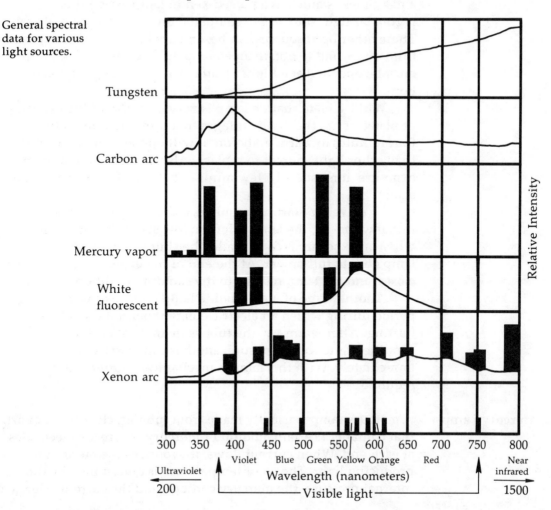

The principal light sources for the exposing of lithographic plate coatings are metal-halide and mercury lamps. Carbon arc and pulsed-xenon lamps are used to a limited extent.

Metal-Halide Lamps

A metal-halide lamp is a mercury-vapor lamp with certain metallic compounds added. Depending on what additives are used, such a lamp can peak (give maximum light energy) at different wavelengths. A typical metal-halide lamp for the graphic arts peaks around 400 to 410 nanometers. The metal-halide lamp is sometimes referred to as the "diazo" type, since it is particularly efficient for the exposing of the diazo type of coatings.

For the exposing of diazo coatings, a metal-halide lamp gives about twice as much actinic light as a conventional mercury-vapor lamp, 2½ to 3 times as much as a carbon arc lamp, and 4 times as much as a pulsed-xenon lamp, when the particular light sources are compared on an equal-wattage basis. These other light sources can be, and are being, used to expose litho plates. But to obtain an equal plate exposure, these lamps must be operated at a higher wattage, or for a longer time, or both.

While a metal-halide lamp is very efficient for the exposing of plates, it has the disadvantages that it requires about two to four minutes to warm up before it will operate, and costs more than other light sources to replace. Also, if turned off after an exposure, it must cool a few minutes before it can be turned on again.

To solve the starting problem, a shutter is used. After the initial warm-up, the lamp is left on low standby power. Then, when an exposure is to be made, the shutter opens while the lamp goes to full power. At the end of the exposure, the shutter closes, and the lamp returns to the standby condition.

Another type of metal-halide lamp requires a warm-up period during which an electric element behind the tube is heating. After warm-up, the tube is in an "instant start" condition; after one exposure, another can be started immediately. With this lamp, a mechanical shutter is not required.

Mercury Lamps

A mercury lamp is usually made from tubular, clear fused quartz that contains a certain amount of mercury. There are electrodes at each end. When current flows, it vaporizes the mercury, producing light. The color temperature is determined by the internal pressure, the mercury content, and the current. Mercury lamps are classified as low, medium, or high pressure, depending on the internal pressure.

Mercury lamps are available that peak in the range from 360 to 370 nanometers, which is in the ultraviolet region. They are most efficient for the exposing of certain photopolymer plates.

The usual mercury lamp requires from one-half minute to one minute to reach full power. If it is turned off after an exposure, it must be cooled about 1½ minutes before it can be restarted. Then the time to return to full power is somewhat shorter. Because of these power variations at the start, a light integrator should be used rather than a timer.

Two variations of conventional mercury lamps are being used in the graphic arts. One is a low-pressure mercury lamp with a specially designed ballast that throws power rapidly into the lamp for instant start. It requires from five to ten seconds to get up to full power; therefore exposures should be regulated with a light integrator. With this system, a hot lamp can be turned off, then restarted immediately. No shutter mechanism is required.

Another variation of the mercury lamp operates at about 90 atmospheres pressure. Such a lamp has thick walls to withstand the high pressure. The lamp must be water-cooled to keep the temperature down. It has instant start and restart. No shutter is required. Since the light does not get up to full intensity for several seconds, plate exposures should be controlled with a light integrator.

Carbon Arcs

For many years, carbon arc lamps were the main source for exposing lithographic plates, and are still being used for that purpose to a limited extent. They provide illumination having a considerable amount of ultraviolet light.

In the graphic arts, the most commonly used carbon arc lamps are made of carbon, tar, and pitch. The white-flame type is copper-coated and contains "rare earth" fillers, usually of the cerium group. The electric current flows from one carbon tip to the other, forming an arc. One of the problems is that color temperature and light intensity vary with fluctuations in line voltage and the condition of the reflector.

It has been realized in recent years that the fumes from carbon arcs are highly toxic. The vapors produced include carbon dioxide, carbon monoxide, ozone, and oxides of nitrogen. Also, the carbon ash liberated may be harmful to the lungs. For these reasons, all carbon arc lamps should be vented to the outside atmosphere.

Because of the problems mentioned and the development of other light sources, the use of carbon arcs has decreased considerably. But a tri-arc carbon lamp is still the best type of light for exposing large deep-etch litho plates in a vacuum frame.

Lasers

Laser beams are being used to a limited extent for the exposure of litho and relief plates. They operate in a different manner from other light sources, as explained in the chapter "Lithographic Plates—Positive-Working."

Treatment of Non-Image Areas

After a plate is exposed, it must be developed to differentiate the image from the non-image areas. Then some kind of treatment is used to make the image areas as ink-receptive as possible. These treatments, which differ from one type of plate to another, are covered in the next two chapters.

The non-image areas of lithographic plates must be treated to make them water-receptive. Areas so treated are said to be *desensitized*—nonreceptive to ink as long as they are kept wet with water.

Four terms are used to describe the surface areas of lithographic plates. These terms are:

hydrophilic: "water-loving"   (water-receptive)
hydrophobic: "water-hating"   (water-repellent)
oleophilic: "oil-loving"   (ink-receptive)
oleophobic: "oil-hating"   (ink-repellent)

The object in litho platemaking is to make the image areas as oleophilic and hydrophobic as possible, and to make the non-image areas as hydrophilic and oleophobic as possible. The best-known method for the desensitization of nonprinting areas is the use of an acidified solution of gum arabic.

Requirements of a Desensitizing Gum

A desensitizing gum must fulfill two functions. First, it must be a hydrophilic material that prefers water to ink on the press. Second, the gum must adhere tightly to the surface of the metal. On the press, a plate is wet continuously by the fountain solution. If the gum is dissolved from the plate, bare metal is exposed and begins to take ink.

Many natural and synthetic materials are hydrophilic. Among these are gum tragacanth, gum arabic, cherry gum, larch gum, mesquite gum, methyl cellulose, hydroxyethyl cellulose, carboxymethyl cellulose, arabogalactan, dextrins, alginates, oxidized starches, polyvinyl pyrrolidone, and polyvinyl alcohol. However, these materials vary widely in their ability to adhere to a metal surface.

Probably desensitizing materials do not react chemically with the metal, but are adsorbed on the surface. A good desensitizing gum such as gum arabic is very soluble in water. When a pressman "washes off the gum," he removes a considerable amount that has been dried on the non-image areas of the plate. But a thin, adsorbed film of gum arabic remains, not removed by water. This film is what desensitizes the non-image areas.

Why Some Materials Desensitize Better Than Others

In the first place, a desensitizing material must be hydrophilic. Most of the substances just mentioned are water-soluble organic materials that contain hydroxyl groups, –OH, in their molecules. So it is likely that these hydroxyl groups are partly responsible for the hydrophilic nature of these materials.

When good, or fairly good, desensitizing agents are examined, most of them are found to be weak organic acids of high molecular weight. For example, gum arabic is a mixture of compounds formed mainly from calcium, potassium, and magnesium ions with arabic acid, a high-molecular-weight carbohydrate containing –COOH groups.

Many organic acids can be expressed with the general formula R–COOH, where R stands for an organic group and –COOH is called a carboxyl group. The potassium compounds of gum arabic can be written R–COOK where K represents potassium.

It is well known that gum arabic does a better job of desensitizing a plate if a solution of it is acidified. When an acid, such as phosphoric acid, is added to a water solution of gum arabic, the calcium, potassium, and magnesium compounds of arabic acid are converted into free arabic acid. One ionic equation is:

$$R\text{–}COOK \; + \; H^+ \text{ (from added acid)} \; \longrightarrow \; R\text{–}COOH \; + \; K^+$$
$$\text{arabic acid}$$

It is believed that the –COOH (carboxyl) groups of arabic acid are responsible for the adsorption to a metal surface. As an acid is added to a solution of gum arabic, lowering the pH, the solution becomes a better desensitizing agent down to a pH of about 3.0. At this point, most of the gum has been converted to free arabic acid. Such a solution desensitizes a metal plate very well; if more acid is added, there is no improvement.

Many materials have been tested as replacements for gum arabic. Many of the more successful replacements have carboxyl groups in their molecules. Some, the alginates, are compounds of sodium, potassium, or ammonium ions with a weak organic acid called alginic acid. On the other hand, hydrophilic materials such as starch, dextrin, and methyl cellulose are very poor desensitizing agents; these do not have any carboxyl groups in their molecules.

While –COOH groups appear to be important in the adsorption of acidified gum arabic to a metal, other groups may do equally well, depending partly on the metal. For example, aluminum and chromium can be desensitized with alkaline solutions of gum arabic, with a pH as high as 9 or 10. What is responsible for adsorption here is not known, but it cannot be the –COOH groups.

Steel offers another exception. A solution containing nothing but phosphoric acid and water can desensitize a steel ink roller so that it will repel ink and accept water. To a limited extent phosphoric acid will also desensitize aluminum and chromium, but it will sensitize copper so that it will accept ink. Measurements at the GATF laboratory with phosphoric acid containing a tracer amount of radioactive phosphorus showed that a considerable amount of phosphoric acid remained adsorbed to aluminum and chromium (after the main part was washed off), while only a small amount remained adsorbed to copper. For some reason, an adsorbed film of phosphoric acid on steel, aluminum, and chromium is preferentially water-receptive.

Chemistry of Gum Arabic

The dried exudation from the gum acacia tree, gum arabic was first used as a plate desensitizer by Alois Senefelder, the inventor of lithography. Nearly 200 years later, it still does more things and does them better than any other plate desensitizing material that has been tested.

Chemically, gum arabic is a mixture of some free arabic acid with mainly calcium and magnesium salts of the acid. An average sample of gum arabic contains about 0.7% of calcium and 0.6% of magnesium, plus much smaller percentages of many other metals.

Putting Plates under Asphaltum

If printing ink is allowed to stand on a plate for several hours, the ink may dry so hard that the plate will not hold fresh ink. So if plates are to be left for several hours or put away for storage, they should be washed out and "put under asphaltum."

There are two ways of doing so. One method is to gum the plate carefully, with a solution of gum arabic. After the gum is completely dry, the ink is removed with an asphaltum solution. This solution is wiped down to leave a thin film over the entire plate.

The other method, which has become more popular in recent years, is to use an asphaltum-gum emulsion. This is an emulsion that breaks easily as it is applied. It deposits gum arabic on non-image areas and replaces ink with asphaltum on the image areas.

Asphaltum is somewhat greasy and preserves the ink-receptivity of the image areas, even after a long period of plate storage. When the plate is to be run again, the pressman goes over the plate with a sponge soaked with water. If the asphaltum layer is thin enough, the water penetrates through the asphaltum and produces a swelling of the gum film in the non-image areas. When this occurs, the asphaltum comes off, leaving a clean non-image area. But asphaltum remains on the image areas, helping them to hold press ink again.

If the asphaltum was applied too heavily when the plate was put into storage, removing asphaltum from the non-image areas may be very difficult. A plate with a dark color, or with heavy streaks of asphaltum, may mean trouble. In this case, do not apply water first. Instead, pour a fresh quantity of asphaltum washout solution on the plate. Work it over the plate with a fair amount of rubbing until the new batch of asphaltum has dissolved the layer that was on the plate. When the old asphaltum is mixed with the new batch, rub off the excess just as if you were putting the plate under asphaltum for the first time. Fan the plate until the new asphaltum film is dry. This new film will now come off the non-image areas very easily when the plate is treated with water.

Miscellaneous Platemaking Problems

Treatment of Sponges

Some chemistry is involved even in the use of sponges. It is desirable not to contaminate lithographic solutions with any chemicals that may come out of new sponges. For example, the synthetic sponges, which often contain a detergent material, should be washed well before using.

Natural sponges may contain a considerable amount of alkaline material. They may also contain small bits of shells from marine animals. These shells consist largely of calcium carbonate, which although not soluble in water, will react chemically with the acid in a desensitizing etch. The result is a partial neutralization of the acid in the etch, reducing its quality as a desensitizing agent.

To prevent trouble of this kind, soak a new natural sponge for ten or fifteen minutes in a 1-fluid-ounce-per-gallon (8-milliliters-per-liter) solution of hydrochloric acid, HCl. This HCl solution will neutralize the alkalinity of the sponge. (Some sponges are so treated before they are sold.)

Tape Marks

Sometimes trouble is encountered with tape marks, caused by the tape used to strip the flat. It was discovered in the GATF research laboratory that this trouble usually develops only when temperature and relative humidity are high, and only with cellophane-backed tapes, which tend to pick up moisture. In contact with a plate, such tapes can cause softening of the coating with resultant tape marks on the plate.

Skin Sensitivity to Chemicals

Some people more than others are sensitive to chemicals that come into contact with their hands and arms. The best treatment is to wash well with soap and water as soon as possible after exposure to the chemicals. Another method is to use rubber gloves. Even with gloves, precautions must be taken. Hands must be clean before putting on the gloves to avoid contaminating their insides. The gloves should be washed well with water before removal.

Many people are sensitive to solutions of ammonium dichromate or potassium dichromate. Ammonium dichromate is one of the materials in deep-etch coating solutions. It is also present in some fountain solution etches. Potassium dichromate is a sensitizer for carbon tissues used to make gravure cylinders and screen process printing stencils.

Skin sensitivity due to dichromates is commonly called "chromic poisoning." It is characterized by skin sores and severe itching. Sometimes people suddenly become sensitive to such solutions after several years of handling them with no trouble. And once you have become sensitive, you usually remain sensitive. So it is advisable to use preventive measures.

7 Lithographic Plates — Negative-Working

Lithographic plates exposed through negatives are called *negative-working plates*. The various types, listed at the beginning of the preceding chapter, are treated in detail in this one.

Many of the things discussed in the previous chapter—anodizing, graining, light sources for exposure, and desensitization of nonprinting areas—are applicable to negative-working plates but need further mention here only briefly.

In general, when a plate is exposed through a negative, the light-sensitive coating is hardened in the image areas; the developer does not attack the hardened coating. But the developer dissolves the coating in the non-image areas, thus exposing the metal in these areas. Finally, a gum solution desensitizes the metal in the non-image areas, so that on the press they will hold water instead of ink.

Automatic plate processors are available for particular classes of plates. Some machines will process only plates of a particular manufacturer. Others will process certain types—diazo plates, presensitized or wipe-on, or certain multimetal plates, for example. Most processors will develop a plate, rinse it, apply a desensitizing film of gum arabic (or an asphaltum-gum emulsion), and dry. A plate thus processed comes out of the machine ready for the press.

Automatic plate processor. *Courtesy of Geiss-America Inc.*

Automatic plate processors offer several advantages. They give more uniform development to all areas of the plate than is possible with manual development. They provide savings in platemaker's time and chemicals used. The chemical saving, in turn, results in a smaller amount of chemicals added to the plant effluent.

Methods are available for the exposing of any negative-working lithographic plate by projection. Projection is particularly suitable for the imposition of a large number of book pages on one plate. A camera is used to reduce camera-ready pages onto 35-mm roll film. The resulting size can vary from one-fourth to one-eighth of original size.

The roll of processed 35-mm film is threaded onto a take-up reel on the projection head. The head also includes a powerful light source and a lens for enlarging the negatives back to the original page size. To get enough ultraviolet light to expose a plate in a short time, it is necessary to use quartz optics. The light source must be well ventilated to keep the film from burning.

By a movement of the projection head or the table on which the plate is mounted, it is possible to expose one page after another. A small computer is programmed with the necessary imposition information. Signals from the computer instruct the projection head to search the roll of film for the particular page to be shot and to move to the exact position on the plate for that page. The projection head is also commanded to rotate so that pages are shot heads up or heads down. The exposure is then made. This process is repeated automatically for all of the pages on one plate.

A system of this kind is very expensive, but there is a great saving in the amount of film required. Manual stripping of page negatives onto a flat is also eliminated.

There are also methods in use for full-size imposition of camera-ready pages onto a piece of film large enough for later exposing of a negative-working litho plate by contact. The pages, arranged in the proper imposition sequence, are mounted one at a time on copyboard pins. Light reflected from the pages goes through a lens onto the film. A small computer is programmed to tell the filmboard in which direction and how far to move before each exposure is made. This method does not save film, but it eliminates manual stripping.

Presensitized Plates

Additive Presensitized Plates

Many litho plates today are *presensitized*. This term means that the light-sensitive coating is applied to the metal by the plate manufacturer. With *additive* presensitized plates, the hardened image areas are made ink-receptive by the addition of an oleophilic resin incorporated in the one-step emulsion developer.

Aluminum or anodized aluminum are the base metals for most of the additive-type plates. Some plates are supplied with a heavy paper back to which aluminum foil is laminated. One plate is offered that has a thin film of chromium electroplated onto an aluminum base.

Most coatings for additive-type plates contain a diazo compound. Since this material decomposes in contact with bare aluminum, it is necessary to give plates a surface treatment. One method is to immerse the plates in a hot solution of sodium silicate, Na_2SiO_3, then wash them with water and seal the layer with a weak acid. The result is the formation of an insoluble film of siliceous material on the surface of the aluminum that separates the aluminum from the diazo coating.

The diazo compound commonly employed is produced from a complicated organic compound called 4-diazo-1,1' diphenylamine. Its structure is:

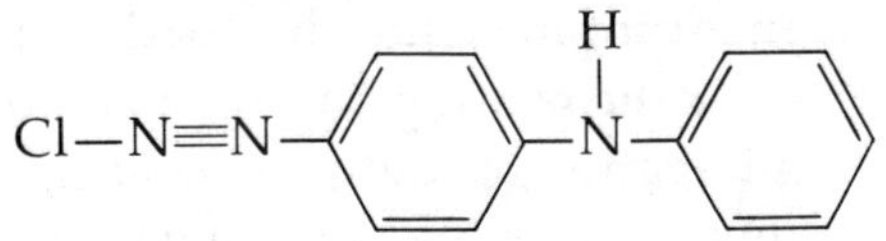

To make a suitable light-sensitive diazo resin, this material is treated with paraformaldehyde in the presence of zinc chloride and sulfuric acid.

Other organic compounds can be used as light-sensitive materials. These include certain azide compounds, hydrazine derivatives, quinone diazides, and esters of quinone. These compounds have very complicated molecular structures.

When a diazo coating is exposed to light, the light causes nitrogen to split from the rest of the molecule. The nitrogen formed escapes as a gas. The remaining portion of the molecules can undergo a variety of reactions. The important thing is that the light-changed diazo coating is not soluble in the developer solution, while the part not exposed is soluble. This condition makes it possible to develop a plate with image and non-image areas differentiated. It is a common practice to expose these coatings to give a solid step 6 on a GATF Sensitivity Guide.

The dark reaction of diazo coatings is very slow if packages of presensitized plates are stored at room temperature. Aging studies have been made on typical negative-working presensitized plates. In this study, it was found that, on the average, plates aged for six months gave about one more solid step on the GATF Sensitivity Guide than did freshly coated plates given the same exposure. In general, modern presensitized plates can still be processed successfully after storage periods of six months to one year.

Additive-type plates are usually developed with a one-step emulsion. This emulsion consists of a water phase containing gum arabic and an acid, and a solvent phase containing an oleophilic resin and a pigment. An emulsion of these two phases is formed. When it is rubbed over a plate, the emulsion breaks, allowing the resin and pigment to be deposited on the hardened image areas. The water phase dissolves the unexposed coating and deposits gum arabic on the non-image areas.

Subtractive Presensitized Plates

With *subtractive* presensitized plates, an oleophilic resin is either incorporated into the coating or is added as a special lacquer over the coating. With a plate of this kind, an exposure through a negative hardens the coating in the image areas. Next, the developer merely removes ("subtracts") the coating from the non-image areas. When the plate is gummed, it is ready for the press.

Photopolymer Presensitized Plates

As press runs grew longer, the demand arose for presensitized plates that would run as long as those made by the deep-etch copperized-aluminum process. This demand has been met by some of the photopolymer presensitized plates, which are tending to replace the expensive and time-consuming deep-etch plates.

The term "photopolymer" has become popular among the manufacturers of litho plates, and it has sometimes been applied indiscriminately to any plate if light exposure through a negative makes the image areas very hard and wear-resistant.

There are two principal mechanisms involved in the production of a photopolymer. One is linear polymerization. Under the influence of ultraviolet and deep-blue light, comparatively low-molecular-weight molecules called *monomers* combine with each other to form long, straight chains. A simple illustration of what occurs is given in the accompanying diagram.

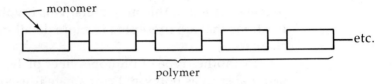

When long chains like this are formed, the coating becomes harder and is insoluble in the developer used to remove the coating from the unexposed area.

The second mechanism is called *cross-linking*. It may occur along with linear polymerization. When this happens, one linear chain hooks onto another by cross-linking until the whole area exposed to light is one giant "molecule." This linkage is illustrated in the accompanying diagram.

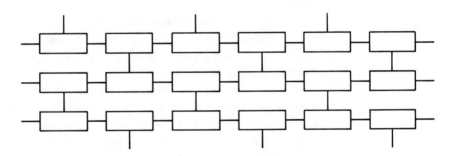

Cross-linking results when new chemical bonds are formed between polymer chains. These bonds can be of any type. For example, unsaturated groups (double bonds) in adjacent polymer chains may form a new carbon-to-carbon cross-link.

$$-C=C- \qquad -C-C-$$
$$\qquad\qquad\qquad\quad |$$
$$-C=C- \qquad -C-C-$$

Some polymers, formed by linear polymerization, will melt when heated sufficiently. These are called *thermoplastic resins*. But if extensive cross-linking is involved, the polymers are harder and do not melt when heated. They are called *thermoset resins*.

Since such plate coatings are proprietary, it is difficult to get exact formulations. However, it is believed that one type uses a combination of light-sensitive acrylate and modified styrene monomers. There is also a *photoinitiator* in the coating. The light first affects the photoinitiator, which, in turn, brings about the polymerization of the monomers. This involves a series of reactions that are presented in more detail in subsequent chapters.

In another type of photopolymer plate, a light-sensitive material such as polyvinyl cinnamate is used for the resin. It is said to be partly polymerized in the original coating. The exposure to light may increase the linear polymerization, but in particular the light causes linear chains to cross-link.

In either case, the image areas are hard and wear-resistant; plates of this kind are giving press runs of from one-half to one million or more.

Following exposure, the plates must be developed. The developer consists of a solvent that will dissolve the unexposed coating but will not dissolve the coating that has been exposed to light.

Photopolymer plates have a much longer press life than diazo plates have. It is claimed that the press life is extended even more if the light-sensitive coating is applied to an anodized aluminum surface.

It is usually recommended that photopolymer plates be exposed to give a solid step 7 on a GATF Sensitivity Guide. It is important to expose these plates to some constant step on a sensitivity guide because the coating thickness is greater than on diazo-type plates and is therefore subject to slight undercutting, particularly of shadow dots. If successive plates are exposed to give the same step on a sensitivity guide, the amount of undercutting will be the same and so the halftone values will be the same.

Wipe-On Plates

The first diazo-type plates were presensitized. Later, it was found that a similar solution of a diazo compound could be wiped over a plate, rubbed down smooth, and fanned dry. Such plates have become very popular. Even if the coating solution is applied with a roller coater, the plates are still referred to as "wipe-on."

The same diazo resin is used as that for additive presensitized plates. It is supplied in powder form, along with a solution in which to dissolve it. Customary practice is to use 3% to 5% of the powder in the solution. The solvent in the solution is water. The solution may also contain a material, such as citric acid, to stabilize the diazo resin for a longer life and a wetting agent to help the coating to be spread more evenly with a roller coater.

Wipe-on plates are usually brush-grained, and many are now being anodized. They must, of course, be treated with a solution of sodium silicate to provide a barrier between the aluminum and the diazo coating, as already explained.

Once the coating has been wiped on, or applied with a roller coater, and dried, the plates are exposed through a negative. They are developed with a one-step emulsion developer exactly as if they were additive presensitized plates, and they are then rinsed.

The final step is the use of an emulsion consisting of an asphaltum solution in one phase and gum arabic and an acid in the water phase. This is such a poor emulsion that the contents in the bottle must be shaken before use. When applied, the asphaltum adheres to the image areas, making them ink-receptive. At the same time, the gum arabic adheres to the non-image areas, making them water-receptive.

As the solid diazo resin ages, it requires a longer time to dissolve. Also, resin stored at room temperature ages faster than refrigerated resin. Press tests have been made with plates having coatings made from diazo resins of different ages. A higher percentage of plate failures occurred with the diazo resins that required a longer time to dissolve. Here are the results:

Age of resin	How stored	Time to Dissolve (minutes)	Press failures (percent)
Fresh		6	0
1 year	refrigerator	10	3.8
8 months	room	13	8.0
1 year	room	20	10.3

These results show that the solid diazo resin should not be kept too long before use, and during that time it should be kept refrigerated.

One manufacturer offers a variation of wipe-on plates. A diazo coating is used that has less diazo in it. As a result, the exposure time is about 65% of that required by the usual wipe-on plates. A thermoset type of resin is incorporated in the developer. After development, the plate is washed, dried, and baked at 450°F (230°C) for 4 minutes. The heat causes the resin to polymerize, becoming very hard and insoluble. After cooling, the plate is gummed to desensitize the nonprinting areas. It is claimed that the press life of this plate is much longer than that of conventional wipe-on plates. The baking process is being used increasingly for certain positive-working plates also. This use is discussed in the next chapter.

Structure of thermoset resin.

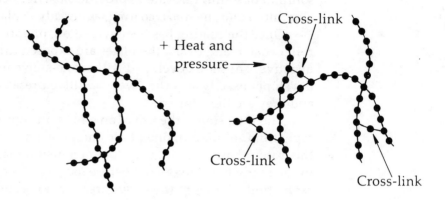

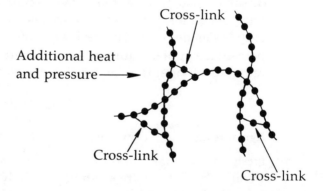

Dry Plates

Conventional lithographic plates are desensitized in the nonprinting areas with a film of gum arabic so that they will accept water instead of ink during printing. Dry plates are planographic plates so prepared that they can be printed without the use of water.

Various advantages have been cited for the use of dry plates, including elimination of the need to constantly monitor and adjust the ink-water balance during printing, less paper waste during press start-up, reduced paper curl, and the ability to print solid, hard halftone dots, especially in dot areas from 50% to 99%.

Countering these advantages, there are also some disadvantages in the use of dry plates. The deposit on the non-image areas is rather soft and easily scratched. The tack of the specially formulated inks tends to be higher than that of usual offset inks, and this tack sometimes results in picking of the paper. Because no water is involved, there is more trouble with static electricity when the relative humidity is low.

A number of background surfaces have been tested. The one mentioned most frequently is a silicone material, a material with low surface energy. One explanation is that the molecules of the ink have a greater attraction for each other than they have for the silicone. This explanation may clarify why the ink does not transfer to the nonprinting areas.

Another explanation starts with the observation that ink usually deposits on the nonprinting areas when the ink rollers are first dropped onto a dry plate. Then, after a number of revolutions, the background cleans up, and printing can begin. During this time, solvent from the ink diffuses into the silicone layer, causing it to swell. The gain in weight is about 5% to 10%. This diffusion forms a weak fluid boundary layer. The split occurs here; so the ink itself does not split and become attached to the background areas.

Plates were found to run clean when the solvent in the ink is soluble in the silicone and were found not to run clean when the ink solvent is not soluble in the silicone. For example, an ink containing the hydrocarbon solvent dodecane, $C_{12}H_{26}$, prints without background toning, apparently because this solvent is able to diffuse into the silicone material on the plate. But the hydrocarbon solvent hexadecane, $C_{16}H_{34}$, will not diffuse into the silicone; inks containing this solvent cause background toning. Using this approach, it may be possible to formulate inks that will print clean and have lower tack values than those employed in the past for waterless lithography.

With several companies working in this field, dry plates may be perfected so that lithographic printing can be carried out satisfactorily without the use of water. In the discussion above, attention was focused on the nonprinting areas. The printing areas also are important. They must adhere firmly to the plate and must cause ink to adhere to them.

Other Negative-Working Plates

Certain Multimetal Plates

Projection Speed Plates

Some multimetal plates are exposed through a negative, and others through a positive. All of these are covered as a group in the next chapter.

Plates with sufficient speed to be exposed by projection contain a silver halide emulsion; areas exposed to light are reduced to metallic silver when the plate is developed. The base is 0.008-inch (0.20-millimeter) thick. It comes in sheets or rolls up to 48 inches (1.2 meters) wide. For a given enlargement of a negative, the exposure time is two to three times greater than that required for film.

These projection speed plates will run for about 5,000 impressions. They are being used for the reproduction of engineering drawings, financial printing, and short-run books.

8 Lithographic Plates—Positive-Working

It is not easy to describe positive-working plates. Some positive-working plates are exposed through positives. Others do not require film. The practice followed here is to call any process "positive-working" if it starts with positive copy, either film or paper, and ends with a positive image on the printing plate, regardless of the intermediate steps that are involved. The various types of plates based on this definition, listed at the beginning of the lithographic plate introductory chapter, are treated in detail in this one.

Many of the things discussed in that introductory chapter, such as anodizing of aluminum, graining, light sources for exposure, and desensitization of nonprinting areas, are applicable to positive-working plates but need further mention here only briefly.

Copperized-Aluminum Deep-Etch Plates

A number of years ago, copperized-aluminum deep-etch plates and multimetal plates were the only ones suitable for long press runs. The introduction of photopolymer negative-working plates and of the "baked" type of positive-working presensitized plates has resulted in competition in the long-run plate field. Because of the time and labor required to make deep-etch plates, the use of these plates is decreasing steadily. But they are still favored for large-size sheetfed presses, long-run web offset publication work, packaging, greeting cards, and labels.

The term "deep-etch" needs clarification. These plates are still essentially planographic, with the etching of the image areas only about 0.0002 inch (0.005 millimeter) deep. With some of the etching solutions in use, it is questionable whether the aluminum base metal is etched at all. But the term "deep-etch" is still used to describe this type of plate.

Cross-section of deep-etch plate.

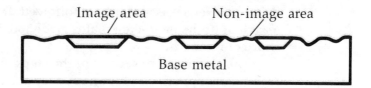

Image area   Non-image area

Base metal

To make a deep-etch plate, ball-grained aluminum is counteretched and then coated—in a whirler—with a light-sensitive coating. (Anodized aluminum is not used for making deep-etch plates.) When the coating is dry, the plate is exposed through a positive. The exposure hardens the coating in the non-image areas but not in the image areas (the opposite of what happens with negative-working plates).

After the plate has been exposed, it is developed with a solution that removes the coating from the unexposed image areas, but does not remove the *stencil*—the light-hardened coating on the non-image areas. The developer bares the aluminum in the image areas, and these areas are next "deep-etched" with another solution.

The deep-etching solution is removed with anhydrous alcohol or some substitute. A copperizing solution that deposits a thin film of copper on the image areas is applied. The step is followed by more alcohol washes to remove the copperizing solution. Then the plate is dried and a lacquer is applied. The lacquer adheres to the copper in the image areas and deposits on top of the stencil in the non-image areas. Next, the lacquer is covered with a developing ink.

At this point, the plate is placed in a tray of warm water and allowed to soak for several minutes. The water softens the stencil so that scrub-brushing removes it along with the lacquer and ink lying over it, thus baring the aluminum in the nonprinting areas. These areas are then treated with a desensitizing etch. The plate is finally gummed with a gum arabic solution.

In recent years, several manufacturers of deep-etch chemicals have modified the materials to reduce the time required to make plates. Use of the alcohol wash and the deep-etching step have been eliminated. One system eliminates the initial counteretching of the metal. Another system uses no desensitizing etch but merely gums the plates at the end. These shortcut methods will make satisfactory plates, if the manufacturer's precautions are followed. It is estimated that at least half of the deep-etch plates made today are being made by shortcut methods.

The chemistry of several of the steps involved in the making of copperized-aluminum deep-etch plates requires more detailed explanation.

Counteretching   The grained aluminum plate is usually treated with a 3-to-4-fluid-ounces-per-gallon (23-to-31-milliliters-per-liter) solution of phosphoric acid. This is called a counteretch. Its purpose is to remove graining sludge and metal oxide before the coating is applied. One of the shortcut methods uses only water for this step.

Coating the Plate   A deep-etch coating usually consists of a water solution of gum arabic, ammonium dichromate, and a small amount of ammonium hydroxide. When gum arabic and ammonium dichromate are mixed in the water solution, they begin to react with each other. It was found in the GATF laboratory that the rate of this reaction slowed as the pH of the solution increased and practically stopped when the pH reached 8.4 or higher. For this reason, deep-etch coatings are made alkaline with ammonium hydroxide to a pH between 8.5 and 9.5.

Exposure to Light   It is not known exactly what happens when a dichromated gum arabic coating is exposed to light. One theory is that the chromium in the ammonium dichromate is reduced from an oxidation number of $+6$ to one of $+3$ (Cr^{+++}). The Cr^{+++} ions then react with the gum arabic. The result is that the coating becomes more or less insoluble by a process similar to the tanning of leather.

The amount of hardening depends in part on the amount of actinic light that reaches the plate. Other factors affecting hardening include the thickness of the coating (the thicker the coating, the more exposure needed), the relative humidity (the higher the relative humidity, the less exposure needed), and the temperature. Most chemical reactions proceed faster as the temperature is raised. Deep-etch developer solutions become more active as the temperature increases. To counter this, the coating must be exposed to light longer for higher developing temperatures.

Dark Reaction and Continuing Reaction of Deep-Etch Coatings   Deep-etch coatings undergo both dark reactions and continuing reactions. If the temperature is 70°F (21°C) or lower and the relative humidity 50% or lower, the dark reaction is fairly slow. Under these conditions, plates being photocomposed can be left on the machine overnight and completed the next morning.

Under conditions of high temperature and high humidity, the dark reaction of a deep-etch coating proceeds rapidly and can lead to trouble. The dark reaction produces some unwanted hardening in the image areas, resulting in a film of partially hardened gum arabic remaining on these areas, even when development seems to be complete. Lacquer will not adhere well to such a residual gum film; the plate may go blind after it is run for a short time on the press. If the platemaker suspects that this may happen, he can often obtain a good plate by doubling or tripling the development time. This increase allows the developer to dissolve the partially hardened gum film in the image areas. If tone values are critical, it will be necessary to expose such a plate longer to compensate for the increased development time.

Development of the Plate

After the coating has been exposed, and prior to development, it is customary to "stop out" areas, such as film lines and tape marks, where the coating is only partly light-hardened. Areas to be protected are painted with a thin film of stop-out solution, and the plate is then fanned until the stop-out is dry.

Water alone cannot be used to develop a deep-etch plate, since water dissolves the light-hardened gum stencil as well as the unhardened image areas. A developer makes use of the fact that, if a water solution contains a large amount of some chemical, other materials will not be as soluble in it.

Developers vary in composition. A typical developer contains a large amount of calcium chloride, $CaCl_2$; some zinc chloride, $ZnCl_2$, or magnesium chloride, $MgCl_2$; and a mild acid, such as lactic acid. The quantities of these substances are adjusted so that the developer will dissolve the unhardened gum coating but not the hardened areas (the part exposed to light).

With the conventional method for making deep-etch plates, a deep-etching solution is applied after development. This solution is similar to the developer except that the solution contains an acid that will attack the base metal. In the shortcut methods, this step is eliminated.

Use of an Alcohol to Clean the Plate

When conventional deep-etch plates are made, some kind of alcohol is used to completely remove the deep-etch solution. The plate is usually washed three or four times with the alcohol to assure that the copperizing solution will react properly with the aluminum in the image areas.

With the shortcut methods, these alcohol washes are eliminated. The deep-etch solution is merely squeegeed from the plate, and some of the remainder is removed with a paper wipe. A special formulation of copperizing solution is then applied.

If an alcohol is used, it can be denatured anhydrous ethyl alcohol, C_2H_5OH, or 99% isopropyl alcohol, or it can be ethylene glycol monoethyl ether. The term "denatured" applied to ethyl alcohol means that a poisonous material such as methyl alcohol has been added to make it unfit for human consumption. The denaturing materials chosen are ones that cannot be removed from the alcohol by distilling it. The distilled alcohol and its vapors are still poisonous.

When two solvents are mixed and then heated, if necessary, to get some of the mixture to vaporize, the vapor usually has a higher percentage of the more volatile solvent than the liquid has. Suppose a solution consists of 25% by weight of liquid A and 75% of the less volatile liquid B. The first vapor to form from this mixture may consist of, say, 40% by weight of A and 60% of B; that is, the vapor is richer in A than is the liquid it came from. As a result, the remaining liquid contains less than 25% of A and more than 75% of B. These proportions continue to change until the last of the liquid to vaporize is almost pure B.

This is true of a litho press fountain solution that consists of, say, 20% isopropyl alcohol and 80% water. As this solution evaporates, the first vapor may consist of 35% isopropyl alcohol and 65% water. As evaporation continues, percentage of alcohol in the liquid gradually decreases. This decrease explains why alcohol must be added occasionally to bring the solution back to 20% alcohol.

At higher concentrations of ethyl alcohol (or isopropyl alcohol) and water, the composition of the vapor gets closer to the composition of the liquid, until they become the same. When a liquid contains 95.5% ethyl alcohol and 4.5% water, the vapor coming from it has exactly the same composition. Similarly, when a liquid contains 91% isopropyl alcohol and 9% water, the vapor coming from it has exactly the same composition.

At still higher concentrations of alcohol, a *reversal* takes place. That is, the vapor contains a little higher percentage of water than the liquid from which the vapor came. As such a mixture continues to evaporate, the last liquid to evaporate is almost 100% alcohol.

This reversal explains why anhydrous alcohol (alcohol with no water in it) or 99% isopropyl alcohol (with only 1% water) is used for the washing of deep-etch plates. The anhydrous alcohol can pick up 4.5% water—and 99% isopropyl alcohol can pick up 8% water—from the water in the deep–etch solution; and all of this water will evaporate, leaving only the water-free alcohol to be the last to evaporate.

If isopropyl alcohol is used and does not dissolve the dried stop-out, this failure can be remedied by adding a small amount of methyl ethyl ketone (MEK) to the alcohol.

Ethylene glycol monoethyl ether does not evaporate as rapidly as the two alcohols and is much less of a fire hazard because it has a flash point (open cup) of 115°F (46°C) compared with about 54°F (12°C) for anhydrous ethyl alcohol and isopropyl alcohol.

The Copperizing Step

A process for the chemical deposition of copper on the image areas of a deep-etch plate was developed to hold the lacquer better, allowing the plates to run longer on the press.

A copper-plating solution must be formulated so that it will not soften or dissolve the hardened gum stencil protecting the non-image areas. One formula developed in the GATF laboratory uses isopropyl alcohol for the solvent, cuprous chloride, and hydrochloric acid. (Cuprous chloride is not soluble in isopropyl alcohol except in the presence of hydrochloric acid.)

When a copperizing solution such as this is applied to a deep-etch plate, the cuprous ions of the cuprous chloride react with the aluminum atoms in the image areas. As a result, the very thin layer of metallic copper is deposited on, and adheres to, these image areas. The ionic equation for the reaction is:

$$3Cu^+ + Al^\circ \longrightarrow 3Cu^\circ + Al^{+++}$$

| cuprous ions | metallic aluminum | metallic copper | aluminum ion |

This is an oxidation-reduction reaction. Three cuprous ions capture three electrons from an aluminum atom and are reduced to metallic copper. At the same time, the aluminum atom is oxidized to an aluminum ion.

This reaction does not continue indefinitely to build up a heavy layer of copper. The cuprous ions in the copperizing solution must react with aluminum atoms in order to be changed to metallic copper. As soon as the chemically deposited copper has completely covered the aluminum, the reaction stops.

Application of Lacquer

When conventional deep-etch plates are made, at least two washes with an alcohol are needed to remove the copperizing solution. With the shortcut methods, a special copperizing solution is used and the alcohol washes are eliminated. However, these methods require the use of a copper neutralizer or image shield to make the lacquer adhere properly to the image areas.

A good lacquer should adhere tightly to the film of copper on the image areas, should be highly ink-receptive, and should be tough enough to resist abrasion on the press. Also, since the lacquer covers the entire plate, the thin film of lacquer on the non-image areas must be penetrable by water so that the light-hardened gum stencil can be scrubbed off.

Most lacquers in use today are of the vinyl type. One resin is a combination of polyvinyl chloride, polyvinyl acetate, and a small percentage of maleic acid. The solvent is methyl ethyl ketone (MEK) or a similar material. The carboxyl groups of the maleic acid are very likely responsible for the good adhesion of this resin to the image areas. Lacquers of this type are not easily blinded by desensitizing etches containing gum arabic.

After a lacquer has been applied and dried, a nonhardening developing ink is rubbed over the plate. This ink is used to increase the ink-receptivity of the image areas.

Scrubbing Off the Stencil

After the developing ink has been fanned dry, the plate is placed in a trough filled with water heated to about 125°F (52°C). After a few minutes, the water penetrates the developing ink and the lacquer, and it begins to swell the hardened gum stencil in the non-image areas. As soon as enough water has been absorbed, the stencil will no longer hold the lacquer and developing ink, which can then be removed with absorbent cotton. Further swelling makes it possible to remove most of the stencil by scrub-brushing the plate. But, on the image areas, the lacquer adheres to the metal, while the developing ink adheres to the lacquer. Thus a plate is produced with image and non-image areas differentiated.

While scrubbing gives the appearance of removing all the stencil, it was discovered in the GATF research laboratory that about 7% to 9% of the total weight of stencil remains on the plate. This remainder is called a "residual stencil." The stencil is hydrophilic (water-loving) and helps to make these plates well desensitized.

The final steps in the making of a deep-etch plate are the use of a desensitizing etch and the gumming of the plate.

Treatment of Waste Material

Excess deep-etch developer and copperizing solution can be collected in a drum to which lime is added. Lime which is calcium hydroxide, $Ca(OH)_2$, neutralizes the acidity of these solutions and also precipitates a considerable amount of the chemicals present. Then the remaining liquid can go into the sewer. Whether such a treatment is necessary depends upon the specifications of the municipal code in the city where the plant is located.

Presensitized Plates

The method of producing an image on positive-working presensitized plates is quite different from the method used on negative-working plates. With negative-working plates, the light makes the coating in the image areas insoluble in the developer, and this hardened coating remains on the plate to hold a lacquer and eventually the press ink.

With positive-working presensitized plates (*not* deep-etch plates), the light has just the opposite effect. The plates are exposed through a positive, so the light acts on the nonprinting areas and does not act on the printing areas. The light-exposed coating is changed chemically so that it becomes soluble in an alkaline solution. When an alkaline developer is applied, the coating is removed from the non-image areas, leaving the unexposed coating to form the image areas.

The base metal for these plates can be aluminum or anodized aluminum. One plate is marketed with a thin layer of chromium electroplated onto the aluminum.

One of the compounds that can be used to form a light-sensitive coating is a diazo derivative of naphthalene, which has the $=N_2$ diazo group and a $=O$ attached in the adjoining, or ortho, position. When this compound is exposed to light in the presence of some water, nitrogen gas is liberated and the original compound is converted into indenecarboxylic acid. There is an in-between step, but the net reaction is as follows:

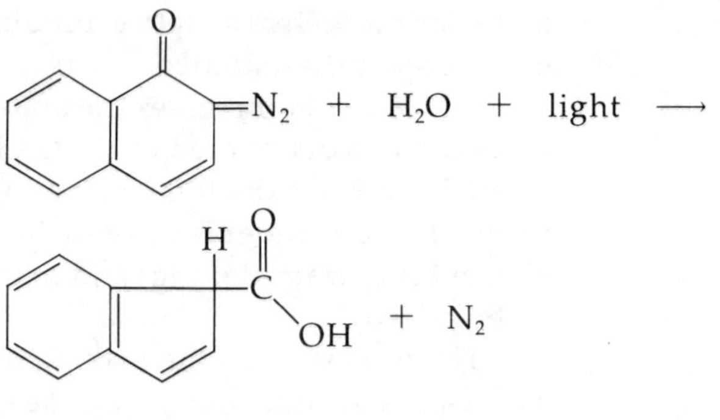

The indenecarboxylic acid is soluble in an alkaline solution, while the original compound is not. A plate can be produced by exposure through a positive because the unexposed coating is oleophilic, or ink-receptive. It is necessary only to gum the plate to desensitize the non-image areas.

The early positive-working presensitized plates had only limited press life; they were used mostly for the proofing of jobs that were printed with deep-etch plates. In recent years, this situation has been changed by the introduction of the *thermoset* type of plates. The light-sensitive materials of these various plates have the same basic structure, but the thermoset-type structure includes a chain of attached atoms that enables the unexposed image areas to be polymerized with heat after a plate has been developed.

These plates are exposed through a positive, with exposure times about 1½ to 2 times as long as are needed with negative-working plates. They are developed with an alkaline developer, for the same reason as that explained above. This is followed with a "finisher" solution to remove the last traces of exposed coating so that the plates will not scum on the press.

After a plate has been dried, it is baked for about five minutes at approximately 450°F (230°C). This baking polymerizes the coating in the image areas and makes it very hard and abrasion-resistant. Baking also makes these areas much less soluble in solvents such as blanket washes. Plates made using a heat-treated thermoset resin are said to be good for press runs from one-half to one million, and they are offering competition to deep-etch plates for many applications.

With the use of coating containing thermoset resins, several manufacturers are confirming the advantages of the baking of plates. The baking process is being used increasingly in printing plants and trade shops. One manufacturer claims that the baking of the thermoset-type of positive-working coating extends plate press life four to ten times. This is much better than can be accomplished with negative-working plates, where baking extends plate life only about 25%.

Positive-working presensitized plates are used to a limited extent in screenless lithography. Plates are exposed through a continuous-tone positive, then developed. To achieve a reasonable tone range, it is necessary to use a plate that will print about eight to ten gray steps when exposed through a GATF Sensitivity Guide. Under magnification, these steps do not print a truly continuous tone, but rather a random, very fine "scum" that increases in amount from one step to another. Similarly, the collotype process, which is also referred to as a continuous-tone process, is not truly continuous-tone either, but consists of a finely reticulated pattern.

Part of the ability to print screenless lithography is due to a coating that gives a number of gray steps when exposed through a sensitivity guide. Also, studies have shown that the grain on the plate is important. In unexposed areas of a positive-working presensitized plate, the coating fills the grains and remains after development, so these areas print solid. With increase in exposure, more of the coating is removed from the valleys of the grain during development, so the amount of coating remaining takes less ink and the tone values become lighter. To prove that grain is important, researchers coated and exposed a smooth plate. When developed, no continuous-tone effect was obtained.

The exposing of plates for screenless lithography is so critical that the method is being used to a very limited extent. But its advantages over the use of a halftone screen have intrigued many people. Screenless lithography has the ability to resolve finer detail, eliminate moiré patterns in multicolor printing, give a higher saturation of pastel colors, and avoid the problem of "50% jump" that is experienced with halftone reproduction.

Diffusion Transfer Plates

Aluminum and paper lithographic plates that are produced by a *diffusion transfer* process are now available.

A photographic paper containing a silver halide is exposed, either by contact or in the camera. This paper negative, as it is called, is placed in close contact with the aluminum or paper plate. The assembly is then passed slowly through a special developer in a diffusion transfer processor. When the paper negative is peeled from the plate, a positive image remains on the plate. Given a treatment to make the image areas ink-receptive, the plate is ready for printing.

The method by which a positive image can be formed on the printing plate involves some interesting chemistry. If the exposed photographic paper were developed in the usual way, a negative of the original copy would be formed: the image areas of the original copy still contain unreacted silver halide in the photographic paper.

In the diffusion transfer process, the processing fluid contains, among other things, a developing agent such as hydroquinone and a fixer such as sodium thiosulfate ("hypo"). The developing agent reacts with the light-exposed areas of the paper, changing them to black, metallic silver. The sodium thiosulfate acts much as it does in any fixing bath, dissolving the unexposed silver halide and causing it to diffuse from the surface of the paper. And since the paper and the lithographic plate are in close contact at this point, the dissolved silver halide transfers to the surface of the plate. This is why the process is called "diffusion transfer."

Something must now happen to reduce the silver halide to metallic silver. With one process, the plate is grained aluminum. Aluminum is a more active metal than silver: aluminum atoms can lose electrons to silver ions, causing the silver ions to be deposited as metallic silver. The ionic equation is:

$$Al^\circ \;+\; 3Ag^+ \;\longrightarrow\; Al^{+++} \;+\; 3\,Ag^\circ$$

If the plate surface is anodized aluminum or paper, a different process must be used. In this case, the surface of the plate is treated with a "nucleated coating." This is gelatin containing small amounts of a metal in a very finely divided (colloidal) state. The metal used could be any metal, such as aluminum or magnesium, that is more active than silver.

The nucleated coating reduces the transferred silver halide to metallic silver, by a process similar to the one described above for aluminum. The reaction involved is an oxidation-reduction reaction. The finely divided metal is oxidized (losing electrons), and the silver ions of the silver halide are reduced to metallic silver (gaining electrons).

By this process, a positive image of metallic silver is formed on the plate. After a short wait, the paper negative is peeled from the plate. While the silver image on the plate looks good, it is not ink-receptive. To make it ink-receptive, an "etch" solution is applied. With one process, this etch contains an oxidizing agent and an organic compound with an oleophilic group. The oxidizing agent converts the silver atoms to silver ions. Then the silver ions combine with the oleophilic group of the organic compound to form an insoluble material that is ink-receptive. Since the gelatin in the nucleated coating on the nonprinting areas is hydrophilic (water-loving), the plate is ready for printing.

Multimetal Plates

Some multimetal plates are exposed through a negative, while others require a positive. Since they are a distinctive type of plate, all varieties will be covered here.

If properly made and if properly handled on the press, a multimetal plate is capable of printing several million impressions. The reason for its long life is that the image and non-image areas are established by two different metals; the holding of image areas is not dependent entirely on a hardened coating or lacquer.

In the manufacture of such a plate, one metal is used for the base. If it is electroplated with a thin layer of another metal, the result is a bimetal plate. If a thin layer of a third metal is electroplated over the second metal, the result is a trimetal plate. And there are even quadrimetal plates, with three electroplated films over the base metal.

The question arises as to what metals are best for the image and non-image areas respectively. The use of contact angles has helped to determine what metals to use. Suppose you place a very small drop of water on a well-cleaned piece of metal. If a tangent line is drawn to the surface of the drop at the point where it touches the surface of the metal, the angle between this tangent line and the surface of the metal is called the "contact angle." The angle must always be measured through the liquid, water in this case. A small contact angle indicates that the metal is easily wet by water. A large contact angle indicates the opposite. Contact angles can vary from about 15° for a metal that is easily wet with water, to about 130° or 140° for a metal that is very poorly wet with water.

Contact angles.

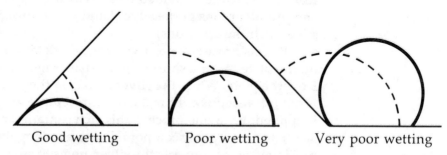

Good wetting   Poor wetting   Very poor wetting

Contact angles can be made using liquids other than water. For example, a study made in a Pira research laboratory in England determined the contact angles of small drops of oleic acid applied to several metals previously immersed in water. This study showed the tendency of a greasy material like oleic acid to displace water from the metal's surface:

Metal	Contact Angle of Oleic Acid
Copper	18°
Aluminum	60°
Chromium	77°
Iron	178°

With oleic acid, the contact angle measurement must be interpreted oppositely to those made with water. These results therefore predict that copper should be a good metal for the image areas of a plate because of the small contact angle. And they predict that aluminum, chromium, and iron (or stainless steel) should be good metals for the non-image areas because of the larger contact angles.

Multimetal plates use the metals predicted by contact angles. Copper or brass is used for the image areas; stainless steel, chromium, or aluminum is used for the non-image areas.

This combination of metals is interesting in another way. It would be very desirable to be able to repair plates that are either scumming or going blind on the press by the use of one chemical that would make the image areas ink-receptive and the non-image areas water-receptive. A solution of nitric acid (HNO_3), a 2%–5% solution of sulfuric acid (H_2SO_4), or a 10%–25% solution of phosphoric acid (H_3PO_4), worked over a multimetal plate, will make the copper image areas ink-receptive and at the same time will desensitize chromium, stainless steel, or aluminum.

Multimetal plates vary in the metal used for the base and in the metals electroplated onto it. But certain procedures are common to all of them. Thus, if copper is the top metal, development of the light-exposed coating must uncover the copper in the *non-image* areas so that it can be etched away to bare the chromium, stainless steel, or aluminum underneath. If chromium is the top metal, development of the light-exposed coating must uncover the chromium in the *image* areas so that it can be etched away to bare the copper (or brass) underneath.

Three types of light-sensitive coatings are employed on multimetal plates. They are:

Type 1. Ammonium dichromate–gum arabic or ammonium dichromate–polyvinyl alcohol. A coating of this type must be applied in the printing plant or trade shop, using a whirler.

Type 2. Presensitized negative-working coating. This type is similar to the coatings used on negative-working presensitized plates.

Type 3. Presensitized positive-working coating. This type is similar to the coatings used on positive-working presensitized plates. (Remember such a coating works in reverse to negative-working types of coating. That is, the part exposed to light is *removed* by the developer, with the coating remaining in areas that were not exposed to light.)

Let's see how these different coatings can be used to make a multimetal plate when the top metal is copper.

Method 1. With a Type 1 coating, expose through a *negative*. The exposure hardens the gum coating in the image areas, and the developer removes it from the non-image areas, so that the copper can then be etched away. (Since even a hardened gum coating is not ink-receptive, the coating must be removed from the non-image areas, too, at a later time.)

Method 2. With a Type 2 coating, expose through a *negative*. The exposure hardens the coating in the image areas, and the developer removes it from the non-image areas. In this case it is not necessary to remove the coating from the image areas.

Method 3. With a Type 3 coating, expose through a *positive*. In this case, the developer removes the coating from the light-exposed non-image areas. Later, heat is used to harden the coating on the image areas for long plate life on the press.

Notice that all the above methods lead to uncovering of the copper in the non-image areas, so that the copper etch that is applied next can remove the copper in these areas to expose the metal underneath.

If chromium is the top metal, the following procedures can be used:

Method 4. With a Type 1 coating, expose through a *positive*. The exposure hardens the coating in the non-image areas, and development uncovers the chromium in the image areas.

Method 5. With a Type 3 coating, expose through a *negative*. In development, the positive-working coating is removed from the light-exposed image areas, uncovering the chromium.

Methods 4 and 5 both lead to the uncovering of the chromium in the image areas, so the chromium etch that is applied next can remove the chromium in these areas to expose the metal underneath.

With the plate metals and method of procedure as the basis, it is now possible to classify the various multimetal plates available. (In the hyphenated series of metals in the following listings, the first metal mentioned is the base; the others are electroplatings in the order given.) Here are the principal classes:

Class 1. Stainless steel–copper, or aluminum-copper, or stainless steel–copper-chromium-copper; Method 1. The completed plate has stainless steel, aluminum, or chromium for the non-image areas and copper for the image areas.

Class 2. Stainless steel–copper, or aluminum-copper; Method 2. The completed plate has stainless steel or aluminum for the non-image areas and copper for the image areas.

Class 3. Stainless steel–copper, or aluminum-copper; Method 3. The completed plate has stainless steel or aluminum for the non-image areas and copper for the image areas.

Class 4. Base metal–copper-chromium, or brass-chromium; Method 4. The completed plate has copper or brass for the image areas and chromium for the non-image areas.

Class 5. Base metal–copper-chromium; Method 5. The completed plate has copper for the image areas and chromium for the non-image areas.

Steps in making a
Class 1 or Class 2
multimetal plate.

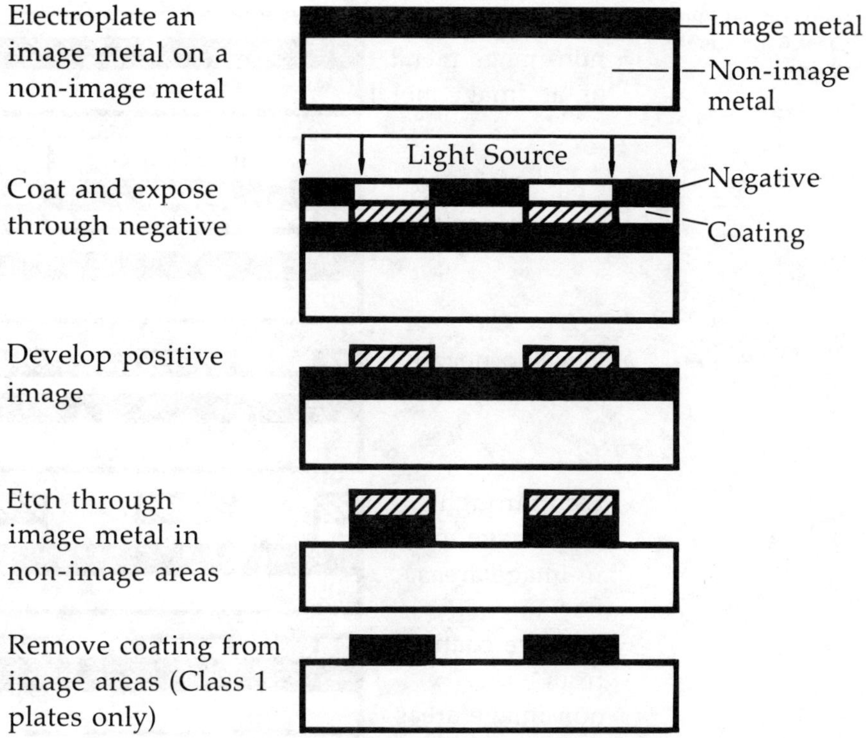

Electroplate an
image metal on a
non-image metal

—Image metal

—Non-image
metal

Coat and expose
through negative

Light Source

—Negative

—Coating

Develop positive
image

Etch through
image metal in
non-image areas

Remove coating from
image areas (Class 1
plates only)

Steps in making a
Class 3 multimetal
plate.

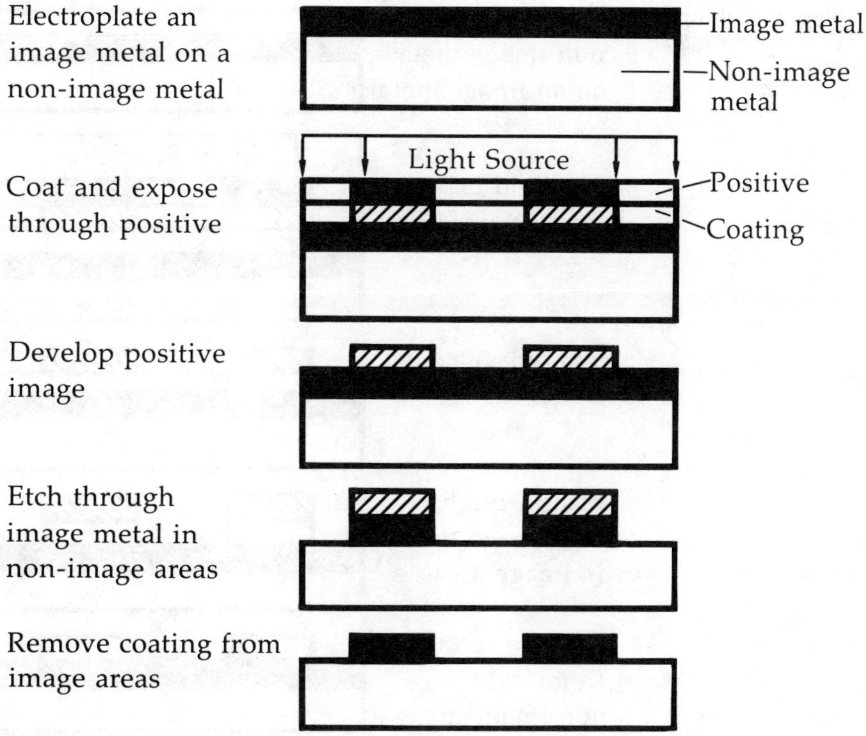

Electroplate an
image metal on a
non-image metal

—Image metal

—Non-image
metal

Coat and expose
through positive

Light Source

—Positive

—Coating

Develop positive
image

Etch through
image metal in
non-image areas

Remove coating from
image areas

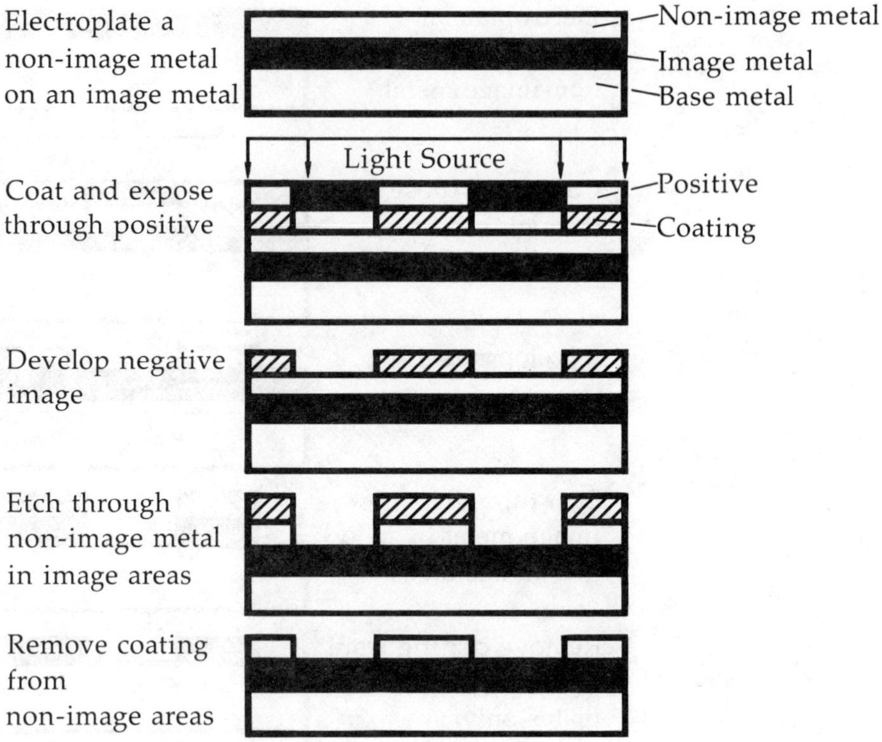

Steps in making a Class 4 multimetal plate.

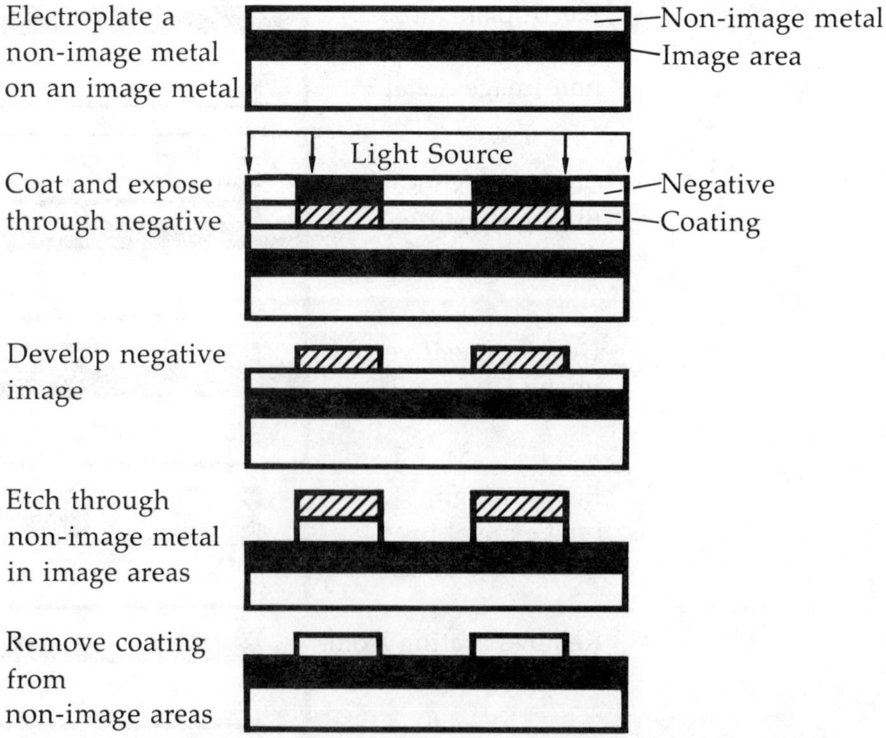

Electroplate a non-image metal on an image metal

Non-image metal
Image metal
Base metal

Coat and expose through positive

Light Source

Positive
Coating

Develop negative image

Etch through non-image metal in image areas

Remove coating from non-image areas

Steps in making a Class 5 multimetal plate.

Electroplate a non-image metal on an image metal

Non-image metal
Image area

Coat and expose through negative

Light Source

Negative
Coating

Develop negative image

Etch through non-image metal in image areas

Remove coating from non-image areas

One other multimetal plate should be mentioned. It consists of an aluminum base electroplated with chromium. A presensitized positive-working coating is used, and the plate is exposed through a positive. The developer removes the coating from the light-exposed non-image areas. Then the plate is gummed and is ready for the press. The method of making this plate differs from the others in that there is no etching of the top metal.

Etches for multimetal plates must be formulated so they will dissolve (oxidize) the top metal but will not attack the metal underneath. An etch containing ferric chloride, $FeCl_3$, is often used to etch copper when the metal underneath is stainless steel. Ferric nitrate, $Fe(NO_3)_3$, may be used to etch copper when the metal underneath is aluminum. With either etch, a copper atom loses two electrons, to form a cupric ion, Cu^{++}, and these two electrons reduce two ferric ions, Fe^{+++}, to ferrous ions, Fe^{++}. The ionic equation is:

$$2Fe^{+++} \ + \ Cu^{\circ} \longrightarrow 2Fe^{++} \ + \ Cu^{++}$$

A chromium etch may contain compounds such as aluminum chloride ($AlCl_3$), zinc chloride ($ZnCl_2$), and hydrochloric acid (HCl). In this case, the hydrogen ions in the etch are reduced to hydrogen gas, and the chromium atoms are oxidized to chromic ions Cr^{+++}. The ionic equation is:

$$6H^{+} \ + \ 2Cr^{\circ} \longrightarrow 3H_2{\uparrow} \ + \ 2Cr^{+++}$$

As noted previously, a Type 1 coating can contain ammonium dichromate and gum arabic, or ammonium dichromate and polyvinyl alcohol (PVA). Coatings made with PVA differ in their development after plates have been exposed to light. A PVA coating must be developed with a spray of water. A developing pad cannot be used, as the light-exposed areas are relatively soft and easily damaged. Following development, the remaining light-exposed areas are hardened by flowing a 3% solution of chromic acid over the plate. Then a solution of paraphenylenediamine is used to blacken the stencil so that pinholes or other defects can be seen easily.

After the chromic acid treatment, the stencil is very hard; there is no problem in applying the etching solution with a deep-etch pad. Indeed, the stencil is so hard that it cannot be removed merely by soaking the plate in warm water and scrubbing with a brush as is customary with a gum arabic stencil.

If copper is the top metal, the hardened PVA stencil is removed with a dilute solution of sulfuric acid, H_2SO_4. If chromium is the top metal, a hot solution of lye, NaOH, is used.

Electrostatic Plates

A tremendous number of small plates for offset duplicators are made by an electrostatic process. Two general methods are used.

In xerography, the photoconductor consists of selenium in a suitable binder, coated permanently on a drum or plate. A corona discharge is used to give the selenium a charge of static electricity. When exposed to camera-ready positive copy, the charge is removed from the exposed areas (non-image), but remains on the unexposed areas (image). These areas then attract and hold finely divided toner particles, which consist of carbon or other pigment treated with a thermoplastic resin. The toned image is then transferred to a heavy paper plate, which, after the toner is fused with heat, becomes a lithographic printing plate.

In another electrostatic process, the paper plate is coated with zinc oxide, ZnO, in a suitable binder. The coating is applied so that the plate will accept a charge of static electricity. After the plate has been charged, the procedure is the same as above except that the image is formed on the plate and no transfer is involved.

Some kind of layer must be used over an aluminum plate, since a charge of static electricity will not remain on a metal such as aluminum. In one process with aluminum, the plates are coated with a layer of zinc oxide. The procedure is much the same as for paper plates made with such a process. The charged plate is exposed to camera-ready copy. The exposure removes the charge from the nonprinting areas (areas exposed to light). Then a liquid toner is used to tone the image areas. The plate is still not ready for printing, since the nonprinting areas are covered with zinc oxide, which is not water-receptive. To correct this condition, a "conversion solution" containing potassium ferrocyanide, $K_4Fe(CN)_6$, is used. This solution converts the zinc oxide to water-receptive zinc ferrocyanide, $Zn_2Fe(CN)_6$.

In still another process, the aluminum plates are coated with an organic photoconductor. After the charging, exposing, and image development with a liquid toner have been accomplished, the plates are placed in a "de-coater." Here a solvent is applied that removes the organic photoconductor from the nonprinting areas. The bare aluminum thus exposed is treated with a solution of gum arabic to desensitize these areas.

Electrostatic plates are more suitable for exposure with an oscillating laser beam, since much less laser power is required compared with that needed for the exposure of presensitized plates.

A modification of the processes described above involves two pieces of equipment—an imager and a heat fuser. On the imager, camera-ready copy is exposed through a lens onto a special film. The film, with a latent image on it, moves to a place where it is toned with a dry toner. The toned image is then transferred to a rubber-base blanket.

The blanket, with the toner image on it, is removed from the drum of the imager and placed on pins on the heat fuser. Here it is brought into contact with any fine-grained, uncoated, aluminum litho plate. The two move together through the heat fuser under some pressure and at a temperature of about 330°F (165°C). This process accomplishes a 100% transfer of the image to the plate and also fuses the toner on the plate to give a long-lasting image. The plate is then gummed manually and is ready for the press.

While one plate is being imaged in the heat fuser, another piece of copy can be exposed in the imager. After a particular image has been transferred from the blanket to a printing plate, the blanket can be reused several hundred times.

Projection Speed Plates

While the exposure time for lithographic plates has been reduced as plate coatings have been improved, the time is still too long in most cases to make exposure in a camera practical. Camera exposure of plates requires use of a *projection speed* type of plate. A large number of plates of this kind are used in camera platemakers.

With a camera platemaker, camera-ready copy is illuminated. The light from the copy passes through a lens system that can be adjusted to give various reproduction sizes. The light then exposes a positive-working projection speed litho plate. Development of the plate occurs inside of the platemaker, and the plate comes out ready for the press.

The chemistry involved in the preparation of a plate of this kind varies with the manufacturer. One type consists of three gelatin emulsion layers on a paper base. Starting from the top, the layers are a prefogged silver halide emulsion, an unexposed silver halide emulsion, and an emulsion containing a photographic developer.

During exposure, the light from the non-image areas of the positive copy penetrates the top layer and exposes the silver halide in the middle layer. The black image areas of the copy do not affect the silver halide in this layer.

Following exposure, the plate is moved into a processor, which contains an activator and a stop bath. The activator penetrates the top two layers and dissolves the developer in the bottom layer. The developer then migrates into the middle layer and reduces the light-exposed areas there to metallic silver. All of the developer is exhausted in these areas, so none can reach the top layer.

In the image areas, the developer migrates through the middle layer and reduces the prefogged emulsion in the top layer to metallic silver. Thus a positive image is formed in this top layer. Since a tanning type of developer is used, the gelatin in the image areas of the top layer is hardened, and these areas become ink-receptive. The gelatin in the non-image areas of the top layer is not hardened, and these areas become water-receptive.

In a previous section in this chapter, the preparation of diffusion transfer plates is explained. The procedure involves exposing a photographic paper, mating it with a specially prepared aluminum or paper plate, and passing the two together through a developer in a diffusion transfer processor.

Two types of projection speed plates are based on the diffusion transfer principle, but neither requires a separate photographic paper. One camera plate consists of two layers mounted on a polyester base. The top layer is a silver halide emulsion. The bottom layer is "nucleated"—it contains a material that can reduce unexposed silver halide to metallic silver.

The light from positive copy, which goes through a lens that allows for enlargement or reduction, is projected onto the plate. The plate then moves into a developing solution containing a photographic developer and also a substance that can dissolve silver halide for diffusion transfer.

The developer produces a negative silver image in the top layer. Then the silver halide solubilizing material in the developer dissolves the silver halide in the unexposed areas of the top layer, and this solution diffuses into the bottom layer. Here the dissolved silver halide reacts with the nucleated material and is reduced to metallic silver, producing a positive silver image in the bottom layer.

The plate then moves to a 115°F (46°C) water wash which removes the top layer. Now the layer with a positive image becomes the top layer. As the plate moves through succeeding operations, it is treated with an activator to make the metallic silver image ink-receptive and is washed with water to remove the activator. The plate is now ready for printing.

The second type of projection speed plate based on diffusion transfer has four layers on a paper base. (The fourth layer simply prevents undesirable light reflections from the base.) After exposure to positive copy, the plate is passed through a diffusion transfer developer. The developer penetrates the top two layers and reduces the light-exposed (non-image) areas of the third layer to metallic silver. The unexposed silver halide in this layer diffuses through the second layer and is reduced to metallic silver by the thin nucleated coating in the surface layer. (This process is explained in the description of the first type of diffusion transfer plate.) The final treatment is with a solution that makes the silver image on the top layer ink-receptive.

Laser-Exposed Plates

With the usual method of making plates, a light source exposes every area of a plate at once, for times varying from about $1\frac{1}{2}$ minutes to 5 minutes, depending on the strength of the light source, its distance from the plate, and the light sensitivity of the plate. When a plate is exposed with a small beam of light from a laser, the light scans the plate very rapidly, while the plate moves slowly under the scanning beam.

With a laser system of this kind, each very small printing unit may receive an exposure of only one or two milliseconds duration. Thus the exposure time is in the neighborhood of 1/100,000 of that used with ordinary light sources. Therefore, to get sufficient exposure, the intensity of the laser beam must be at least 100,000 times as great, providing that the reciprocity law continues to hold. (And apparently it remains reasonably valid in this case.)

Laser-exposing systems are now in use for the exposing not only of presensitized and wipe-on litho plates but also of relief plates and films with a silver halide emulsion.

One such laser platemaking system uses two platens. Pasted-up copy (such as a full newspaper page) is placed on one platen, and the unexposed litho plate on the other. During exposure, both platens move slowly, with identical speed.

The copy is "read" by an economical low-power (2 milliwatt) helium-neon laser, which operates in the red region of the visible spectrum. This laser rapidly scans across the copy, making a complete scan for every 0.001 inch (0.025 millimeter) that the copy moves.

At the same time that the "read" laser is scanning the copy, a "write" laser is scanning the printing plate (or film). Various lasers are available that could be used for plate exposing; a typical one is a 15-watt argon-ion laser.

In some way or other, the information from the "read" laser must tell the "write" laser whether to expose each little area or not to expose. The mechanisms for doing so are complicated; the following is a simplified version of what happens in the system being described.

If light has been reflected from the copy, it is picked up by a row of fiber-optic light-pipes which transfer this light to photomultiplier tubes. The output of these tubes goes to a digitizing station, and then to a modulator.

When the modulator receives a signal indicating that light has been reflected from a non-image area of the copy, the energy of the argon-ion laser is deflected, preventing the beam from reaching the plate. When the modulator receives a signal indicating that no light has been reflected from the copy (the beam having struck an image area), the laser is commanded to pass light to the plate. In this way, non-image and image areas are differentiated on the plate exactly as they appear on the pasted-up copy.

It must be kept in mind that a new small area is evaluated for this "go–no go" condition every couple of milliseconds as the argon-ion laser rapidly scans a plate. And several scans are required to complete the letters of one line of type or the larger halftone dots. But every thing proceeds so rapidly that a full-sized newspaper plate is exposed in approximately two minutes.

After a plate has been laser-exposed, it is developed and gummed as if it has been exposed with a conventional light source. At present, most litho plates that are being exposed with a scanning laser beam are the type commonly called "negative-working" plates; that is, the areas exposed by the laser become the image areas of the plate. But since no negative is involved, and since positive copy is converted to a positive image on the plate, the laser platemaking system is a "positive-working" process according to the definitions used in this book.

One advantage of laser exposing is that the signals obtained from the scanning of the copy can be used to make a plate in the same machine, and at the same time can be sent to some distant location to make a duplicate plate. Or, by changing the signals, a negative can be produced on film. When this negative is developed, it can be used to make a conventional litho or relief plate.

Comparison of argon-ion laser output to mercury vapor lamp output and plate sensitivity.

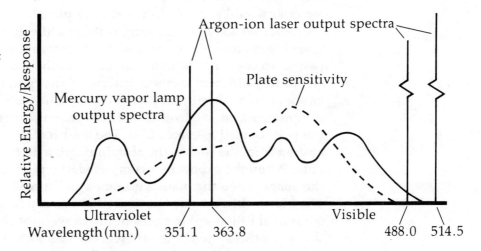

There are four main lines in the output spectrum of an argon-ion laser. Two are in the ultraviolet at 351.1 and 363.8 nanometer wavelengths. The other two are in the visible range at 488.0 and 514.5 nanometer wavelengths. In addition, the energy output of the ultraviolet lines is low compared with that of the visible lines. A 15-watt argon-ion laser contributes only from 1½ to 2 watts in the ultraviolet. Yet present printing plates are insensitive to visible light and only moderately sensitive to wavelengths of the ultraviolet laser lines.

For these reasons, it has been necessary to use a laser with considerable power in order to get sufficient exposure of a plate. Work is active at present to improve this situation. It may be possible to develop other lasers that will have more of their energy available for the exposure of present plates. The plate manufacturers are also endeavoring to produce plates that will work more efficiently with laser exposure. Such an accomplishment will require either developing a coating that is more sensitive to the argon-ion ultraviolet lines or developing a coating that will be more sensitive to visible light. Several experimental plates have shown a big advance toward the solving of this problem. One company is supplying a presensitized photopolymer plate that is five times as fast as a conventional plate. The heat developed by the laser beam also helps to harden the plate coating.

One facsimile transmission system now employs a 15-milliwatt helium-neon laser in the transmitter and a 4-watt argon-ion laser in the recorder. Conversion to a flat-field recorder would permit a litho printing plate to be exposed.

Another laser platemaking system, while employing the same type of low-power helium-neon laser as the others to scan pasted-up copy, produces an image on a litho plate by means of an entirely different method. Instead of an argon-ion laser, it uses a yttrium-aluminum-garnet (YAG) solid-state infrared laser. A nonsensitized anodized aluminum plate is covered with a nonphotosensitive-coated film. The laser transfers the oleophilic coating from the film to the aluminum plate in the image areas only. When the exposure is completed, the plate is heated to fuse the image. Then the plate is gummed and is ready for the press. The film is either discarded or used as a negative to make additional lithographic plates in the conventional way.

With this system, the problem of mating the laser wavelengths to the peak-wavelength sensitivity of the plate's coating has been eliminated.

The field of laser-exposed plates is in a state of change. Equipment improvements are being made; new lasers and new lithographic plates are being investigated. This activity will undoubtedly result in improvements making laser-exposed plates more competitive with other platemaking methods, particularly for newspaper and other plant requiring a large number of plates to be prepared in a short period of time.

9 Relief and Gravure Image Carriers

A variety of methods are employed to produce the nonlithographic image carriers, and the chemistry involved differs from one to another. Letterpress uses metal, plastic (photopolymer), and duplicate plates. Flexography uses both photopolymer and duplicate plates. Gravure cylinders are made of copper.

Relief Plates

Letterpress and flexographic plates are similar in that the image areas are raised, permitting the ink rollers to cover only those areas. Such plates are called *relief* plates. They are generally exposed through a negative. The light hardens the coating of the image areas on the metal plates. The plates are developed to remove the coating from the unexposed, non-image areas. Then an acid solution is used to etch the non-image areas to the desired depth.

With plastic plates, the procedure is somewhat different. Light through the negative hardens the image area plastic all the way through to the base. Then a washout solution is used to remove the unexposed plastic from the non-image areas.

Magnesium and Zinc Relief Plates

The use of zinc relief plates has declined drastically. The decline is due partly to regulations limiting the amount of zinc salts that can be sent into a sewer system. When zinc plates are made, they are etched with a solution of nitric acid, HNO_3.

The light-sensitive coating on metal plates is called the *top* or *enamel*. For zinc and magnesium plates, a "cold top" enamel is used. This usually consists of polyvinyl alcohol (PVA) sensitized with a dichromate. After exposure through a negative, the coating is developed with a spray of water. Then a chromic acid solution is used to harden the exposed coating further, so it will resist the acid etching solution. Finally, the coating is baked at about 350°F (177°C). The plate is then etched.

Very few magnesium plates are made this way today. Over 90% of magnesium plates are supplied with a presensitized coating, which consists of polyvinyl cinnamate. Light through a negative hardens this coating in the image areas, and the unexposed part is removed by inserting the plate in a special trichloroethylene vapor degreaser. This solvent has the structural formula:

$$\underset{\text{ClC}=\text{CCl}_2}{\overset{\text{H}}{|}}$$

A vapor degreaser consists of a closed tank with the liquid on the bottom. The liquid is heated; the vapors rise and change to liquid again in the upper part of the tank. In this case, the pure liquid flows over the plate and dissolves the unhardened coating. The mixture of liquid and coating returns to the bottom of the tank.

Following development of a presensitized magnesium plate, no baking is required. The plate is descummed with a dilute nitric acid solution to clean the non-image areas so that etching will proceed uniformly.

Etching of magnesium plates is carried out in machines equipped with paddles that throw the etching solution onto the plate. Etching solutions contain 14%–22% of 42° Baumé nitric acid by volume, and the bath is maintained at 85°–130°F (30°–54°C).

A *powderless etching* process is used. In this process, banking materials are added to the bath. The purpose of these additives is to form a film on the shoulders of the image areas to prevent undercutting as the metal is etched deeper.

Mechanism of powderless etching.

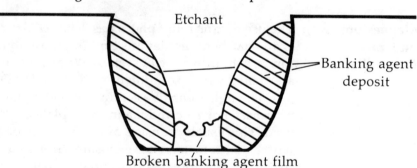

Etchant

Banking agent deposit

Broken banking agent film

The additives must accomplish two things. At least one additive must adhere to the sidewalls, and the combination of materials must produce a film that will protect the sidewalls from further etching. An early combination consisted of a surface-active agent and an oil. The surface-active agent became adsorbed to the sidewalls, and the oleophilic (oil-loving) end of the molecules held the oil.

Several improvements have been made in additives for this process. Some of them contain five or more ingredients. It is claimed that all of the ingredients used in one additive are biodegradable. The materials used are complicated organic compounds, such as isostearic acid, saturated fatty acids with eight to sixteen carbon atoms in their molecules, coupling agents such as glycol ethers—to keep the solution clear—and anionic surface-active agents.

The chemical reactions of magnesium etching are as follows:

$$4Mg^\circ \;+\; 2NO_3^- \;+\; 10H^+ \longrightarrow$$
$$4Mg^{++} \;+\; N_2O \;+\; 5H_2O$$

$$Mg^\circ \;+\; 2NO_3^- \;+\; 4H^+ \longrightarrow$$
$$Mg^{++} \;+\; 2NO_2 \;+\; 2H_2O$$

The solid magnesium is oxidized by the nitrate ions, NO_3^-, of the HNO_3 to form magnesium ions that are soluble in the etching solution. The nitrogen atoms of the NO_3^- ions are reduced to N_2O or NO_2. These reactions also consume the hydrogen ions present in HNO_3. Nitrogen dioxide, NO_2, in particular is toxic when operators are exposed for extended periods of time to quantities over five parts per million. Therefore, etching machines are equipped with hoods and blowers to remove these vapors.

The question arises as to why the additives in the etching bath can prevent etching at the sidewall while allowing it to occur at the bottom of the etched cavity. One theory is that the force of the splashing etch removes the banking film from the bottom areas. This may be part of the answer. But the differential heat theory, as follows, is the explanation most widely accepted today.

When magnesium is etched with nitric acid, heat is evolved—in the amount of about 850 British thermal units per ounce (30 kilojoules per gram) of magnesium dissolved. According to the differential heat theory, the additives do not adhere well to a hot surface, so they do not adhere where the metal is being etched, and therefore the etching proceeds. But the sidewalls are cooler, so the additives can adhere there and prevent further etching.

As magnesium plates are etched, nitric acid is consumed, so more must be added. At the same time, the concentration of magnesium ions in the bath keeps increasing. This increasing concentration creates what is called a *mass action effect*, resulting in a decrease in the rate of etching. Finally, the etching bath must be dumped.

The proper disposal of spent etching baths is becoming increasingly important because of city and federal regulations. The magnesium in the bath is not harmful—all it does is make water harder—but the acid must be neutralized. This neutralization is accomplished by adding sodium hydroxide,

NaOH, or sodium carbonate, Na_2CO_3 (soda ash). Most sewer codes will accept effluents with a pH of 5.5–6.0, so it is not necessary to go to the neutral point of pH, 7.0. With such treatment the magnesium remains in solution, since it does not precipitate until the pH reaches 9.0.

For exceptionally long runs, magnesium plates can be electroplated first with a thin film of copper and then chromium. A process for depositing a very thin film of nickel without the use of an electric current has also been developed. Magnesium press plates are immersed for about a half hour in a solution that contains several ingredients, including basic nickel carbonate, $2NiCO_3 \cdot 3Ni(OH)_2 \cdot 4H_2O$. Metallic nickel deposits on the magnesium by an oxidation-reduction displacement reaction, as follows:

$$Mg^\circ \ + \ Ni^{++} \ \longrightarrow \ Mg^{++} \ + \ Ni^\circ$$

Copper Relief Plates

The light-sensitive coating for copper photoengravings is a "hot top" enamel. It usually contains fish glue and some egg albumin, and is sensitized with potassium dichromate, $K_2Cr_2O_7$. After exposure through a negative, the photoengravings are developed with water. This removes the coating from the unexposed areas. The remaining coating, the *resist*, is then set by heating to temperatures of 550°–650°F (285°–345°C).

Copper plates can also be presensitized with a positive-working coating. This coating works similarly to that of positive-working presensitized litho plates. A plate is exposed through a positive. The developer then removes the coating that has been exposed but does not remove the unexposed coating.

With the powderless etching process for copper, it is common to give a plate two etches—one for more-deeply-etched line work and another for the flat-etched halftone work. This etching is easy to accomplish with a presensitized positive-working coating. The following steps are used:

1. Expose the plate through a positive of the line work, with halftone areas masked out with paper.

2. Develop the plate. Development removes the coating from all parts of the plate except where there is line work and where there are masked-out halftone areas.

3. After the plate is dried, expose it this time through a positive of the halftones, with the line work masked out. But do not develop the plate again at this stage.

4. Etch to the desired depth for the line work. (The halftone

areas are still protected by the coating.) Then clean the plate and dry it.

5. Now develop the plate again for the halftones only. After drying, burn in the coating at 350°F (177°C).

6. Finally, give the plate a flat etch for the halftones.

Copper plates are descummed with dilute hydrochloric acid, HCl, prior to etching. This removes any cupric oxide, CuO, which is soluble in HCl. The molecular reaction is:

$$CuO \quad + \quad 2HCl \quad \longrightarrow \quad CuCl_2 \quad + \quad H_2O$$

The plates are etched with a 28%–45% solution of ferric chloride, $FeCl_3$. The ionic reactions are:

$$Fe^{+++} \quad + \quad Cu° \quad \longrightarrow \quad Fe^{++} \quad + \quad Cu^+ \quad (\text{cuprous ion})$$
$$Fe^{+++} \quad + \quad Cu^+ \quad \longrightarrow \quad Fe^{++} \quad + \quad Cu^{++} \quad (\text{cupric ion})$$

Oxidation and reduction are involved in both reactions. In the first one, ferric ions are reduced to ferrous ions, and the copper is oxidized from metallic copper, $Cu°$, to cuprous ions. In the second reaction, the ferric ions react with the cuprous ions and oxidize them to cupric ions.

A powderless etching process for copper plates was developed by the Platemakers Educational and Research Institute. The mechanism for the protection of sidewalls is somewhat different from that for magnesium plates. The additives to the etching bath are derivatives of thiourea. The prefix "thio" indicates that the molecules contain sulfur as a substitute for oxygen. Thus the structural formula for urea is:

$$\begin{array}{c} H_2N \\ \diagdown \\ C\!\!=\!\!O \\ \diagup \\ H_2N \end{array}$$

and the structural formula for thiourea is:

$$\begin{array}{c} H_2N \\ \diagdown \\ C\!\!=\!\!S \\ \diagup \\ H_2N \end{array}$$

The etching bath additives react with cuprous ions, Cu^+, to form an insoluble film on the sidewalls. This film protects the sidewalls from further etching.

Because cuprous ions are involved in sidewall protection, a minimum of 2 ounces per gallon (15 grams per liter) of copper must be present in the etching bath. Then a bath works satisfactorily until the copper increases to 4.6 ounces per gallon (35 grams per liter). At this point, half of the bath is dumped and replaced with fresh bath fluid containing ferric chloride and the additives. The amount of copper in a bath can be checked by spectrophotometric analysis.

The disposal of spent etching baths presents problems. The baths can be neutralized with sodium hydroxide, NaOH (caustic soda), to precipitate out the copper. But this also precipitates out the iron as a mixture of hydrated iron oxides, which are slimy and very difficult to filter out. They rapidly plug most filter screens. The same problem is encountered in the treatment of spent etching baths from the production of copper gravure cylinders. The best answer at present is to arrange for a disposal company to collect such spent baths.

Plastic (Photopolymer) Letterpress Relief Plates

A number of photosensitive plastic plates are now available for the production of letterpress relief plates. Some of these plates are used for commercial magazine printing, while others are used mostly for the direct printing of letterpress newspapers. Some are suitable for the making of masters from which stereotype mats are rolled. Others are used on offset presses in an offset letterpress system sometimes called "dry offset" or "letterset."

Photopolymer plates use a resin that is photosensitive. Some of these plates have a combination of two or more such resins. The plates are exposed through a negative. This exposure causes the resin or resins to harden all the way through the thick coating. The hardening is accomplished by the polymerization of the resin molecules. They combine with each other, both by joining end-to-end to form chains and by cross-linking between the chains. This process ties the molecules together, making these areas hard. It also makes them insoluble in the washout solution.

To accomplish this polymerization in a reasonable length of time, the coating contains a small percentage of a material that accelerates the reaction. Most types of photopolymer plates contain a *photosensitizer*. A typical photosensitizer is benzophenone. Its formula is:

or $(C_6H_5)_2CO$

The photosensitizer absorbs ultraviolet light. This causes the photosensitizer to be changed to an *excited state:* some of the electrons in the outer energy level are raised to a higher energy level. Then various things can happen; one is that these energetic molecules can cause the carbon-to-carbon double-bond linkages in the resins to open up. When this happens, the resin molecules begin to link together.

When the excited photosensitizer opens one of these carbon-to-carbon double bonds, it loses its energy to the resin molecule and returns to its original state. Then it can again become excited by ultraviolet light and be able to act on another double bond of the resin. In this way, a small amount of photosensitizer can bring about the polymerization of a large amount of resin. One of the photopolymer plates uses only 1% of benzophenone; most of the remainder consists of the resins.

Various light-sensitive resins are used, depending on the type of plate. One plate uses a form of nylon. Another type uses acrylate resins. Certain other plates are made with a mixture of urethane-based polyene and tetrathiol. These are complicated substances with this feature in common: they all have carbon-to-carbon double bonds so situated in the molecules that they can easily link together when these double bonds are opened.

The mechanism of polymerization for another type of plate is somewhat different. These plates are composed of a combination of an acrylate-type monomer (resin), a binder (such as polymethyl methacrylate), and a photoinitiator. Some plates may also contain a small amount of a plasticizer to ensure plate flexibility.

A *photoinitiator* accelerates the polymerization of the monomer by ultraviolet light, but does so in a way different from that of a photosensitizer. When the photoinitiator absorbs ultraviolet light, it splits apart to form two *free radicals.* These free radicals bring about the opening of the double bonds of the monomer, allowing polymerization to proceed. (This process is explained in more detail in Chapter 11, "Chemistry of Inks.") The monomer also combines with part of the binder to form a *copolymer.*

Systems such as this are "oxygen-sensitive"; that is, oxygen can terminate the polymerization process. For this reason, some types of these plates are stored in an atmosphere of carbon dioxide, CO_2. The large excess of carbon dioxide replaces the oxygen on the surface of the plates and thus eliminates the terminating effect of oxygen when the plates are later exposed.

Another method used with these plates is to give a pre-exposure through a green-colored filter sheet. This sheet removes most of the ultraviolet light that is responsible for polymerization, but allows some of the monomer to combine with the oxygen present. Then the filter is removed, and the plate is exposed as usual through a negative. With thinner versions of these plates, no carbon dioxide storage or filter pre-exposure is needed.

Following exposure, these plates are washed out in the non-image areas with an alkaline aqueous solution. The plates in several other systems are washed out with an aqueous solution. One washout solution consists of alcohol and water. These solutions must be formulated so that they will dissolve the unhardened parts of a plate.

One process used with the plate made with a urethane-based polyene and tetrathiol mixture does not involve any chemistry. The light-sensitive material used to create the plate has a consistency of heavy honey. Light hardens this material in the image areas but leaves it semiliquid in the non-image areas. This semiliquid material is then blown off the plate with a blast of air. The material recovered can be mixed with new material and reused.

Flexographic Photopolymer Relief Plates

Until recent years, flexographic printing was done with rubber plates. To make a rubber plate, it is necessary first to make a metal or phenolic photoengraved plate. This is used to produce a matrix from which the rubber plate is molded.

A lot of flexographic plates are still made from rubber, but there are now several companies producing photopolymer flexo plates. These plates contain ingredients similar to those used in letterpress relief plates. They contain a light-sensitive resin and a small amount of either a photoinitiator or a photosensitizer. But the processed plates are more flexible, like rubber plates. This relative lack of hardness is measured by the durometer. Most rubber plates have a durometer reading of about 50. The hardness of photopolymer flexo plates is in the same region, with readings of 40–60. In contrast to this, the durometer reading of letterpress plastic plates is about 70–80.

It is the cross-linking of polymer chains that produce a hard plate, such as a typical letterpress polymer relief plate. With the flexo plates, the amount of cross-linking is less, so the plates are softer, with a lower durometer reading.

After exposure, the non-image areas must be washed out. As with letterpress plates, a solvent must be used that will dissolve the unhardened material. Some of the systems use an aqueous solution. The plates of one type are washed out with perchloroethylene. This solvent has a boiling point of 250°F (121°C). It is a derivative of ethylene; its formula is $Cl_2C{=}CCl_2$.

Photopolymer flexo plates are better than rubber ones for jobs requiring close register, since a photopolymer does not stretch as much as rubber. In fact, commercial work rivaling the best four-color letterpress or lithographic work has been produced with these plates. They run as long as—or longer than—rubber plates. There is no problem printing with alcohol-based or water-based flexo inks. However, some solvents, such as ketones and aromatic hydrocarbons, attack these plates. Such solvents should be eliminated from the inks and from the reducer used in the pressroom to adjust the viscosity of the inks.

Duplicate Plates

All of the plates described previously are original plates: if two or more are needed from the same negative, the entire process must be repeated. It is also possible to make an original photoengraving on magnesium or copper, or on certain photopolymer plates, from which a matrix is molded and used to mold several *duplicate* plates. (Electrotypes are also duplicate plates, but are produced by a different method.)

Materials suitable for the production of duplicate plates include natural rubber, synthetic rubbers, vinyl resins, and polypropylene. Natural and synthetic rubbers are compounded with powdered sulfur. When this soft mixture is molded under pressure and heat, in contact with a matrix, the rubber is *vulcanized*, becoming much harder. This is a polymerization reaction that is catalyzed by sulfur.

Buna N is one type of synthetic rubber. It is produced by the polymerization of butadiene, $CH_2{=}CH{-}CH{=}CH_2$, and acrylonitrile, $CH_2{=}CH{-}C{\equiv}N$.

A process has been developed for making duplicate newspaper plates using polypropylene. Propylene, with the formula $H_3C{-}CH{=}CH_2$, can be polymerized to produce polypropylene. An original of each page is made, using a magnesium photoengraving. From this, a matrix is molded. Then the matrix is used in an injection molding machine to make duplicate polypropylene press plates.

Polypropylene is a thermoplastic resin: it is a solid at room temperature, but it can be melted with sufficient heat. After a press run and removal of ink from these plates, they can be ground up and reused because of this thermoplastic nature of polypropylene.

Structure of thermoplastic resin.

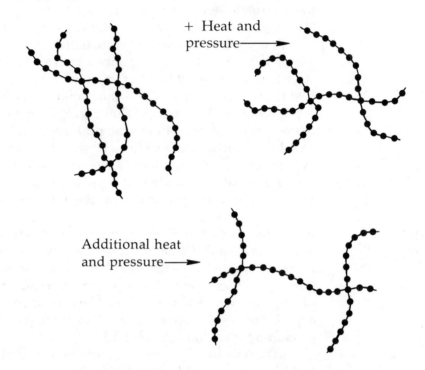

+ Heat and pressure——→

Additional heat and pressure——→

Electrotypes are another form of duplicate plate. The original is usually a photoengraved copper plate. An impression of this original is made with hot vinyl plastic. The impression is then sprayed with silver to make it electrically conductive. It is placed in a bath and plated electrically with copper or nickel to produce a thin shell. This shell is then stripped from the plastic and backed with molten metal.

The plastic with silver on it forms the negative pole, or cathode, in the electroplating bath. The metal ions in the bath combine with electrons on the cathode and are reduced to uncharged metal. The reduction reaction is:

$$Cu^{++} \ + \ 2e^- \ \longrightarrow \ Cu^\circ$$

Methods of Preparing Gravure Cylinders

Gravure is an intaglio process, so some method must be used to produce image areas that are below the surface of the copper cylinder. Such methods include the use of carbon tissue, silver halide–gelatin emulsion on polyester, presensitized photopolymer on polyester, direct engraving, the electronic scanner engraving machine, and epoxy resin.

Carbon Tissue

Carbon tissue, sometimes called gravure pigment paper, is actually available with a base of either paper or film. The base is coated with pigmented gelatin. The gravure printer or trade plant obtains the material already coated. It has long life if properly stored.

Gelatin is an animal protein material, obtained from connective tissues, cartilage, and hides. Proteins consist of a mixture of amino acids. There are eighteen amino acids present in gelatin, five of which constitute about 80% of the total. They are:

Glycine	27.5%	$H-\overset{\displaystyle H}{\underset{\displaystyle NH_2}{C}}-\overset{\displaystyle O}{C}-OH$

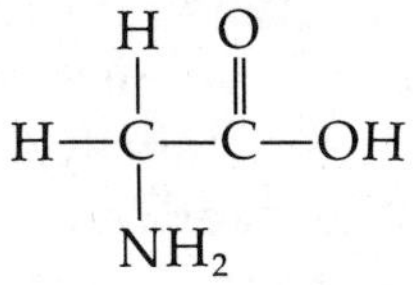

Glycine — 27.5% —

$$\begin{array}{c} H \quad O \\ | \quad \parallel \\ H-C-C-OH \\ | \\ NH_2 \end{array}$$

Proline — 16.4 —

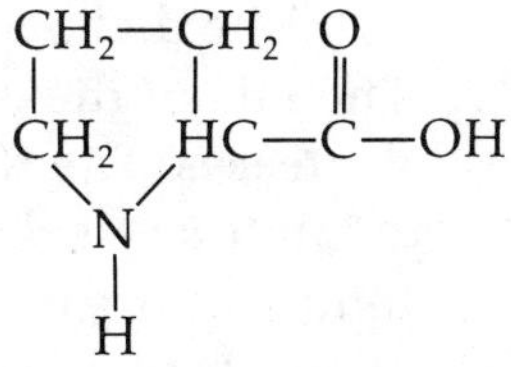

$$\begin{array}{c} CH_2-CH_2 \quad O \\ | \qquad\quad | \quad \parallel \\ CH_2 \quad HC-C-OH \\ \diagdown \ \diagup \\ N \\ | \\ H \end{array}$$

Hydroxyproline — 14.1 —

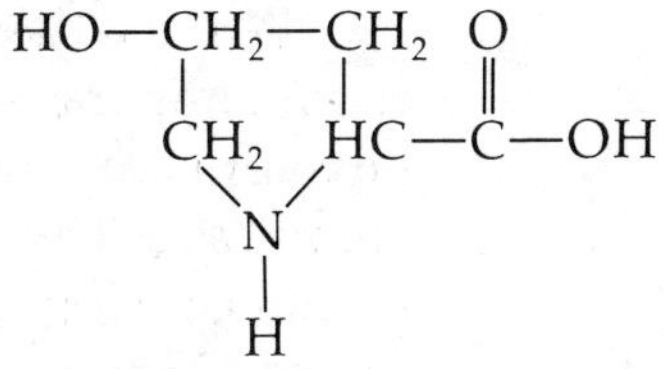

$$\begin{array}{c} HO-CH_2-CH_2 \quad O \\ | \qquad\quad | \quad \parallel \\ CH_2 \quad HC-C-OH \\ \diagdown \ \diagup \\ N \\ | \\ H \end{array}$$

Glumatic acid — 11.4 —

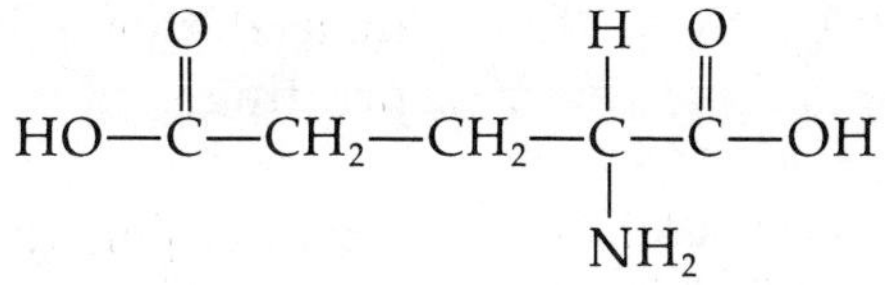

$$\begin{array}{c} O \qquad\qquad\qquad H \quad O \\ \parallel \qquad\qquad\qquad | \quad \parallel \\ HO-C-CH_2-CH_2-C-C-OH \\ | \\ NH_2 \end{array}$$

Alanine — 11.0 —

$$\begin{array}{c} O \\ \parallel \\ CH_3-CH-C-OH \\ | \\ NH_2 \end{array}$$

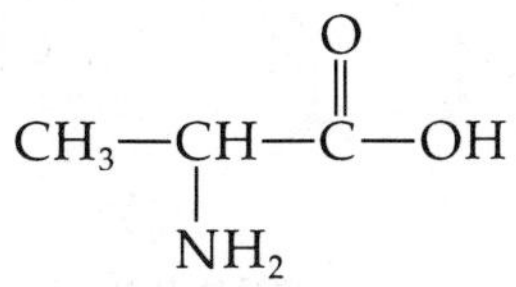

Amino acids will react chemically with either bases or other acids. The –COOH group in the molecules makes them acids, while the –NH$_2$ or the –NH group makes them bases. Such acid-base compounds are called amphoteric. Gelatin is hydrophilic ("water-loving") because of the $-NH_2$ groups, but hardened gelatin is hydrophobic ("water-hating") partly because of the $-CH_2$ groups.

Gelatin can absorb water, which causes the gelatin to swell. The percentage increase in weight due to absorbed water can reach 500% or more. When gelatin has absorbed a certain amount of water, it will melt at a temperature of about 95°F (35°C). This property of gelatin is important in the preparation of gravure cylinders with carbon tissue.

When it is desired to make a gravure cylinder, the carbon tissue is sensitized by immersion in a 3½% solution of potassium dichromate, $K_2Cr_2O_7$—4.7 ounces per gallon (35 grams per liter). When removed from this solution, the carbon tissue is squeegeed onto a thermoplastic plate or ferrotype tin to give it gloss and to allow it to dry.

The dichromated gelatin is now subject to dark reaction. The rate of the dark reaction decreases as the temperature decreases. The rate is about 7% per day at 70°F (21°C), but only 7% in four weeks at 40°F (4°C). Because of this effect of temperature, it is customary to store sensitized tissues in vaporproof envelopes in a refrigerator until they are ready to be exposed.

When a tissue is to be exposed, it is first allowed to come to room temperature. During this time, it is kept in the vaporproof envelope, so moisture from the air does not condense on the cold tissue. The tissue is given two exposures. One is through a screen consisting of transparent lines and opaque square dots, 150 or 175 to the inch (5.9 or 6.9 per millimeter). During the subsequent etching step, these screen lines are not etched; instead, they provide "lands" to support the doctor blade in printing.

Steps in making a gravure cylinder using carbon tissue.

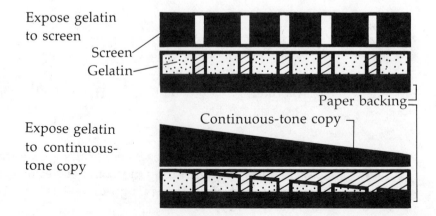

Expose gelatin to screen

Screen
Gelatin

Paper backing

Continuous-tone copy

Expose gelatin to continuous-tone copy

Steps in making a gravure cylinder using carbon tissue. (continued)

Apply gelatin to copper cylinder, with paper backing stripped away

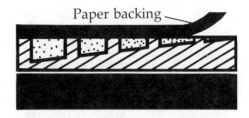

Dissolve unhardened gelatin

Etch cylinder

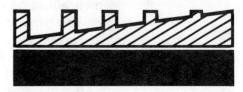

Remove resist

The second exposure is through a continuous-tone positive. The screen establishes the size of the little cells, while the continuous-tone-positive exposure determines the depth to which the cells will be etched. In a different method, one exposure is made through a continuous-tone positive and another through a halftone positive having a lateral dot formation with varying dot sizes.

Exactly what happens when dichromated gelatin is exposed to light is still a subject of some controversy. It seems that the light reduces the chromium, which has an oxidation number of +6 in $K_2Cr_2O_7$, to Cr^{+++}. Then the Cr^{+++} ions attach to the –COOH groups of the amino acids of gelatin, creating cross-linking. In simple terms, the light causes the gelatin to harden and its melting point to increase to over 200°F (93°C).

In order for this light-induced reaction to occur, it is necessary for the gelatin to contain a certain amount of water. The gelatin of the carbon tissue appears to be dry, but it actually contains about 10% to 12% water by weight. With this amount, the reaction with light proceeds very well, while a completely dry film of sensitized gelatin, as well as one completely swollen with water, is insensitive to light.

Carbon tissue, exposed but not developed, is subject to continuing reaction. This proceeds for about an hour after exposure is completed. If several tissues are to be applied to one cylinder, continuing reaction can be equalized by allowing all of them to stand for an hour before they are mounted.

After exposure, the carbon tissues are transferred under pressure to a gravure cylinder that has been wet with water to promote adhesion. The cylinder is then revolved in a bath of hot water. The paper or film is peeled off, leaving the exposed gelatin layer on the cylinder. As the cylinder continues to revolve in the hot water, the unhardened gelatin is washed away, leaving the hardened portions on the cylinder.

After development is complete, the cylinder is cooled by rotating it in cold water. Then the resist must be dried. Alcohol is often used to speed up the drying and ensure its uniformity. It has also been determined that the use of alcohol results in a decrease in penetration time, particularly when two strengths of ferric chloride are used in the etching step.

Some alcohols are suitable for use on a gelatin resist, while others are incompatible with it. Methyl alcohol, CH_3OH, can be used but should not be since it is too toxic. Isopropyl alcohol, $(CH_3)_2CHOH$, is satisfactory; and several formulas of denatured ethyl alcohol, C_2H_5OH, can be used.

After staging, the cylinder is ready to be etched. Etching is done with a solution of ferric chloride, $FeCl_3$, which etches copper. The ionic reaction is:

$$2Fe^{+++} + Cu^\circ \longrightarrow 2Fe^{++} + Cu^{++}$$

Thus, the ferric ions are reduced to ferrous ions, while the copper is oxidized to cupric ions.

At present, most gravure cylinders made with carbon tissue are etched with one strength of ferric chloride solution, of 40–44° Baumé (specific gravity 1.38–1.44).

The thinnest areas of gelatin are penetrated first, so these areas are etched the deepest and produce the shadow tones. The thickest areas are penetrated last by the etching solution, so they are etched the least and produce the highlight tones. Many other tones are created between these two.

Silver Halide–Gelatin Emulsion on a Polyester Film Base

Years ago, the carbon tissue method was the predominant method for the creation of images on gravure cylinders. It is still used in many plants. But several other methods have since been introduced. One of these is the use of a *silver halide–gelatin emulsion* on a polyester film base. It comes ready to use, with no refrigeration required. It is not subject to either dark reaction or continuing reaction.

Exposure is made much the same as with carbon tissue. Then the film is developed in a two-part photographic developer. The first solution contains either pyrogallol or pyrocatechol as the developing agent. When the film emerges from this solution, no visible effect can be seen. But an image appears immediately when the film enters the second solution, which contains sodium carbonate, Na_2CO_3. The image is then fixed in a fixing bath containing no hardener.

In Chapter 5,"Chemistry of Photography," structural formulas are given for the two common developing agents hydroquinone and metol. The active groups in the molecules of these compounds are in the 1,4 (or para) position. With pyrogallol and pyrocatechol, the active –OH groups are in the 1,2 (or ortho) position. Here are their structural formulas:

1,2,3-trihydroxybenzene, or pyrogallol
(also called pyro or pyrogallic acid)

o-dihydro benzene, or pyrocatechol
(also called catechol)

When exposed film is developed, metallic silver is produced in the light-exposed areas. But this is much less important than what happens to the gelatin in those areas. Pyrogallol is a tanning-type developer, hardening the gelatin in the areas exposed to light. This effect is the same as that obtained by the light-hardening of dichromated-gelatin on carbon tissue.

The developed film is transferred to a gravure cylinder that has been wet with water. Then the film base is stripped off manually. At this point, the emulsion on the cylinder is covered with a water-impermeable membrane. It is usually necessary to lay down several pieces of film on one gravure cylinder. The membrane prevents the first sheets transferred from beginning to be developed by the water before all sheets are transferred.

After all pieces of film have been laid down and the film base has been stripped off, the membrane is dissolved with diacetone alcohol. Its formula is:

$$H_3C-\overset{\overset{\displaystyle CH_3}{|}}{\underset{\underset{\displaystyle OH}{|}}{C}}-CH_2-\overset{\overset{\displaystyle O}{\|}}{C}-CH_3$$

This solvent is a combination of an alcohol (an organic compound with an –OH group) and a ketone (with general formula R–CO–R′), but gets its name from the fact that it is produced from two molecules of acetone.

The cylinder can now be rotated in hot water to dissolve the unhardened gelatin. The rest of the process is the same as that described for carbon tissue, except that two or three different strengths of ferric chloride are customarily used during the etching step.

Presensitized Photopolymer on a Polyester Film Base

Another gravure cylinder-making material consists of a high-contrast *presensitized photopolymer* on a polyester base. When this is used, fewer steps are required to make a gravure cylinder. However, the method is useful mostly for the reproduction of line work or of illustrations exposed only with gravure halftone positives. Areas on the cylinder are either etched or not etched; variable-depth etching of cells is not obtained.

The film is usually exposed first through a conventional gravure screen and then through a line positive. Or a single exposure can be made through a gravure halftone positive. The coating hardens in the areas exposed to light (the non-image areas). The film is then applied, emulsion side down, to a gravure cylinder that has been wet with water. It is not necessary to develop the film prior to laydown.

After all films have been mounted, the film base is stripped off, any necessary staging is done, and the cylinder is ready to be etched. No hot water treatment is necessary. One strength of ferric chloride solution can be used for etching, but it is common to use two strengths. The etching rate increases rapidly as the temperature of the etch increases, but the etching rate decreases slowly with time.

Direct Engraving In all of the preceding methods, a light-sensitive coating on paper or film is exposed and then laid down on the cylinder. In *direct engraving,* a light-sensitive material is coated directly onto the cylinder and is dried.

The coating is exposed in the same way as described above for high-contrast presensitized photopolymer. Exposure hardens the coating in the light-exposed areas. Next, the cylinder is rotated in a machine containing a solvent that dissolves the unexposed coating. After staging, the cylinder is ready to be etched with a ferric chloride solution.

Direct engraving does not produce the long tone scale required for illustrations. It is used mostly in the packaging field.

The Electronic Scanner Engraving Machine The *electronic scanner engraving machine* scans a photoprint, which can be either a positive or a negative. The electrical signals from the scanning unit operate a rapidly moving diamond point that digs cells into the copper cylinder. Their size and depth vary according to the signals received.

To make a good gravure cylinder by this method, it is important that the copper have a uniform hardness across and around the entire cylinder. The copper must also be uniformly ductile. (A material that is ductile is one that can be drawn out without breaking. Ductile is the opposite of brittle.) These characteristics are obtained by the use of proper copper-electroplating equipment and certain additives in the plating bath. If these requirements are not met, there is often excessive wear on the diamond stylus that creates the cells.

In an early model of such equipment, bromide prints are mounted on one cylinder. As the cylinder rotates, the prints are scanned and the varying amount of light is converted into electrical signals that instruct the diamond point at another cylinder to dig cells into the copper press cylinder.

Another method is now offered that eliminates the need for bromide prints. The output of a color scanner is converted into digital information that is fed into a computer for storage. In this step, originals can be enlarged or reduced and cropped as desired. A page layout is made, and information about where each page is to be placed on the printing cylinder is also fed into the computer. All of this information then flows electronically to the unit that operates the diamond point.

Epoxy Resin   Another system that is being developed for the engraving of gravure cylinders makes use of epoxy resin and employs a laser to etch the cells.

Two steps are involved. The initial preparation of a cylinder can be carried out at any time. Then the cylinder is etched when it is needed for the press.

In the first step, a copper cylinder is coated with a light-sensitive emulsion, exposed all over with a gravure screen, developed, and then etched so that all the cells are deeper than necessary for a subsequent laser-etching process. After the preliminary etch, the cells are filled with an epoxy resin, which is cured and honed to make the surface smooth. The cylinder can be stored until the time it is to receive its laser etch.

All of the information for preparation of a cylinder is stored in a computer. The computer instructs a carbon dioxide laser to remove part of the resin from certain cells. The result is the production of image cells with variable area and depth.

The laser etching of epoxy resin requires less energy than if copper is etched, and is also faster. Any pages with last-minute information can be inserted later.

10   Chemistry of Paper

The making of paper is a very ancient art. It was invented by the Chinese about A.D. 100. At first, it was used only for handwriting, but after the invention of printing, paper was also printed upon. Now many different papers are produced, designed specifically for letterpress, lithography, and gravure.

Papermaking

Paper was first made by hand. Of course, this practice was costly and time-consuming. The paper machine was invented early in the nineteenth century; since then, hand methods have almost disappeared. Some paper is made from cotton linters or cotton and linen rags, but about 98% is produced from various kinds of wood.

Groundwood, or Mechanical Pulp

To make groundwood pulp, the bark is removed from the logs. Then the cut logs are forced by hydraulic or steam pressure against a revolving grinding stone in the presence of water. This treatment converts the wood into a pulp consisting of minute particles of both fibrous and nonfibrous portions of the wood. The nonfibrous materials deteriorate when left for some time in contact with air, so paper made from this kind of pulp lacks permanency.

Groundwood pulp does not make as strong a paper as can be made with chemical pulps. For this reason, groundwood is mixed with other pulps. Newsprint, for example, contains about 80% groundwood pulp and 20% chemical pulps. Besides newsprint, groundwood pulp is used extensively for wallpaper, paper towels, and lightweight catalog and publication papers. It is unexcelled in its ability to produce papers with high opacity, smoothness, and ink receptivity.

Thermo-mechanical Pulp

Thermomechanical pulp (TMP) is being used more and more to make paper or paperboard in which the presence of nonfibrous material is not objectionable.

To make TMP, wood chips or sawdust are first softened by steam and then subjected, under pressure, to the defibering action of a disk-type refiner. The fibers produced in this way are more completely separated from each other and suffer less damage than those produced by the conventional groundwood pulp process.

Compared to groundwood pulp, TMP is cleaner and stronger. Compared to chemical wood pulp, it gives much higher yield of fiber, uses little or no chemicals, and creates no water or air pollution.

Increasing amounts of TMP are being used to produce newsprint. (In fact, papers of 100% TMP have been run satisfactorily.) A smaller percentage of chemical wood pulp is required, since paper with TMP has greater strength than paper with groundwood pulp.

Chemical Pulps

In the production of chemical pulps, the fibrous material in the wood is separated from the nonfibrous by a chemical process. The fibrous material is cellulose, with the formula $(C_6H_{10}O_5)_n$. Cellulose is one of the carbohydrates. It has a much higher molecular weight than starches and sugars, which are also carbohydrates. Nonfibrous materials make up about 50%–55% of the weight of wood. They include about 23%–30% of a binding material called lignin, which is a complicated mixture of phenolic materials; 7%–24% of complicated cellulose-like materials called hemicelluloses; and a small amount of mineral salts. Wood also contains a small percentage of resin, or pitch; the percentage varies considerably, depending on the particular species of wood.

Manufacture of Chemical Wood Pulp

To make chemical wood pulp, logs are usually first debarked. Then they are reduced to small pieces by means of a chipper. (It is much easier for the chemicals to react when the wood is in the form of small chips.) The chips are then cooked in large digester tanks, where they come in contact with chemicals that react with the nonfibrous materials. It is in this step that the methods for the production of chemical pulps differ.

During digestion, the chips are converted into a soft pulp, which consists mostly of cellulose fibers. Most of the nonfibrous materials are dissolved in the chemical solution. The pulp is then washed to separate it from the chemical solution.

At this stage, the pulp is still dark in color and has undigested knots mixed with it. The knots are screened out, and the pulp is then bleached to make it white. After the pulp has been refined in beaters or refiners, it is ready to go into the papermaking machine.

The Sulfate Process for Making Wood Pulp

The sulfate, or kraft, pulping process is now used to make most chemical pulp. This process produces high-strength fibers from almost any variety of wood. It produces pulp at a reasonable cost, and it also provides a means of generating energy through the recovery of the chemicals used. The main disadvantage is the low fiber yield—less than 50% of the wood processed.

The cooking liquor for the sulfate process is a solution of sodium hydroxide, NaOH, and sodium sulfide, Na_2S. Some of the nonfibrous materials are dissolved by the NaOH. Others decompose upon being heated, forming acids. These acids react with the base NaOH to form compounds that are soluble in water. The NaOH also reacts with the resins in the wood, forming water-soluble soaps. Thus, in one way or another, the nonfibrous materials are dissolved and separated from the cellulose fibers.

As sodium hydroxide is consumed, the sodium sulfide reacts with water to produce more sodium hydroxide. The reaction is:

$$Na_2S \ + \ H_2O \ \longrightarrow \ NaHS \ + \ NaOH$$

Thus the sodium sulfide acts as a reserve supply of NaOH, decreasing the initial amount required. Since too much NaOH can attack the cellulose fibers somewhat, this lesser requirement is one reason why paper made from sulfate pulp is strong.

The first kraft paper was produced in 1909. Initially it was used only for such things as wrapping paper, paper bags, and corrugated cartons, where whiteness was not demanded but where strength was important. Bleached kraft pulp appeared in the 1930s. This pulp had a brightness in the low 80s. In 1950, the first chlorine dioxide multistage bleaching plant was built for producing pulp with a brightness in the high 80s. Many fine papers are now made with sulfate pulp.

The Sulfite Process for Making Wood Pulp

The sulfite process was developed about 1882. Woods commonly used for making pulp by this process include spruce, hemlock, balsam, and fir. Since most of the resins in the wood are not dissolved, this process is limited to woods that are low in resin content.

A solution of calcium acid sulfite (calcium bisulfite) and some sulfur dioxide is used to reduce wood chips to wood pulp. To make sulfur dioxide, powdered sulfur is burned. The reaction is:

$$S \ + \ O_2 \ \longrightarrow \ SO_2$$

To make calcium acid sulfite, the sulfur dioxide gas is passed up through a tower containing limestone, $CaCO_3$. Water comes down through this tower. The following reaction occurs:

$$2SO_2 \ + \ CaCO_3 \ + \ H_2O \ \longrightarrow \ Ca(HSO_3)_2 \ + \ CO_2 \uparrow$$

The calcium acid sulfite remains dissolved in the water, along with some excess sulfur dioxide.

This solution is pumped into a digester tank. Steam is introduced, and the digesting of the chips is carried out at an elevated temperature and pressure. During the digestion process, the lignin in the wood combines with the calcium acid sulfite to form a compound, called calcium lignosulfonate, that is soluble in the hot solution. At the same time, most of the cellulose-like materials are converted into sugars that are also soluble in the hot solution. What remains undissolved is the pulp, consisting largely of cellulose fibers.

Because the calcium liquor presents severe waste disposal and stream pollution problems, calcium is being replaced with magnesium, ammonium, or sodium acid sulfites. Liquor from these bases can be easily burned to generate energy. When magnesium or sodium acid sulfites are used, it is possible to recover the chemicals for reuse.

Bleaching the Pulp

To make white paper, pulp must be bleached. Different bleaching systems are used. In one, chlorine gas is passed into the pulp–water mixture. The chlorine reacts with the small amount of lignin still remaining. The chlorinated lignin is then removed by treatment with caustic soda, NaOH. The final bleaching is carried out with calcium hypochlorite, $Ca(OCl)_2$, which is produced by passing chlorine gas into a water solution of calcium hydroxide, $Ca(OH)_2$. The NaOH and $Ca(OCl)_2$ mixture oxidizes the small amount of colored materials in the fibers to colorless materials. By this process, the pulp becomes nearly white.

The above is an example of multistage bleaching involving three stages. Bleaching of sulfate pulp uses more than three stages, with chlorine dioxide, ClO_2, being used in the final stages to improve the brightness.

The brightness of groundwood and TMP pulps is increased by bleaching them with hydrogen peroxide, H_2O_2, or sodium peroxide, Na_2O_2. Sodium and zinc hydrosulfites are also used to increase the brightness of these pulps.

The newest development is the bleaching of pulps with oxygen. This method has been used abroad for several years; the first installation in the United States was in 1974. Oxygen bleaching, compared with that using chlorine or compounds of chlorine, results in less pollution. Use of oxygen bleaching, originally very limited, is expected to increase.

Stock Preparation

Following bleaching, the pulp-water slurry is adjusted so it contains about 5% fiber and 95% water. Two types of stock preparation systems are used. In one, the stock is treated first in a beater and then in a Jordan conical refiner. This system is a batch process. In high-production mills, continuous stock preparation is employed, consisting of disk-type refining followed by conical refining. As part of stock preparation, other materials are added, including fillers, coloring materials, and internal size (material that affects water and abrasion resistance and related properties).

Jordan conical refiner.

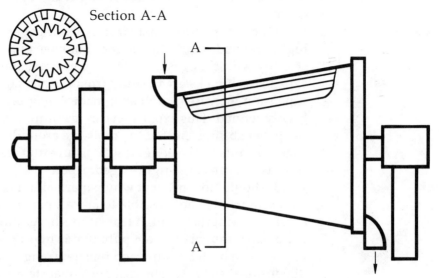

Section A-A

What happens to the cellulose fibers during stock preparation has an important effect on the characteristics of papers of various types. The beaters and refiners roughen the individual fibers and fray their ends; this condition is desirable. When such fibers are made into paper, the fibers interlock to make a strong paper. Blotting paper, on the other hand, is made from unbeaten pulp; it is quite weak.

Secondly, the beating is assumed to break down the water-resistant outer wall of the fibers, thereby exposing the inner fibrils. This effect is called *fibrillation*. Once it takes place, the fibers take on water and swell. This effect is called *hydration*. The longer the refining process continues, the more the fibers are hydrated, and the stronger the resulting paper becomes.

Different types of papers are refined to different extents, depending on how the paper is to be used. This varies from little or no refining for making blotting paper to prolonged refinement for making a transparent paper, such as glassine.

Almost every paper that is made is a compromise; it is important to understand the problems facing the papermaker. As the amount of refining is increased, the paper produced has higher bursting strength, tensile strength, and folding endurance, due to the greater internal bonding of the fibers. There is also an increase in sheet density, hardness, rattle, and resistance to pick during printing.

These qualities are advantages, unless a high-bulk paper is desired, or one with little rattle. On the other hand, there are some disadvantages to increased refining. As the amount of refining is increased, the tear strength and opacity of the paper decrease.

One of the unfortunate things about paper made from highly refined pulp is that it does not have as good dimensional stability with changes in moisture content. Paper always expands as it picks up moisture from the air. The amount of expansion increases with paper made from pulp that has been highly refined. This expansion can result in wavy-edged paper if the paper absorbs most of the moisture around the sides of sheets or rolls. If the edges lose moisture, the resulting contraction can cause tight-edged paper.

It should now be clear why papermaking is a compromise. For example, it is not possible to make a paper that has both high bursting strength and high tear strength. As another example, bond papers are made from pulp that is highly refined; such papers have high bursting and tensile strength, but have poor dimensional stability. Since dimensional stability is important for offset papers, the pulp is refined only enough to produce paper that will have enough strength to resist the pull of the ink during printing.

Fillers and Coloring Materials

Materials called fillers are added to the pulp during stock preparation. Printing papers may contain 15%–25% of fillers by weight. Other papers, designed for strength and rugged use, such as bond and ledger papers, may contain only 2%–6% of fillers.

The three materials most commonly used for fillers are clay, a naturally occuring alumino-silicate; titanium dioxide, TiO_2; and calcium carbonate, $CaCO_3$. The principal reasons for adding fillers are to increase opacity, brightness, and smoothness and to reduce ink strike-through. Fillers also improve texture and feel, and make the paper more dimensionally stable.

There are also some disadvantages. As the percentage of filler increases, the burst, tensile, and tear strengths decrease. Folding strength and stiffness of paper also suffer. So here is another area where the papermaker must compromise.

Some fillers have special properties. Thus titanium dioxide—more expensive than clay—is unexcelled for increasing the brightness and opacity of papers. Papers in which calcium carbonate is used have an excellent affinity for ink. Calcium carbonate also contributes to paper permanency, since its alkalinity helps to neutralize any acidity in the paper.

Microscopic plastic spheres, or "plastic pigment," are used to a limited extent in the coatings of lightweight coated papers for higher bulk with less basis weight and with high gloss and brightness.

Besides fillers, coloring materials are added in small amounts to make paper whiter or brighter. Thus a blue coloring material helps to overcome the slight yellow color of the pulp. Fluorescent dyes, called optical brighteners, are often used. The action of these brighteners depends on ultraviolet light. Paper containing them will glow when viewed under a "black light" (ultraviolet radiation without visible light) in a dark room. These papers have maximum brightness when viewed on clear, bright days. Their brightness will be lower when viewed under incandescent lamps.

The term *brightness* has been referred to several times. This term relates to the *whiteness* of paper, but the two terms do not have identical meanings. Whiteness is defined as the extent to which the surface of a paper reflects light of all wavelengths, as compared with an ideal surface. Brightness is measured by comparing the amount of light of a single, prescribed wavelength in the blue region of the spectrum reflected from a pad of the paper with the amount reflected from a block of magnesium carbonate, which is assigned a brightness of 100.

Brightness of newsprint ranges from the high 50s to the low 60s. Many bleached white papers will range from 78 to 85, and a small number of very bright papers will measure as high as the low 90s. Higher brightness papers cost more to manufacture.

Paper Sizing

Both internal and surface sizing are used with many papers. For internal sizing, rosin size is added to the fiber mix just before it goes to the paper machine. Rosin is one of the materials obtained, along with turpentine, from pine trees. It is a complicated material, acid in nature. Rosin size is prepared by boiling rosin with soda ash, Na_2CO_3, or caustic soda, NaOH, dissolved in water. These chemicals react with the rosin acids to form soaps. These soaps act as an emulsifying agent to keep the rest of the rosin in a finely divided state.

The rosin size is then "set" by adding papermakers' alum, which is aluminum sulfate, $Al_2(SO_4)_3$. This material is acid; enough is added to bring the pH of the fiber slurry down to 4.0–4.5. This acid converts the rosin soap back into free rosin in a very finely divided colloidal form. This becomes fixed on the cellulose fibers in tiny globules, and when the paper is later dried on the dryers of the paper machine, these globules sinter, or fuse together. Paper made this way usually has a pH between 4.5 and 6.0.

Besides rosin size, synthetically produced sizing agents are used. No alum is required, and the paper so produced is neutral or slightly alkaline. Such a paper is more permanent than acid papers, because alum causes deterioration of paper within a few years.

Papers with internal sizing are said to be "hardsized." Such papers are not waterproof, but possess some resistance to wetting by water or by water-based inks.

The Papermaking Process

After the pulp-water mixture has been refined to the desired extent, and the fillers, coloring material, and size have been added, the mixture is ready to be made into paper. It is diluted with water to make a slurry that contains only about ½% to 1% of cellulose fibers.

Fourdrinier papermaking machine.

This dilute slurry is pumped to head boxes on the wet end of a Fourdrinier papermaking machine. It is spread out on a fine bronze or plastic screen (called "wire")—about 65 meshes per inch (2.6 meshes per millimeter)—which moves along rapidly. A large amount of the water drains downward through the screen, leaving the interlocked fibers on top of the screen. After the screen has advanced a short distance, suction boxes remove more water, and a web of paper is lifted from the end of the screen. This web still contains a large amount of water; the purpose of the rest of the papermaking machine is to remove a considerable amount of this water. It is removed by passing the web first between rollers and then over large heated cylinders. At the end, the web is passed between heavy steel calender rolls to smooth it, and it is then rolled up.

Surface Sizing

At one point in the drying train, a unit is installed to add a surface size. To do this, a water solution of dextrinized starch, other special starches, or animal glue is used. The remaining heated cylinders dry this surface sizing.

Surface sizing seals the surface fibers. Such sealing increases the surface bonding strength, so the paper does not have as great a tendency to pick on the press. Surface sizing also increases ink holdout. In the case of writing papers, it gives a superior surface for writing with a pen and for ease in erasing.

Surface sizing varies in amount and kind of ingredients, depending on the end use. Thus a surface-sized letterpress sheet may not run well on an offset press. And paper sized for sheetfed offset may not run well on a web offset press—or vice versa.

Felt and Wire Sides

Paper produced on a Fourdrinier papermaking machine has a wire side and a felt side. The wire side, of course, is the side in contact with the moving wire on the wet end of the machines. The other side is called the felt side—because it comes in contact with a felt material during the drying of the web—or the top side.

The wire side has a higher percentage of fibers oriented in the machine direction than does the felt side. As a result, the wire side has a more pronounced grain direction. The wire side also has the impression of the wire mesh left in its surface. This produces a diamond-shaped pattern, easy to see on some papers and difficult to see on others. The wire pattern has been reduced greatly by the use of plastic instead of bronze wires on the papermaking machine. The felt side is generally preferred for printing when only one side of the paper is printed.

In recent years, twin-wire paper machines have appeared. In 1976, when there were about twenty of these in North America, most of them producing newsprint, the first twin-wire machine for the production of fine paper began operation in the United States.

In the twin-wire forming of paper, a jet of fibers dispersed in water enters the converging zone of two wires. Water drains simultaneously from both sides of the web being formed. Paper made this way has a more even distribution of fibers in its structure and has essentially two wire sides.

Multi-ply paperboard has been made on twin-wire cylinder machines for years, but these machines are limited in speed. The new twin-wire formers are operating at speeds in excess of 3,000 feet (900 meters) per minute. It is claimed that newsprint produced on a twin-wire former prints with less linting, particularly on web offset presses.

Supercalendered Paper

A *supercalender* is a machine designed to increase the smoothness of either coated or uncoated paper. It contains a series of rollers that are alternately steel and cotton or paper. The cotton or paper rollers are made by threading disks of the material onto heavy shafts, putting the disks under hydraulic pressure, and fastening them with steel heads.

The paper passes—under considerable pressure—between several pairs of these rollers. They impart a higher finish to the paper. Paper treated in this way is called supercalendered paper.

Basis Weight of Papers

With the premetric system in the United States, basis weight is the weight in pounds of 500 sheets (one ream) of a particular size. The trouble is that this basis size varies, depending on the type of paper or board. It is 25″ × 38″ for book and offset papers, 25½″ × 30½″ for index, 17″ × 22″ for bond and ledger, etc. Therefore, the basis weights of different papers do not represent the true relationship of weight per unit area.

There is only one metric basis weight for any kind of paper or board. It is the weight, in grams, of one sheet that has an area of one square meter. Thus the unit of measure is grams per square meter (g/m^2).

A factor (F) can be used to convert premetric basis weights to metric basis weights, or the reverse. The equations for doing this are:

$$\text{premetric basis weight} \times F = \text{basis weight in } g/m^2$$

$$\frac{\text{basis weight in } g/m^2}{F} = \text{premetric basis weight}$$

The value to use for F depends on the premetric basis size for a given class of paper or board. The values of F for various size classes are given in the accompanying table.

Class of Paper or Board	Basis Size (inches)	F
Bond, Ledger	17 × 22	3.76
Blotting	19 × 24	3.08
Index	20½ × 24¾	2.77
Cover (Antique, Coated)	20 × 26	2.70
	22 × 28	2.28
Bristol, Plate Vellum	22½ × 28½	2.20
Index	25½ × 30½	1.81
Bristol, Smooth Vellum	22½ × 35	1.78
Kraft, Manila, Newsprint, Tag	24 × 36	1.63
Book, Offset	25 × 38	1.48
Postcard	28½ × 45	1.10

Using these factors, the metric basis weight of a 50-lb. offset paper is:

$$50 \times 1.48 = 74 \text{ g/m}^2$$

For a 20-lb. bond paper, it is:

$$20 \times 3.76 = 75.2 \text{ g/m}^2$$

Conversion to a fixed basis-weight unit makes comparison much easier. A 20-lb. bond paper is a little heavier than a 50-lb. offset paper.

Coated Papers and Special Papers

Coated papers are referred to as film-coated, matte-coated, or enamels. They differ as to the amount of coating and how it is treated after it is applied.

Film-Coated Papers

Instead of applying surface sizing, the sizepress on the papermaking machine can apply a pigmented coating. The binder is either starch or, for offset paper, a mixture of starch and synthetic binder so that the coating will not dissolve in the fountain solution. The amount of coating is considerably less than is used on fully coated papers. But even this small amount of coating improves the smoothness of halftones.

Matte-Coated Papers

Matte-coated papers are used in offset printing. They are not supercalendered, and therefore retain their brightness and opacity—some of which are lost in supercalendering. Inks printed on matte-coated paper have a higher color strength than when printed on uncoated paper.

Enamel Papers

Enamel papers are coated with a slurry of water, pigment, and binder and are supercalendered. This treatment creates a smoother surface and increases opacity. The dried coating weight varies from about 10 to 20 lb./ream on a 25″ × 38″ basis size (15–30 g/m^2). A particular basis weight of a coated paper includes the weight of the base stock and the coating. The base stock provides most of the strength, so a 60-lb. coated paper is not as strong as a 60-lb. uncoated paper.

Pigments used in coatings include: clay; precipitated chalk, $CaCO_3$; blanc fixe, $BaSo_4$; titanium dioxide, TiO_2; and plastic spheres.

Several different materials have been used as binders for coatings. Casein, a protein material prepared from soured skim milk, was once one of the principal binders, but growing demand for milk as food has limited casein's use in paper. One replacement is soy protein. In some coatings, starch is used alone or in a mixture with synthetic binders such as polyvinyl alcohol and polyvinyl acetate. Coatings with synthetic binders are more pliable, fold with less cracking, and cut with cleaner edges during trimming and slitting.

Paper can be coated either "on-machine" or "off-machine." A roll or blade coater can be installed about one-half to two-thirds of the way down the drier section of the papermaking machine. The first on-machine coaters used rollers. However, they imparted an "orange-peel" pattern to the coated surface. In 1956, the blade coater was introduced; this is now the major method for producing coated paper. With this method, an excess of coating is applied to the paper web prior to the time it passes under the blade. The blade removes the excess, leaving an amount of coating that depends on how the blade is set.

The coating applied by blade coating contains 50% to 70% solids. With such a high solid content, less water is applied to the paper. Blade coating fills the valleys in the paper surface; the result is a very smooth, coated surface.

For many years, it was less expensive to apply coating on the papermaking machine than with an off-machine coater. This condition changed with the introduction in the 1950s of off-machine blade coaters with speeds of from 2,000 to nearly 5,000 feet per minute (600–1,500 meters per minute). With these high-speed coaters, paper can often be coated as cheaply off the machine as on. The finest-quality coated papers may be double-coated—first on-machine and then off-machine.

The pH of coatings (usually 7.5–8.5, sometimes as high as 10.0) is considerably higher than the pH of uncoated papers (4.5–6.0). Inks with drying-oil varnishes dry faster on such alkaline coatings.

In general, colored inks appear grayer ("dirtier") on uncoated paper than on coated paper. They also may not have the same hue (shade). A magenta ("process red") appears warmer (meaning more toward red and away from blue) on uncoated paper than on coated paper. A spectrophotometric curve of such a magenta, proofed on coated and uncoated paper, shows almost equal reflectance in the green and red portions of the spectrum, but lower reflectance in the blue part of the spectrum for the ink on the uncoated paper. Because of the lower reflectance of blue, a magenta appears less blue, or warmer, on uncoated paper.

Cast-Coated Papers

To make a cast-coated paper, a special coating is applied. While the coating is still wet, it is brought into contact under pressure with a polished chromium surface. This procedure causes the coating to dry with a very high gloss. The process is somewhat like making glossy photo prints by rolling the right type of coated photo paper onto a ferrotype plate under pressure.

Wet-Strength Papers

Most papers lose almost all of their strength when wet completely with water. A wet-strength paper is one that maintains at least 15% of its dry tensile strength when wet with water. Some may maintain 50% or more.

Wet strength is imparted by the addition of about 3% of a melamine-formaldehyde or urea-formaldehyde resin to the papermaking furnish. They serve as a bonding material for the cellulose fibers.

Why do these materials impart wet strength? When wet with water, individual cellulose fibers do not weaken. However, a loss of fiber-to-fiber bonding strength occurs. The resins help to prevent this loss. One theory is that a reaction takes place between the resin and the fibers, forming a chemical linkage that is not destroyed by water.

Wet-strength papers are used for special purposes where they must resist the application of water. These include hand towels, industrial wipes, table covers, wet-type sandpaper, wallpaper, garbage bags, beer labels, and photographic paper. Wet-strength papers are not necessarily water-repellent. Some, such as those used for paper towels, are in fact very water-absorbent.

One of the problems the papermaker encounters is the difficulty in recycling the in-process waste from wet-strength paper.

Some Properties of Paper

Only a few of the properties of paper are discussed here. These include water in paper and the effect of the relative humidity and temperature of the air, the printing consequences of grain in paper, and the effect of pH of paper or coating on the drying of inks. Some other properties of paper are treated in Chapter 12, "Chemistry in the Pressroom."

Water in Paper

Paper appears to be dry, but usually contains about 4% to 6% (by weight) of water. This is called hygroscopic water, meaning that it is not combined chemically with the cellulose fibers.

If a sheet of paper is exposed to air of a certain temperature and relative humidity, it will either lose water to the air or gain water vapor from the air until it reaches an equilibrium with the air. When this state is reached, the sheet will remain indefinitely without losing or gaining water if the temperature and relative humidity of the air remain constant. But if *either* the temperature or the relative humidity of the air changes, the sheet will begin to gain or lose water again. This statement is important because some people emphasize the importance of relative humidity and neglect the effect of a change in temperature.

When single cellulose fibers are completely dry and are then wet with water, they may change as much as 30% in diameter, but only 1%–2% in length. Since each cellulose fiber changes size as it absorbs or loses water, the whole sheet of paper will likewise expand or shrink. This can lead to misregister of color work printed on single- or two-color litho presses. If sheets are on a pile, or if a roll of paper is involved, absorption of water from the air leads to wavy edges. On the other hand, if water is lost from the sides of sheets or the ends of rolls, the result is "tight-edged" paper.

A skid or roll of paper brought into a pressroom from a cold warehouse should be left wrapped until it comes to room temperature. This conditioning may require one to seven days, depending on the volume of the paper and the initial difference in temperature between the paper and the pressroom. If the cold paper is unwrapped at once in the pressroom, it cools the surrounding air. As this air is cooled, its relative humidity increases. If the increase is great enough, it will cause water vapor from the air to be absorbed into the sides of the sheets or the roll. The result is wavy-edged paper.

Temperature conditioning chart.

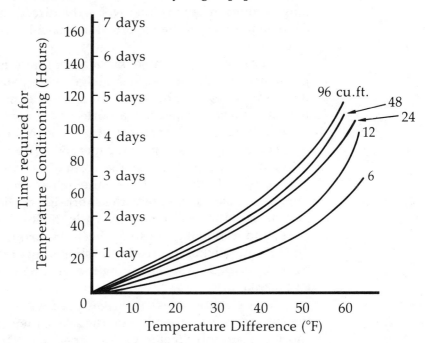

For the best performance of paper, it is desirable to have the pressroom air-conditioned. Adequate air conditioning includes control of both temperature and relative humidity.

The idea of "relative humidity" of paper needs explanation. If a paper is in equilibrium with air of, say, 45% relative humidity, then it is said to have a relative humidity of 45%. It would be better to include the air temperature in such a reference. If the specified relative humidity exists at 70°F (21°C), then a completer description is "45% relative humidity, 70°F" paper.

It would be desirable to be able to purchase paper already in equilibrium with the pressroom relative humidity and temperature, but it is difficult for paper mills to supply such paper. Therefore a properly air-conditioned room is important for providing a situation closer to the ideal than is possible when conditions are allowed to vary widely from day to day.

Several instruments are available that can be used in a pressroom to determine the difference between the relative humidity of the air and that of a skid of paper.

Grain in Paper   Individual cellulose fibers are longer than they are wide. When paper is formed, considerable crisscrossing and interlocking of these fibers takes place. But there is an overall tendency for the long dimension of the fibers to be aligned in the direction of the long dimension of the paper web—the direction of the web movement through the papermaking machine (machine direction).

This fiber alignment is the cause of grain in paper. The grain direction is parallel to the edge of the paper web. Because moisture causes the fibers to swell more in diameter than in length, a sheet of paper that absorbs water may expand from two to eight times as much across the grain as in the grain direction.

For the reason just given, paper to be printed by lithography is usually cut so the grain direction is the long way of the sheets. In this way the smaller expansion is in the long dimension. On a litho press, the short side of the sheet usually goes around the press cylinder, while the long side lies across the cylinder. When grain-long sheets are printed, any expansion due to water pickup is greater the short way of the sheet and can be compensated for by changing the packing under the plate and blanket.

Some sheetfed presses are equipped with roll sheeters. If the cut sheets feed directly into the press, they are printed grain short. Certain roll sheeters are designed to cut the sheets and then turn them 90° before they are fed into the press. In this case, grain-long sheets are printed.

In the case of most but not all web presses, the printing is grain-short. But this circumstance is not a problem here, since the web passes rapidly from one printing unit to another, with little opportunity for loss or absorption of moisture. A few web offset presses have a cutoff that is longer than the web width; on such presses, printing is grain-long.

Effect of pH on Ink Drying   Whether the pH of paper or coating affects ink drying depends on the type of ink. The pH of the paper is not involved in the drying of heatset or ultraviolet-curing inks. It also has little or nothing to do with the fast setting of a "quickset" type of ink. The pH does have a considerable effect on the drying time of inks containing varnishes that dry by oxidation and polymerization. This effect on drying includes the final hard drying of quickset inks. The following discussion is concerned only with these types of inks whose drying is affected by pH.

If something has a pH of 7.0, it is neutral. Most uncoated papers are slightly acid, with a pH range of 4.5–6.0. The pH of coatings on coated paper is on the alkaline side, ranging usually between 7.5 and 8.5, but sometimes going as high as 10.0.

Other things being equal, the drying time of a particular ink on uncoated paper increases as the paper pH decreases (becomes more acid); the drying time decreases as the pH increases. In one test, an ink printed on uncoated paper dried in 4 hours on paper with a pH of 7.1, 5 hours when the paper pH was 5.3, and 18.5 hours when the paper pH dropped to 4.4. Thus, as the paper becomes more acid, the drying time of the ink increases.

In the case of coated papers, the drying time of inks is determined only by the pH of the coating, and not that of the base stock. In one test, an ink printed on a coating with a pH of 7.5 dried in 7.3 hours, on a coating of pH 8.0 in 4.8 hours, and on a coating of pH 8.7 in 4.6 hours. Thus, as the pH of the coating becomes more alkaline, the drying time of the ink decreases.

Besides the formulation of the ink, other factors are involved in drying time. As the relative humidity of the air in the pressroom increases, ink drying time increases considerably. In some cases, it may take twice as long for an ink to dry after there is a considerable increase in the relative humidity. Also, a highly acid fountain solution will retard the drying of litho inks containing varnishes that dry by oxidation and polymerization.

Effect of coating pH and relative humidity on ink drying.

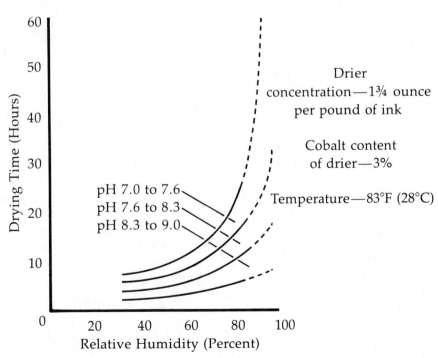

Other Properties of Paper   There are many other properties of paper that are important to the papermaker and the printer. These include tensile strength, bursting strength, folding endurance, tearing resistance, stiffness, internal bond strength, porosity, density, opacity, brightness, curling tendency, pick resistance, and ink absorbency. Instruments for the measurement of many of these properties are available.

11   Chemistry of Inks

The composition of inks varies greatly depending on whether an ink is to be used for lithography, letterpress, gravure, flexography, or screen printing. Within some of these categories, the inks are different for sheetfed or web presses. They also differ depending on whether they are to be dried at room temperature or the drying is to be accelerated by the use of heat in a dryer, ultaviolet light, infrared radiation, or a beam of electrons. And often they must be formulated for special purposes, such as resistance to scuffing or to fading on exposure to light and for use in contact with various kinds of foods. Because of all of these variations, the manufacture of inks has become a complicated business, requiring much skill.

The fundamentals of ink components, drying methods, and properties are first presented mainly in terms of lithographic inks. Special considerations concerning the inks of other processes are treated at the end of this chapter.

Inks for lithographic printing contain a pigment or mixture of pigments, a varnish or mixture of varnishes, usually a drier, and sometimes an extender, solvents, and modifiers. These ingredients are blended by the inkmaker to produce inks that will print to the required density, transfer properly over rollers and finally to the material being printed, and dry with the required rapidity.

While other things are involved, it is mainly the choice of varnish, or *vehicle*, that makes the ink suitable either for sheetfed or web offset printing. The varnish is responsible for making a sheetfed ink "quickset," or making an ink that will dry rapidly with ultraviolet light or set rapidly with infrared radiation. The varnish, plus solvent in some inks, is what makes an ink semifluid. One of its functions is to transport the pigment from the ink fountain to the material being printed. The varnish is also responsible for the binding of the pigment to the material being printed.

Varnishes must be chosen so they wet the pigment particles. Wetting means that the varnish molecules form an adsorbed film around the pigment particles. If a pigment is not thus wet by the varnish, the ink will be very short (not able to form a string) and dry. Generally the wetting of pigments by varnishes increases somewhat as an ink ages.

Pigments   A wide variety of pigments is available for use in printing inks. Most of these pigments are usable in inks for every process, although a few of the pigments are suitable only for lithographic inks, and a few others are suitable only for nonlithographic inks.

In lithography, rather thin films of ink are deposited. In general, film thickness varies from about 0.0001 to 0.0002 inch (3 to 6 micrometers). This is a thinner film than is usually deposited by other printing processes. To obtain sufficient color strength on the printed material, lithographic inks must be more highly pigmented than most other inks.

Ink film applied to the paper according to the printing process. *Courtesy of Coates Bulletin #44*

Offset lithography	0.00008″	(0.002 mm or 2 μm)
Letterpress	0.00020″	(0.005 mm or 5 μm)
Gravure	0.00050″	(0.013 mm or 13 μm)
Screen (thin film)	0.00125″	(0.032 mm or 32 μm)
Screen (thick film)	0.00250″	(0.064 mm or 64 μm)

It is convenient to divide pigments into these classes: carbon black, white inorganic pigments, colored inorganic pigments, and organic pigments.

Carbon Black

Black inks are made with carbon black. Since more black ink is used than any other color, it is the most important pigment.

Chemically, carbon black consists mostly of elementary carbon, a small percentage of ash (mineral matter), and a somewhat higher percentage of volatile matter—mostly hydrogen and oxygen.

To produce carbon black by the furnace combustion process, natural gas (or a mixture of gas with various liquid petroleum fractions) is burned with an insufficient amount of air in a chamber lined with firebrick. The furnace is filled with flames, and its temperature rises to 2,300–2,600°F (1,260–1,430°C). The materials that leave the furnace consist of carbon monoxide, hydrogen, nitrogen, water vapor, and suspended particles of carbon black. They are cooled with a water spray. The carbon black is separated with electric precipitators and cyclone collectors.

White Inorganic Pigments

The most important white pigment is titanium dioxide, TiO_2. It is used to make white inks, or as an opaque extender. No other white pigment has the hiding powder of titanium dioxide.

Calcium carbonate, $CaCO_3$, is used with a varnish to make an *extender*. An extender is a material that can be added to an ink to reduce color strength. Calcium carbonate is made by a reaction between a solution of sodium carbonate and one of calcium hydroxide. The reaction is:

$$Na_2CO_3 \ + \ Ca(OH)_2 \ \longrightarrow \ CaCO_3 \ + \ 2NaOH$$

Other white pigments, such as alumina hydrate, blanc fixe, gloss white, magnesia, and zinc oxide, are seldom if ever used in modern lithographic inks.

Colored Inorganic Pigments

The principal colored inorganic pigments used in lithographic inks are the iron blues. While the iron blues have different shades, they are essentially the same chemically, consisting of ferric ferrocyanide. They are produced by pouring a solution of potassium or sodium ferrocyanide into a solution of ferrous sulfate. A light-blue precipitate of ferrous ferrocyanide is formed. The reaction is:

$$K_4Fe(CN)_6 \ + \ 2FeSO_4 \ \longrightarrow \ Fe_2[Fe(CN)_6] \ + \ 2K_2SO_4$$

The light-blue precipitate is converted into a deep-blue precipitate of ferric ferrocyanide (iron blue) by the addition of HCl and an oxidizing agent such as sodium dichromate, $Na_2Cr_2O_7$, or sodium chlorate, $NaClO_3$. The net effect of this reaction is to oxidize the ferrous ion, Fe^{++}, to ferric ion, Fe^{+++}. The oxidation changes the precipitate to ferric ferrocyanide, $Fe_4[Fe(CN)_6]_3$. The different shades of iron blue are produced by changing the acidity of the solution, the temperature, and the time of heating during the oxidation.

The iron blues are lightfast and have high tinctorial strength, though it is not as great as that of some organic blue pigments. Iron blues are not affected by dilute acids, but alkalies destroy their color. They may be mixed with most other pigments, except those which are reducing agents or are alkaline in nature. The iron blues include Prussian blue, bronze blue, Milori blue, and Chinese blue.

Molybdated chrome orange is a deep reddish orange pigment that is not used in lithographic inks but is employed for letterpress and flexographic inks. It precipitates out when a solution of sodium chromate, sodium molybdate, and sodium sulfate is added to a solution of lead nitrate. The composition of this pigment varies, but it can be represented by the formula:

$$27PbCrO_4 \ \cdot \ 4PbMoO_4 \ \cdot \ PbSO_4$$

In the past, other colored inorganic pigments have been used, such as the chrome yellows, chrome orange, and chrome green. These have been replaced almost completely by various organic pigments.

Organic Pigments

Organic pigments possess a number of advantages. They provide a wide selection of colors. Many have high color strength, and inks made with them print clean tones. Most of them do not have high specific gravity. They generally consist of very small particles. These characteristics lead to inks with good working properties. Most organic pigments are easily wet by varnishes; in fact, they prefer to be wet by varnishes rather than by water. Most of them are easy to grind, and produce inks that are low in abrasion.

There are problems with some organic pigments. A few produce inks that are short; it is necessary to remedy this condition with the proper varnish or extender. Some sublime because of the heat generated in the delivery pile. When a pigment sublimes, part of it changes from solid to vapor. The vapor may penetrate several nearby sheets, producing on them, when the vapor condenses to a solid again, a tint of the pigment color. The tinting is undesirable in most printing. However, to make the textile heat transfer printing process work, it is necessary to use pigments that sublime.

Many organic pigments produce transparent inks. These are used for process colors. But if opacity is required, an opaque white must be added. If a pigment and the varnish into which it is ground have nearly the same index of refraction, a thin film of the resulting ink is transparent. If the index of refraction of the pigment and varnish are widely different, a thin film of the resulting ink is opaque. The refractive index of a material is determined by the angle through which a beam of light is bent as it leaves the air and enters the material.

The chemistry of organic pigments is very complicated. Most of such pigments are derivatives of benzene, naphthalene, or anthracene. They are all carbon ring compounds, and some contain four or five rings in one molecule. In addition, the molecules contain certain groupings of atoms that are responsible for the pigment color. Examples of such groupings are $=C=NH$, $-CH=N-$, and $-N=N-$. These color-forming groups must be in such positions in the molecules that the electrons can reposition themselves. When white light strikes a film of ink containing an organic pigment, there is a resonance of the electrons within these groups. As they change back and forth rapidly between these positions in the molecules, some of the wavelengths of the white light are absorbed. The color, then, is due to the wavelengths that are *not* absorbed by the resonating groups but instead are reflected to the viewer's eyes.

Azo pigments are one group of organic pigments. They are made by a chemical reaction between a derivative of benzene and a derivative of naphthalene, and they contain the —N—N— color-forming group. Azo pigments include toluidine red, Hansa yellow, para red, permanent orange, diarylide yellow, and naphthol AS. A large number of these pigments are available.

Azo dye pigments are produced by the conversion of certain dyes into pigments. Lithol rubine and Red Lake C are important members of this class of pigments.

Basic dye pigments are made by the reaction of certain basic dyes with phosphomolybdic acid or phosphotungstic acid. The resulting pigments have good fastness to light, yet still have strong, brilliant colors. Pigments in this group include the rhodamines, Victoria blue, and the red, violet, blue, and green Fanal pigments.

The phthalocyanine pigments include cyan blue and cyan green. Copper phthalocyanine is called phthalocyanine blue, or cyan blue. Two shades are produced; one called red-shade cyan blue, and the other green-shade cyan blue. The green-shade cyan blue makes an excellent cyan for process color work. If chlorine is introduced into the molecules of cyan blue, the result is a brilliant green pigment, called cyan green. This too is produced in two shades. All the phthalocyanine pigments are fast to light and alkalies. Inks made with them dry easily. The only disadvantages of phthalocyanine pigments is that they are somewhat hard to grind.

A number of organic pigments can be prepared as flushed pigments. The pigment is usually prepared by precipitating it out of a water solution. The mixture is then filtered and washed to separate the pigment from most of the water. The water still present in the wet pigment filter cake can be removed by a process known as flushing. The wet pigment is mixed with a viscous varnish, such as a heat-bodied linseed oil, in a large dough mixer. The varnish gradually replaces the water attached to the pigment surface. The water that is forced away from the pigment surface collects during the mixing operation and can be poured off by tilting the dough mixer. The rest of the water is removed by hot mixing, by hot grinding on an ink mill, or by vacuum distillation. The mixture remains very short until practically all of the water is removed, and then it suddenly changes to the consistency of an ink. The flushed pigment is sold in this form to the ink maker.

Flushed inks have advantages and disadvantages. Excellent dispersion of the pigment particles, high color strength, considerable finish, and low moisture content are definite advantages. Some of the disadvantages are a lack of flexibility in vehicle formulation, the requirement of a relatively large inventory to insure uniformity of color, an insufficient opacity for many uses, and a number of color and body changes that occur during manufacture and storage. Some pigments, such as alkali blue, dry to a hard horny texture, with reduced color strength, when prepared as a dry pigment. Such pigments are best prepared by the flushing process. But certain heat-sensitive pigments are not suited to this process and must be air-dried at low temperatures to avoid color changes.

It is estimated that 90% of present-day inks are made using flushed pigments. Many organic pigments are being flushed with a urethane alkyd varnish. The use of such flushed pigments improves the fast-setting properties of quickset inks.

Varnishes

The varnish, or vehicle, is the part of an ink in which the other materials—pigments, driers, and modifiers—are suspended or dissolved. Great progress has been made in the manufacture of varnishes that enable inks to give high scuff resistance or to dry very rapidly.

Today, many types of varnishes are produced, including oil, alkyd, urethane-modified, resin-oil, and resin-solvent varnishes. Besides these, there are special varnishes for inks that dry with ultraviolet light or electron beams, and for inks that dry on various types of plastic films.

Drying-Oil Varnishes

The chemistry of drying oils is explained in Chapter 4, "Chemistry of the Compounds of Carbon." The main drying oils used to produce varnishes for lithographic and letterpress inks are linseed oil, soybean oil, safflower oil, and china wood oil (tung oil). These oils are made into varnishes by bodying (stiffening) them with heat at various temperatures for various lengths of time. The longer they are heated, the greater is the viscosity of the varnish that is produced.

Drying-oil varnishes are used only to a limited extent in present-day inks. But the drying oils or the fatty acids derived from them are used to make other types of varnishes, such as alkyd, quickset, and gloss.

Alkyd Varnishes   Alkyd varnishes are used in inks for letterpress, lithography, and screen printing. They are the main varnishes used to make inks for metal decorating. Inks made with alkyd varnishes dry quite rapidly, and the dried films are tough, with good scuff resistance.

One way to make an alkyd varnish is to chemically combine phthalic anhydride (phthalic acid minus a molecule of water) with glycerin and the fatty acids derived from some drying oil. A typical reaction (not balanced) is:

$$
\text{(phthalic anhydride)} + \begin{matrix} H_2C-OH \\ | \\ HC-OH \\ | \\ H_2C-OH \end{matrix} + \begin{matrix} \text{fatty acids} \\ \text{from drying} \\ \text{oil} \end{matrix} \longrightarrow
$$

$$
\text{alkyd varnish} + H_2O
$$

If a high proportion of fatty acids is used, the result is called a long-oil alkyd varnish. This is the type normally used for the preparation of inks.

Urethane Alkyd   Varnishes   Urethane alkyds are not true alkyds, but are commonly given this name. Urethane has the formula:

$$
H_2N-\overset{\overset{\displaystyle O}{\|}}{C}-O-C_2H_5
$$

It will react with a drying oil to form a urethane-modified drying-oil varnish. Such varnishes have good pigment wetting characteristics and are used in lithographic sheetfed inks. They are not used much in metal decorating inks, as they tend to yellow when baked.

Rosin-Modified   Phenolic   Varnishes   Under proper conditions, phenol and formaldehyde react to produce an insoluble resin, such as Bakelite. If rosin or a rosin ester is added to the phenol and formaldehyde, and the mixture heated, a solid resin is formed. The rosin introduces oil solubility and, when it is heated with a drying oil, makes the resin suitable for use in an ink varnish.

Varnishes Made   with Rosin   Esters   One method of making a rosin ester is to react rosin with pentaerythrital. Pentaerythrital is a solid with a melting point of 504°F (262°C). Its formula is $C(CH_2OH)_4$. That is, each molecule consists of one carbon atom surrounded by four CH_2OH groups. To make an ink varnish, the rosin ester is dissolved in a high-boiling-point hydrocarbon solvent. One that is commonly used has a boiling-point range of 460–520°F (238–271°C).

Varnishes Made with Rosin and Maleic Anhydride

Rosin and maleic anhydride combined, with heating, produce a resin. Maleic acid has the structural formula:

$$\underset{\displaystyle HOOC-\overset{\displaystyle \overset{H}{|}}{C}=\overset{\displaystyle \overset{H}{|}}{C}-COOH}{}$$

This acid can be treated to remove one molecule of water from each molecule of the acid. The result is called maleic anhydride (anhydride meaning "minus water"), with the structural formula:

$$
\begin{array}{c}
H \qquad\qquad H \\
\diagdown\qquad\quad\diagup \\
C\!=\!C \\
\diagup\qquad\quad\diagdown \\
O\!=\!C\qquad\quad C\!=\!O \\
\diagdown\qquad\diagup \\
O
\end{array}
$$

To make varnishes for gloss inks and quickset inks, a rosin–maleic anhydride resin is heated with a drying oil to produce a resin-oil type varnish. To make a resin-solvent varnish for heatset inks, the resin is dissolved in a hydrocarbon solvent.

Varnish Made with Hydrocarbon Resins

Hydrocarbon resins are produced by refining the material that remains when petroleum is distilled to make gasoline, fuel oil, etc. They are also recovered from oil-bearing shales. These resins can be dissolved in a hydrocarbon solvent to produce an inexpensive varnish.

Gloss Inks

What makes an ink glossy is the varnish that is used. Rosin-modified phenolic and rosin–maleic anhydride varnishes are commonly used. Due to the presence of drying oil in such varnishes, they polymerize in the presence of air, to make the ink dry on the paper. The rosin–maleic anhydride varnishes do not give quite as much gloss, but there is less tendency for the dried inks to yellow than when resin-modified phenolic varnishes are used.

Quickset Inks

The varnishes used in quickset inks vary from one ink manufacturer to another. The varnishes often used include rosin-modified phenolic, urethane alkyd, and rosin–maleic anhydride. Besides these resins, the varnishes contain a high-boiling-point hydrocarbon solvent.

Heatset Inks

For heatset inks, typical varnishes are those made with rosin esters and rosin–maleic anhydride. Varnishes made with hydrocarbon resins are also employed. These varnishes are made with high-boiling-point hydrocarbon solvents, and so it is not necessary to add a drier to the inks. Sometimes a small amount of drying oil is added to a rosin–maleic anhydride varnish to improve the grease resistance of the dried ink.

It has been customary to employ about 40% of the weight of a heatset ink as solvent, including the solvent in the varnish and the extra solvent added to adjust ink viscosity. Such inks are still being used on web offset presses. One improvement to produce low-odor, low-smoke heatset inks is to use hydrocarbon solvents purified with hydrogen gas. Another change has been the development of new varnishes that made it possible to reduce the solvent content of the inks to 28%–30%. Using such inks has helped to reduce air pollution.

The newest heatset inks incorporate water to replace part of the hydrocarbon solvent. Web offset inks may contain 12%–15% water; heatset letterpress inks may contain up to 25% water. Usually, the sum of the water and hydrocarbon solvent is about 38%–42%. These inks containing emulsified water help considerably to reduce air pollution.

Another development is the use of a cosolvent that becomes volatile when the ink is heated. A resin is used that is not soluble in the hydrocarbon solvent. By the use of a cosolvent, the resin becomes soluble, and a good varnish can be produced. When inks containing such a varnish are heated in the press dryer, the cosolvent evaporates (along with much of the hydrocarbon solvent also), while the resin precipitates.

Vehicles for Ultraviolet Inks

An ink formulated for drying with ultraviolet light usually contains a mixture of vehicles. These include oligomers, multifunctional acrylates, and monofunctional acrylates. Such inks also contain a material called a photoinitiator. Since all of these materials are involved in the drying process, they are described in the "Mechanism of Ink Drying" section of this chapter.

Varnishes for Drying with Electron Beams

A beam of electrons is a powerful means for the drying of coatings or inks that are formulated with special photosensitive varnishes. This method is being used for the drying of coatings on chipboard, furniture, and some parts of automobiles. Work is being done to modify the equipment for use on printing presses. Such units must be carefully shielded to absorb X rays that are produced.

In general, the photosensitive varnishes used in inks intended for electron-beam drying are similar to those used in ultraviolet (UV) inks. One difference is that no photoinitiator is required. Several ink companies have formulated such inks and are testing their ability to be dried with laboratory electron beam equipment.

Printing on Plastics

There are two main types of inks for printing on plastics. One type is the "aggressive" inks, which contain a solvent that softens the plastic surface, allowing the ink to adhere. The other type is the "nonaggressive" inks, which do not attack the surface but adhere to the surface because of mechanical and chemical bonding.

A particular type of ink must be used with a particular type of plastic. Thus polystyrene and sometimes vinyl plastics require an aggressive ink. (However, some vinyl fabrics become too fragile when printed with an aggressive ink. In these cases, a nonaggressive ink must be used, even though it does not bond as well to the vinyl.) Nonaggressive inks are formulated for polyethylene, polypropylene, and polyester. In order to obtain ink adhesion on polyethylene and polypropylene, the surface must first be treated with a corona discharge. The extruder of the films usually applies this treatment, but it is sometimes done in the printing plant on the press. Most plastic films are printed by flexography or gravure.

Overcoatings

An overprint varnish is one type of coating that can be applied over printed inks. But the term "overcoating" or "press coating" as used here refers to the use of a water- or alcohol-based film-forming coating solution to cover the wet ink. Such a solution must not dissolve the inks, and the solvent in the overcoating must be volatile.

The use of an overcoating allows inks without solvents to be used on web presses to avoid air pollution. Overcoating can also be used on sheetfed presses, where it has found application particularly for the printing of board. The overcoating is dried rapidly with an air blower or mild heat. After overcoating, printed board can be stacked high on a sheetfed press delivery pile without setoff or blocking; no antisetoff spray is needed. Sheets can be die-cut only a few hours after printing.

A typical overcoating contains about 30% of some resin. One resin is an alcohol-soluble form of the propionate ester of cellulose. In this case, the solvent consists of about 70% alcohol and 30% water. Water-soluble acrylic resins are also being used.

Work to be overcoated can be printed with conventional inks if they are formulated without waxes or silicones. (The presence of such materials prevents the overcoating from forming a complete film over the wet inks.) When printed sheets are protected with an overcoating, they can be handled within a few minutes, even though the inks may require several hours to dry. There is no problem with the recycling of sheets printed in this way.

As an alternative to water- or alcohol-based overcoatings, a clear, ultraviolet-curable coating may be used over wet or dry UV inks. This is being done on web offset presses. Such a coating is also being used to a limited extent over wet conventional sheetfed inks, but this use results in the loss of gloss with some inks. A better method is to allow the sheetfed inks to dry, and then apply the UV varnish.

While overcoatings of one type or another have several advantages, they have the disadvantage of greater cost. This is not important in sheetfed operations, since the cost is less than that of an overprint varnish. But when a fast-moving web must be completely covered on both sides, the cost is high. The cost of overcoating compared with the cost of using UV inks varies depending on the percentage coverage of the UV inks.

Another overcoating method, resembling thermography, has been developed. Conventional inks are first printed and then, with the printed material moving in an enclosed chamber, are dusted with a clear resin powder. The resin sticks to the wet ink; the excess resin is removed by suction and reused. Then the paper passes under an infrared dryer that fuses the resin over the ink. Printed material treated this way can be handled and packaged immediately, even though the inks under the fused resin require several hours to dry.

This method has the advantage that the resin covers only the printed areas, not the entire sheet. Only enough resin is used to protect the inks; an embossing effect such as is obtained in thermography is not acquired. At present, the method is being used on slow-moving, narrow-width web presses.

Driers

An ink containing varnishes with a drying oil usually dries very slowly. A drier is a material that is added to such inks to accelerate their drying. Supposedly, the drier is not changed chemically. Therefore it acts as a catalyst to speed the oxidation and polymerization of the varnishes.

Chemical Composition of Driers

The best driers are compounds of cobalt, manganese, or zirconium. These metals combine with organic fatty acids to form soaps that are soluble in the varnishes. Octoate soaps are now the most used because of their low odor. Octanoic acid has the formula $C_7H_{15}COOH$; a cobalt octoate drier has the formula $(C_7H_{15}COO)_2Co$.

Other driers are cobalt, manganese, or zirconium resinates, linoleates, soyates, and naphthenates. Driers vary from about 6% to 12% in their content of metal. A 6% cobalt drier contains 6% of the metal cobalt, so it doesn't matter whether it's a cobalt octoate or a cobalt naphthenate.

Amount of Drier Needed

As more drier is added to an ink, the ink dries faster. The rate of drying increases rapidly with the first small additions of drier. As more drier is added, its effect on decreasing the drying time is less. A point is finally reached at which the addition of more drier decreases the drying time very little or not at all.

Effect of drier content on ink drying.

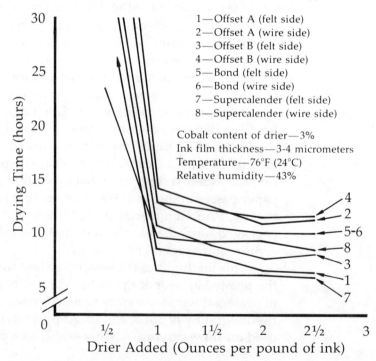

1—Offset A (felt side)
2—Offset A (wire side)
3—Offset B (felt side)
4—Offset B (wire side)
5—Bond (felt side)
6—Bond (wire side)
7—Supercalender (felt side)
8—Supercalender (wire side)

Cobalt content of drier—3%
Ink film thickness—3-4 micrometers
Temperature—76°F (24°C)
Relative humidity—43%

Suppose we want an ink that will dry on the slab in four hours. The amount of drier needed to accomplish this will depend on the nature of the drier (cobalt, zirconium, etc.), on the drying properties of the varnishes in the ink, and on the pigments that are present. An ink with certain colored pigments may dry in four hours when it contains 0.5%–1% of a 12% cobalt drier, while a black ink may require 1%–2% of the same drier for the same drying speed. An ink containing only an iron blue pigment will dry satisfactorily with no drier.

The reasons for these variations in drying are not certainly known. It is believed that some pigments adsorb more drier molecules on the pigment surface than others do. This adsorption inactivates the drier, making it necessary to use more drier when such pigments are present. The additional drier ensures that sufficient active drier remains to dry the ink in a reasonable length of time.

Drier Dissipation

As inks containing drying oils age in the can, the drying time often increases. This effect is called *drier dissipation*, or "drier kill-off." The drier, being nonvolatile, can't leave the ink, so something must happen to make the drier inactive. It is likely that the pigment slowly adsorbs more and more drier as the ink ages in the can, making the drier more inactive.

If an ink has suffered drier dissipation, the remedy is to add more drier just before the ink is used on a job.

Feeder Driers

Sometimes it is possible to formulate an ink so that part of the dissipated drier will be replaced with new drier. This is the purpose of *feeder driers*. Compounds such as cobalt borate, manganese borate, and magnesium perborate can serve as feeder driers. These compounds are only slightly soluble in varnishes containing drying oils. As part of the original drier is dissipated, some of the feeder drier dissolves in the varnish to replace it. It is claimed that by using the proper amount of a feeder drier, the drying rate of certain inks can be held almost constant over a period of two or three months.

Modifiers

Some inks are made with nothing but pigment, varnish, and drier. Usually, however, small amounts of other materials, called modifiers, or compounds, are also included. These are ingredients such as antiskinning agents, wax compounds, reducers, solvents, etc.

Antiskinning agents are added to some inks to help prevent skinning of the ink in the ink fountain and on the press rollers.

Such agents will not prevent the ultimate skinning of the ink, but they can in many cases increase considerably the time required for an ink to skin. The addition of an antiskinning agent to an ink always increases its drying time somewhat. A good antiskinning agent is one that increases the skinning time greatly without much increase in drying time.

Various wax compounds are sometimes used to reduce the tack of an ink and to give more rub resistance to the dried ink. The addition of a wax compound shortens the ink. Some wax compounds will come to the top when the ink dries and will prevent good trapping of the next color. Other wax compounds can be used in the first-down ink without any trouble regarding the trapping of the next color.

Petroleum solvents are sometimes added to reduce the tack of an ink. A light varnish, such as a 00 litho varnish, will also reduce ink tack. It is much easier to reduce the tack of an ink than it is to increase it. Tack can be increased somewhat by the addition of a No. 7 or No. 8 litho varnish, or by the addition of a heavy gloss varnish.

Magnesia, a mixture of hydrated magnesium carbonate and magnesium hydroxide, is sometimes added to an ink to shorten and stiffen it.

Modifiers such as these must be handled intelligently or they can cause more harm than good. In general, they are used only in small amounts in order to make necessary modifications in the properties of an ink. Modern practice is to add any necessary modifiers at the ink manufacturing plant. Thus inks supplied to the printer are ready to be run on the press.

Mechanisms of Ink Drying

There are several ways of drying inks, depending on the type of varnish and whether the drying is accelerated by the use of a gas-fired dryer, infrared radiation, ultraviolet light, microwaves, or electron beams.

Drying by Absorption

Ink for printing newspapers consists mainly of carbon black dispersed in a petroleum solvent similar to kerosene. With such inks, drying is obtained by the absorption of the solvent into the newsprint. These inks never dry hard—the reason that newspaper ink rubs off easily onto hands or clothes.

Drying of Inks Containing Varnishes with Drying Oil

The drying of inks containing drying oils is accomplished by a polymerization of the varnish molecules, aided by oxygen from the air. This explanation is true for the straight drying-oil varnishes, the alkyds, the urethane alkyds, and the gloss varnishes.

After the ink is printed, there is first an *induction period*. During this time there is no absorption of oxygen and no increase in ink viscosity. It is assumed that the drier is reacting with natural antioxidants present in the varnish.

At the end of the induction period, the ink begins to absorb oxygen from the air, and the viscosity of the ink consequently increases. One theory assumes that the drier first absorbs oxygen from the air and then transfers it to the drying oil. The drier is then back in its original state, ready to absorb more oxygen. This theory explains how a small amount of drier can finally bring about the oxidation of a large amount of drying oil.

It is believed that the oxygen adds on to the double bonds of the molecules of the drying oil to form peroxides. The amount of peroxides formed increases to a maximum and then decreases. In other words, there is first *peroxide formation* and later *peroxide decomposition*. Water, H_2O, is one of the by-products of peroxide decomposition.

While peroxides are forming and particularly while they are decomposing, polymerization is taking place. This causes a rapid increase in the viscosity of the ink film. Aided by the opening of the double bonds by oxygen, drying-oil molecules hook together at these points. This type of polymerization is called *cross-linking*.

The next stage is *gel formation*. The partly polymerized varnish can be considered to be colloidal particles that are dispersed in the unchanged varnish. As the amount of these colloidal particles increases, they combine with the liquid portion to form a gel. (For example, gelatin dessert is a gel after it sets.) Gel formation is the manner of *setting* of the ink.

After the ink's gelation, oxygen continues to be absorbed, and the viscosity increases further until a hard, dry film is obtained. The final stage is called *film deterioration*. This stage may continue, at a continually decreasing rate, for a week or two. During this time the ink film becomes harder and more rub-resistant. Some of the by-products formed during film deterioration are water, carbon dioxide, acetic acid, and formic acid.

During the phases of drying, some of the varnish molecules split into molecules that are small enough to leave the ink film as vapor. It is these volatile materials that create the odor of the dried ink.

Drying of Quickset Inks

Typical varnishes for quickset inks contain a resin, drying oil, and a high-boiling-point hydrocarbon solvent. The inks usually contain some free solvent in addition to that present in the varnish. The total solvent content is about 15%.

When a quickset ink is printed on paper, some of the solvent is absorbed into the paper. This causes the ink film to increase in viscosity and leads to fairly rapid setting of the ink. The oil is absorbed into the coating of coated paper faster than into an uncoated paper. For this reason, inks are more quicksetting on coated papers than on uncoated.

While inks of this type set fairly rapidly, they are not dry. The drying process may take several hours, and the mechanism of oxidation and polymerization is the same as that described for the drying of inks containing varnishes with drying oils.

There have been great improvements in quickset inks for sheetfed lithographic presses; many present inks set much faster than earlier inks did. While the formulation of these inks is proprietary, it is believed that they contain pigments that have been flushed with a quickset-type varnish. Furthermore, new resins are used to make quickset varnishes that are barely soluble in the solvent. When the ink deposits on the paper and only a small amount of the solvent is absorbed into the paper, the resin precipitates and the ink is set. The balance of the drying takes place by oxidation and polymerization over a period of a few hours.

Setting by Infrared Radiation

Infrared radiation accomplishes the rapid setting of inks. So the term "infrared drying" is not correct, although it will probably continue to be used.

Inkmakers are using different approaches to the formulation of inks for infrared setting. One is to use inks similar to quickset inks except for a smaller amount of drying oil in the infrared inks. Infrared radiation helps to drive the ink solvent into the paper rapidly, causing the resins in the varnishes to precipitate. This action results in the fast setting of the inks. They may become smear-free in 30 seconds to a minute. Then drying continues by oxidation and polymerization over a period of several hours.

Recently, special varnishes became available that react with one type of cross-linking when exposed to infrared radiation. These inks are also rapid-setting. In addition, it is claimed that they acquire close to permanent hardness in about two hours, particularly if a temperature of 130–140°F (54–60°C) is maintained in the delivery pile. While there is cross-linking of the resins in the varnish, there is no problem with the recycling of paper printed with the inks.

Infrared dryers have been improved greatly. Many sheetfed printers are using them to reduce or eliminate antisetoff spray powder and yet to allow jobs to be backed up rapidly. Two types of infrared dryers are manufactured. The type most popular in the United States is nearly "color-blind" (meaning that yellow inks set almost as rapidly as black inks), while the type most popular in Europe is not color-blind. One color-blind infrared dryer operates at 1,100–1,200°F (about 600–650°C). At this temperature, it emits radiation in wavelengths of from 0.00009 to 0.00016 inches (2.2 to 4.0 micrometers), a range that corresponds closely to the natural frequency of vibration of the molecular bonds of resin-based varnishes.

Drying of Heatset Inks

As mentioned before, resin-solvent varnishes are used in heatset inks. These inks also contain free solvent for viscosity adjustment, and some of them now contain a certain percentage of water.

Inks of this type are used for web offset and web letterpress. When the printed web passes through the dryer, the heat causes the solvent and water to evaporate. However, the heat also causes the resins to soften, so the inks are still not dry. As the web emerges from the dryer, it passes over chill rollers that cool it to a temperature of about 90°F (32°C). This rehardens the resins to complete the drying. The entire drying process occurs in a second or less.

Not all of the solvent is removed from the inks. It is estimated that about 5%–15% of the weight of the dried ink film consists of solvent. But from a practical point of view the inks are dry and jobs are ready to be trimmed and collated.

How Ultraviolet (UV) Inks Dry

The development of inks that dry in a second when exposed to high-intensity mercury vapor lamps was a remarkable achievement of inkmakers, in view of the complicated chemistry of the process. Other ink systems dry by the slow process of oxidation and polymerization of drying oils, or by absorption of solvent into the paper, or by evaporation into the air. The drying of UV inks is entirely different. The liquid vehicle in the ink is rapidly polymerized by the UV light, and the polymerized material is solid; the ink is dry.

There are three steps involved in a polymerization reaction. The first step is *initiation*, or getting the process started. The second is *propagation*. In this step polymerization proceeds rapidly. The third is *termination*. Certain materials can interfere with the propagation step, causing polymerization to terminate before it is completed, or requiring more UV energy to accomplish it.

The polymerization process is started by the action of UV light on an ingredient called a photoinitiator. This is a very active material, requiring far less UV energy to activate than would be required to activate the molecules of the vehicle. The UV light breaks apart the molecules of the photoinitiator to form what are called *free radicals,* which in general are very reactive chemically. They bring about a rapid polymerization of the vehicle.

For illustration consider the simple molecule of methane, CH_4, with the structure:

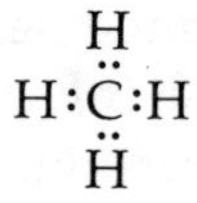

$$H:\overset{\displaystyle H}{\underset{\displaystyle H}{\overset{\cdot\cdot}{C}}}:H$$

If this molecule could break apart to form:

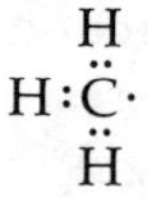

$$H:\overset{\displaystyle H}{\underset{\displaystyle H}{\overset{\cdot\cdot}{C}}}\cdot$$

and $\cdot H$, then each part would be neutral (not electrically charged), but neither would be satisfied with this situation, since neither would have a full complement of electrons. In this case, $CH_3\cdot$ and $\cdot H$ would be free radicals.

Photoinitiators split in this way when exposed to UV light. Several suitable substances can be used. One of these is benzoin methyl ether. When it is exposed to UV light ($h\upsilon$), the following reaction occurs.

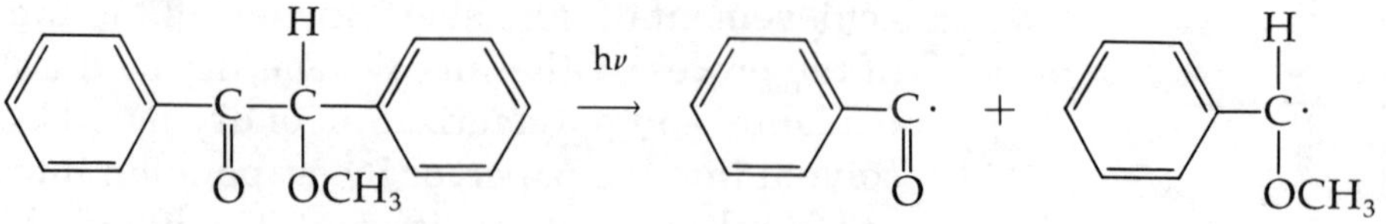

benzoin methyl ether   benzaldehyde radical   methoxy toluyl radical

That is, each molecule of benzoin methyl ether splits to form two free radicals.

One of the ingredients of a typical UV ink vehicle is called an *oligomer.* An oligomer is a partly polymerized material. It is produced by the reaction of certain substances with acrylic acid.

Acrylic acid has the formula:

$$\overset{\displaystyle H \quad H}{\underset{\displaystyle}{HC{=}C{-}COOH}}$$

Notice that the molecules contain a double bond between two carbon atoms. Oligomers are produced by the reaction of acrylic acid with a polyester, a combination of polyester and urethane, or an epoxy. (The formulas are complicated.)

Oligomers are not necessarily fast-curing; they are used in UV ink vehicles to promote adhesion, tensile strength, and flexibility in the cured film.

Another ingredient prepared by the chemical reaction between some substance and acrylic acid is one called a *multifunctional* acrylate. The term "multifunctional" refers to the two or three acrylic double bonds in its molecules. This type of compound is a true monomer. It has a lower viscosity than the oligomers, and has a fast cure speed. Examples are pentaerythritol triacrylate, trimethylolpropane triacrylate, and hexanediol diacrylate.

If the viscosity of the mixture of an oligomer and a multifunctional acrylate is too great for a satisfactory ink, a small amount of a *monofunctional acrylate* is added. Such a compound has only one acrylic double bond in its molecules, and has a low viscosity. As little of the monofunctional acrylate as possible is used in a UV ink, since it reduces curing speed.

The description of these ingredients makes it possible to explain how rapid polymerization is obtained. The active free radicals, produced when the photoinitiator is exposed to UV light, cause the double bonds of the acrylic acid part of the oligomer and multifunctional acrylate to open and the parts to begin hooking onto each other in a process called cross-linking. When this proceeds nearly to completion, the ink is solid, or dry. This is the *propagation* step in the polymerization process.

Finally, there is the *termination* step in the polymerization process. If, for example, something else reacts with the free radicals, they become inactive, and the process terminates. If only part of the free radicals reacts with such an inhibitor, then more UV energy must be used to accomplish polymerization of the vehicle in the necessarily short time available.

One inhibitor is the oxygen of the air that is adsorbed on the surface of the wet inks. It has been stated that 20 times as much UV light is required to create polymerization of the surface layer of ink, because of the oxygen, as that required for the ink below the surface.

One method for attacking this problem is to pass sheets wet with UV inks through a chamber filled with nitrogen gas. Satisfactory drying is said to be obtained with considerably less UV energy. This process is in use for the drying of inks on sheets of metal and also on offset printing paper webs that are traveling at a fairly low speed.

Drying with Microwaves

Microwave drying is being used now only for special applications, but work is continuing to broaden the things that can be done with it.

Microwaves, like visible light, are a form of electromagnetic radiation. The wavelengths of microwaves are much longer than those of visible light. Microwaves may be defined on the basis of frequency, or the number of cycles (waves) per second. The unit employed is the megahertz (MHz), which is one million cycles per second.

It is important to understand that microwaves can bring about drying only if the material to be dried contains molecules that are polar in nature—that tend to align themselves with a magnetic field. When a polar material, such as water, is exposed to microwaves, the molecules try to line up with the microwave field. If the microwave frequency is 2,450 MHz, the polarity of this field is reversing 2,450 million times per second, generating heat through molecular friction. If drying can be accomplished merely by the loss of water, the material dries. Thus, water-based glue can be dried in this way. There is the possibility that water-based inks, or inks whose liquid portion is some other polar material, can also be dried with microwaves.

Properties of Inks

Inks differ according to the materials used to formulate them. Inks usually have some odor. They may be "long" or "short." They exhibit what is called "tack," which can vary considerably from one ink to another. Some have greater stability on press ink rollers than others. Occasionally, inks will "fly," or mist. Sometimes the pigments in the ink will flocculate, or bleed into the lithographic fountain solution. All such characteristics of a substance are known as its *properties.*

Length of Inks

A *long* ink is one which can be stretched out into a long string when it is pulled away from the ink slab with an ink knife or a person's finger. A *short* ink breaks sooner under the same conditions. Usually an ink is long because it has good flow characteristics.

As an ink is worked more and more on the slab, it becomes longer. This is related to the breaking down of the internal forces in the ink. Different inks vary in the amount of increase in length with working. Since they vary with the amount of working, two inks should be compared for length only after they have been worked on the slab for an equal length of time and with equal force.

An ink must have sufficient length so that it will not back away from the ink fountain rollers and will give good distribution on the ink rollers.

Tack of Inks

Tack is a measure of the stickiness of an ink. It can be measured roughly by the pull on one's finger, wet with a thin film of ink on the slab, when it is pulled quickly away from the slab. Tack manifests itself during printing in the power required to drive the rollers of the ink-distributing system and the pull required to separate the paper from the printing areas of the rubber blanket. Excessive ink tack results in excessive consumption of power, generation of heat in the rollers, and picking or tearing of the paper.

In measuring tack, both surfaces must first be wet by the ink. When the two surfaces are pulled apart rapidly, the film of ink between them splits. Usually about half of the ink adheres to each surface. An exception occurs when ink is transferred from blanket to paper. In this case, more than 50% is transferred to the paper. This greater transfer is due to the absorption of some of the ink vehicle, or solvent, into the paper, which increases the tack on the paper side.

It was found in the GATF research laboratory that the force required to split an ink film when it is printed on paper is almost twice as great as that required when splitting from smooth metal.

Instrument Measurement of Tack

While people in the ink business are adept at measuring the tack of inks with "an educated finger," the best method is the use of an instrument specially designed for tack measurement. Such instruments have rotating rollers, on which a fixed amount of ink is distributed. The tack of the ink produces a pull, or torque, on one of these rollers. There is some kind of device, depending on the particular machine, for determining the amount of the torque. In this way, it is possible to get a *tack number*.

These instruments are used by inkmakers to check the tack of manufactured inks so that any necessary changes can be made. Tack readings vary, depending on the instrument used and the speed of the rollers. The tack of sheetfed ink is often measured at 800 revolutions per minute (rpm) and that of web offset ink at 1,200 rpm. Therefore, stating that an ink has a tack of, say, 16 is meaningless without further specification. However, the use of a tack-measuring instrument is valuable for the comparison of tacks of inks measured at the same speed on a particular instrument.

Importance of Tack

If the tack of an ink is too high, it may cause picking of paper or the pulling of coating from coated paper. If it is too low, drying problems, low gloss, and poor sharpness of dots may result. Inks for four-color, wet-trapping process work are adjusted so that the first-down ink has the highest tack, and the succeeding colors have progressively lower tack. This adjustment is made so that the inks printed later will trap well on the inks printed first.

A set of inks for four-color process work has a certain tack sequence as received from the ink maker. But, once the inks are on the press, several things begin to happen that either increase or decrease the tack of each ink. Unless such changes occur the same with each ink, it is possible that the tacks can be altered to the extent that poor trapping results.

With inks containing solvent, there is some evaporation of the solvent, and tack increases. Some of the solvent may be absorbed into rollers or blankets, and tack increases further. As the press operates, the ink rollers heat, heating the ink, and tack decreases. As one ink is printed on paper, a little of the solvent and vehicle is absorbed into the surface of the paper; this absorption increases the tack of the printed ink film.

On lithographic presses, the printing plates are kept moist with water. Some of the water becomes emulsified in the ink, and some is present on the surface of the ink. The amount of water present in and on an ink changes the tack considerably.

Because of all of these variables, the tack sequence can be altered. It is correct to say that, in order to get good trapping, the tack of the first-down ink on the paper should be higher than the tack of the second-down ink at the time it deposits on the first-down ink. Unfortunately, there is no way to determine these tack values. If poor trapping is observed, then one ink or another must be changed by making use of the known ways to increase or decrease tack on the press.

The tack of inks has been altered through the years. When ink varnishes were heat-bodied drying oils, and lithographic plates were not as good as they are now, it was common to use inks with tack numbers varying from 25 to 30 (at 800 rpm). Later, when quickset inks were developed, it was possible to produce inks with tacks varying from about 16 to 25 for sheetfed printing. If the tack was reduced much below 16, the inks became "soupy" and did not print sharp.

The newest development is the so-called "low tack" inks for sheetfed printing that have tack readings varying from 16 down to 10. They differ from previous inks in that they have a heavy body brought about by using gel varnishes, but they also have a low tack. So it is no longer true that a heavy-bodied ink must have a high tack.

Generally, the tack range of inks must be decreased as press speeds increase. Thus the tack of web offset press inks is quite low. Higher tacks are required in general for sheetfed offset press inks. However, low-tack inks may perform satisfactorily on sheetfed presses that operate at higher speeds.

Ink Flying   Sometimes an ink will fly on the press. Ink flying means that thousands of tiny ink particles leave the ink roller and form a mist in the pressroom air. Flying usually happens when the ink is a very long one. The speed of the press is involved also. If an ink is on the borderline, it may not fly at low press speeds, but may start to do so as press speed is increased.

Ink flying.

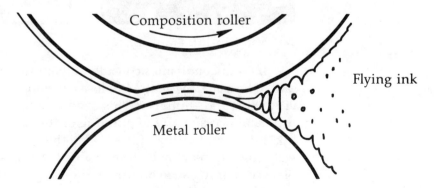

Composition roller

Flying ink

Metal roller

To understand ink flying, you must know what happens when ink films separate on rapidly rotating ink rollers. High-speed flash pictures have shown that, just after the ink has passed through the nip between two rollers, it forms thousands of tiny filaments, or threads. These threads get longer, until their length is about ten times their diameter at the instant they break in two. Then they decrease in length very rapidly and merge with the main body of ink on each of the two rollers. In an ink that flies, these threads may string out to one-eighth inch (three millimeters) before breaking. Then some of them break in two or more places. In this way, free-floating ink particles are produced.

Emulsification of Water in Inks

You have heard the statement that "ink and water don't mix." This is not strictly true. It is true that water does not dissolve in ink; but tiny droplets of water become dispersed in ink when the ink is run on a lithographic press. This produces a water-in-ink emulsion. Even a good litho ink will emulsify about 25%–30% of its weight of water.

Emulsification of water in ink and ink in water.

Water-in-ink emulsion

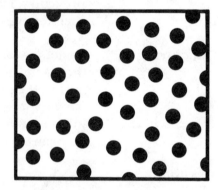

Ink-in-water emulsion

If an ink emulsifies considerably more water than this, it is said to be *waterlogged*: the ink loses its good body and becomes very short and "buttery." This condition leads to a washed-out print and occasionally to blinding of the image, stripping of the ink rollers, and piling of the ink on the rollers and plate. A waterlogged ink may be responsible for gum streaks when a plate containing such an ink on the image areas is gummed up.

While an ink that picks up too much water is definitely a poor ink, inks that emulsify only a small amount of water are not good either. In explanation, it is supposed that water not only emulsifies in the ink but is present to some extent as surface moisture as well. Under normal conditions, this small amount of surface moisture helps to keep halftones open. But if the ink emulsifies only a small amount of water, then more is left as surface moisture, and the printing has a "snowflaky" appearance due to failure of ink to reach small areas that are protected by water.

Lithographic inks should be printed using as small an amount of water as possible—just enough to keep the nonprinting areas from beginning to accept ink. In this way, the amount of water emulsified in the ink is kept an an acceptable level, with only a small amount of surface moisture on the ink.

If water is completely emulsified in an ink, its tack increases compared with that when no water is present. Surface water, on the other hand, greatly reduces the apparent tack of the ink. In GATF tests, tack readings dropped to about half the original value as soon as the dampening rollers were put onto the plate. This drop was due to the tack-reducing effect of the surface moisture. The effect largely disappeared by the time the ink reached the paper, since the ink had lost most of its surface moisture.

Press Stability of Inks

The press stability of an ink refers to the number of hours that the ink will stay open on press rollers. There are two main reasons that inks get heavy and sometimes dry on the rollers. One involves inks with drying-oil varnishes. If left too long, such inks will oxidize and polymerize, leading to drying. The other involves inks with a considerable percentage of solvent. If the rollers get hot, such inks can lose enough solvent into the air that they dry on the rollers.

Press stability is often a compromise. For example, the press stability of inks with drying-oil varnishes decreases as the amount of drier in the ink is increased. But it may be desired to use this extra drier so that the printed ink will dry faster. There is a definite trade-off when web heatset inks are used. If inks are formulated with solvent having a somewhat lower boiling point, they dry with less dryer heat but have poorer press stability. The use of water-cooled ink rollers helps this situation considerably.

The ideal, of course, is to have inks that will stay open for days on press rollers but will dry almost immediately when they are printed. The ultraviolet inks come closest to meeting this ideal.

Pigment Flocculation and Bleeding

A good pigment consists of very tiny particles. These are dispersed through the varnish when the ink is ground on an ink mill. If something happens that causes these particles to clump together to form fewer but larger particles, the pigment is said to *flocculate*. Flocculation happens primarily when a lithographic

Pigment
flocculation.

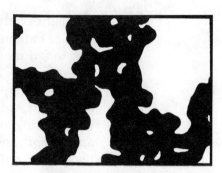

Pigment dispersed,
ink relatively fluid

Pigment flocculated,
ink no longer fluid

ink comes in contact with water on the press. If a pigment
flocculates, the ink becomes very short, or pasty. This condition
may lead to stripping of the ink from the ink rollers and piling
on rollers and plate. Luckily, most pigments do not flocculate.

Why some pigments flocculate may be explained as follows:
Pigment particles are surrounded by an adsorbed film of varnish
molecules. This condition usually remains so even after the
fountain solution becomes emulsified in the ink. Some
pigments, however, prefer water molecules to varnish
molecules. In the presence of water, these pigments lose the
varnish molecules and take on an adsorbed film of water
molecules. The pigment particles then become more polar, since
water molecules are highly polar. Polar particles have an
electrical attraction for each other. Therefore, many of the
pigment particles join to form a much larger particle: the
pigment flocculates.

Pigments for lithographic inks must be chosen so that they
do not bleed into the water fountain solution—they must not be
soluble in water or in dilute acid solutions. This requirement is
no problem with letterpress or screen printing inks; a phloxine-
type pigment, for example, can be employed in a letterpress ink.
But such a pigment is risky to use in a lithographic ink.

Flexographic Inks

Flexographic inks are fluids with low viscosity. In general, they
are formulated with pigments (or dyes), resin-solvent varnishes,
plasticizers, and solvents. Many of the pigments already
discussed in connection with lithographic inks are also used in
flexographic inks.

Several kinds of resins are used to make the resin-solvent
varnishes. These include shellac, vinyl, resin-modified maleic,

polyamide, rosin esters, and nitrocellulose. Shellac is a naturally occurring material. Many of the early flexo inks were made with it, but it is now very expensive and is used mainly for inks to print on styrene.

A number of solvents are employed to dilute particular inks, depending on the resin used in the ink varnish. The principal ones are:

Name	Formula	Boiling Point °F	Boiling Point °C
Anhydrous ethanol	C_2H_5OH	173.1	78.4
Hexane	C_6H_{14}	155.7	68.7
Normal-propyl acetate	$CH_3-COOC_3H_7$	214.9	101.6
Isopropyl acetate	$CH_3-COOC_3H_7$	191.1	88.4
Ethyl acetate	$CH_3-COOC_2H_5$	171.0	77.2
Normal-propanol	C_3H_7-OH	207.0	97.2
Isopropanol	C_3H_7-OH	180.3	82.4

Besides these, the following solvents are used to some extent:

Name	Formula	Boiling Point °F	Boiling Point °C
Heptane	C_7H_{16}	187.0	86.1
Toluene	$C_6H_5-CH_3$	231.1	110.6
Cellosolve	Ethylene glycol monoethyl ether	High	
Naphtha	Hydrocarbon mixture	243–293	117–145

The ink manufacturer recommends a "normal" solvent, or mixture of solvents, to be used for "normal" running speeds on the press. If a press is running fast, then a "fast" solvent is used, so that it will evaporate faster when the ink is printed on the substrate. If a press if running slowly, a "slow" solvent is used.

A few examples are given below to show (a) typical resins or resin mixtures used, (b) solvents or solvent mixtures used for "slow," "normal," and "fast" operation, and (c) the principal substrates on which the ink will adhere well.

Ink Ingredients Related to Substrate

Resins	Solvent Mixtures			For principal substrates
	Slow	Normal	Fast	
Polyamide and nitro-cellulose	Anhydrous ethanol; normal-propanol (high percentage)	Anhydrous ethanol, 80%; normal-propanol, 20%	Anhydrous ethanol, 90%; normal-propanol, 10%	Polyethylene Polypropylene Polyester, coated Paper Board Nylon Glassine Cellophane, coated with polyvinylidene chloride
Nitro-cellulose and rosin-modified maleic	Anhydrous ethanol; normal-propyl acetate; normal propanol	Anhydrous ethanol, 85%; normal-propyl acetate, 15%	Anhydrous ethanol; normal-propyl acetate; ethyl acetate	Cellophane, moisture-proof Cellophane, PVDC-coated Polyethylene Polyester, coated Paper Board Glassine
Vinyl	Small amount cellosolve added to normal mixture	Anhydrous ethanol, 50%; normal-propyl acetate, 30%; nitro-paraffin, 20%	Small amount ethyl acetate added to normal mixture	Polyester, coated Polyester, uncoated Nylon Cellophane PVDC-coated
Shellac	Small amount cellosolve added to normal mixture	Anhydrous ethanol, 65%; normal-propyl acetate 35%	Part of normal-propyl acetate replaced with ethyl acetate	Styrene

As you can see, particular solvent mixtures are used with certain resins to produce inks that will adhere well to certain substrates. If you check the boiling points of the solvents, you will see that in the "slow" solvents, something has been added that has a higher boiling point than that of the "normal" solvents. The opposite is true of the "fast" solvent mixture.

You will also notice that the solvents used in flexo inks have fairly low boiling points. Therefore they can be vaporized from the printed inks with a dryer temperature of 120°F (49°C) or lower. This is below their boiling points, but they have a sufficiently high vapor pressure at this temperature to achieve rapid vaporization.

So far, we have been talking about flexo inks that employ a mixture of organic solvents. In recent years, water-based flexo inks have been developed, and are widely used for printing on paper and paperboard. They are also employed to a limited extent for printing on foil and certain plastic films. The solvent in such inks consists of about 80% water and 20% solvents such as glycols and alcohols.

The mechanism of flexographic ink drying is the same as that of heatset offset ink drying except that solvents with much lower boiling points are used in flexo inks. When the solvents are vaporized, the solid resin remains to hold the pigments and to bind the ink to the substrate. The inks contain no driers, and drying by oxidation and polymerization is not involved.

Gravure Inks

Gravure inks, like flexographic inks, are fluids with low viscosity. They are formulated with pigments, resin-solvent varnishes, plasticizers, and solvents. Many of the pigments already discussed in connection with lithographic inks are also used in gravure inks.

The mechanism of gravure ink drying is the same as that of heatset offset ink drying except that solvents with much lower boiling points are used. When the solvents are vaporized in the dryers, the solid resin remains to hold the pigments and to bind the ink to the substrate. The inks contain no driers. (Rotogravure news inks require no heat, as they dry by absorption.)

Publication gravure inks are used to print long editions on coated or uncoated paper. Here ink cost is a factor, so relatively inexpensive resins are used for the resin-solvent varnishes. These include ester gums, calcium and zinc resinates, and some hydrocarbon resins.

With gravure packaging inks, other resins and solvents are used, depending on the material to be printed. There are about ten types of such inks, designated with letters, such as B, C, D, E, etc. Some of the resins employed, depending on the ink type, are RS nitrocellulose, SS nitrocellulose, chlorinated rubber, and vinyl.

The inks are thinned at the press with a mixture of solvents suitable for use with a particular type of ink. The solvent mixture can also be varied in accordance with the desired rate of evaporation. As an example, consider a type E gravure packaging ink. The resin used is SS nitrocellulose. One ink manufacturer suggests the following solvent mixtures for various evaporation rates:

Slow	Regular	Fast
1 part normal-propyl acetate	2 parts ethyl acetate	1 part ethanol
1 part ethanol	2 parts ethanol	4 parts ethyl acetate
	1 part toluene	

Thinners used for other types of gravure packaging inks include some of the solvents mentioned above as well as lactol spirits, naphtha, heptane, isopropyl acetate, methyl ethyl ketone (MEK), and others.

As a gravure ink is printed, the solvents in the ink remaining in the ink pan gradually vaporize. The percentage of the more volatile solvent in the vapor phase is higher than the percentage of that solvent in the ink. For example, if the solvent mixture in the ink contains 10% ethyl alcohol and 90% toluene, the first vapor from this ink will consist of 46% ethyl alcohol and 54% toluene because ethyl alcohol is correspondingly more volatile than toluene. As vaporization continues, the vapor gradually consists of less and less than 46% ethyl alcohol because its percentage remaining in the ink is less and less than 10%.

Finally, the viscosity of the ink in the pan increases enough so that a makeup solvent mixture must be added. The idea is to use a makeup mixture that will bring the percentage of each solvent in the ink back to its original amount. The manufacturers of gravure inks supply recommended makeup mixture specifications.

To keep the ink printing density constant, it is important to control the viscosity of the ink in the pan. Various viscosity instruments are available for checking this. Many gravure presses are equipped with devices that control ink viscosity automatically.

Screen Printing Inks

Screen printing inks must be formulated to adhere well to a wide variety of substrates. Therefore a number of different types of inks are needed. Some dry by solvent evaporation; others dry by the slower process of oxidation and polymerization of the varnish. One type polymerizes with heat.

In general, the inks contain pigments (or dyes), varnishes, and usually solvents. Some contain driers; others do not. Certain inks are supplied ready to be printed, but it is more customary that they require addition of some solvent to bring them to the desired consistency. The screen printer must know what solvents are compatible with the resins in a particular type of ink.

One type of ink is referred to as *lacquer*. Such inks use nitrocellulose as a base, with various ketones for solvents. Lacquers can be thinned with lacquer solvent. They dry by solvent evaporation, requiring twenty to forty minutes in the air or a few seconds in drying equipment. They are used for printing on paper, paperboard, foil, book covers, wood, and certain plastics.

Modified ethyl cellulose can also be used as a base. Inks of this type are usually not referred to as lacquers. They usually contain mineral spirits or aliphatic naphtha with a high flash point. They dry by solvent evaporation. Some formulations will air-dry in five minutes or less, but most require twenty to forty minutes. They are used mostly for printing on paper and paperboard.

Gloss enamel inks are made with a long oil alkyd varnish. They contain a cobalt drier, and dry by oxidation and polymerization. They are used principally for printing on paperboard, treated polyethylene, and metal.

When good adhesion and solvent resistance are required on certain difficult surfaces, an epoxy ink is used. This employs an epoxy resin, a catalyst to set the resin, and solvents such as glycol ethers. With a two-phase ink, the catalyst is added to the ink and is mixed in well. The mixture is allowed to stand for thirty to thirty-five minutes as an induction period. Then the ink can be used for about five to six hours before it begins to gel. Single-phase inks are also available.

Two-phase epoxy inks will dry at room temperature, but single-phase inks must be baked for curing. Typical curing procedures are to bake 3 minutes at 400°F (200°C), or 7 minutes at 350°F (175°C). Epoxy inks are used for printing on glass, metals, ceramics, and certain plastics such as phenolics, polyesters, and melamines. Such inks are not recommended for outdoor displays or for printing on paper.

Most screen printing inks for printing on plastics dry by solvent evaporation. A small number dry by oxidation and polymerization. A particular type of ink must be used for a particular plastic. In some cases, the solvent in the ink softens the surface of the plastic to achieve bonding. With inks that dry by oxidation and polymerization, the bond is mechanical in nature.

As an example, for printing on a vinyl substrate, the ink contains polyvinyl chloride and solvents such as cyclohexanone, isobutyl ketone, and diacetone alcohol. For printing on acrylics, on cellulose butyrate, and on styrene, a modified acrylic lacquer is used. Inks of this type also dry by solvent evaporation. With other plastics, epoxy inks are used.

Most screen printing inks contain pigments, not dyes. It is estimated that 80%–90% of the inks use opaque pigments. Transparent pigments are used if process color work is to be printed. Some inks are made with pigments that fluoresce. A fluorescent material is one that absorbs some of the shorter wavelengths of radiation and emits light of longer wavelengths. This light is emitted only while the material is receiving these shorter wavelengths. Fluorescent pigments have a limited life, although it has been increased from that of earlier products. The fluorescent materials should not be mixed with other pigments, as such mixture reduces the fluorescence greatly.

Dyes are used only in inks that are to be printed on textile material. Some of these inks use water instead of organic solvents, along with binders such as gum arabic, dextrin, glue, and casein.

Cotton garments, such as T-shirts, can be printed with a 100% solids ink containing plastisol resins. The ink dries when the resins are polymerized with heat. Two methods are used. In one method, the garments are printed directly with this ink, then heat-cured for 3 minutes at 300°F (150°C). In another method, the printing is done on transfer release paper, which is then heated, with additional heat being applied as the printing is transferred to the garment.

Inks that dry with ultraviolet light are being used to a very limited extent in screen printing. They are being employed for printed circuit work, metal decorating, and to a minor extent for printing on glass and paper.

The solvents used in screen printing inks vary in solvent power, boiling range, flash point, and relative rate of evaporation. Screen printers often classify solvents as fast, medium, or slow in evaporating. A relative evaporation rate system uses 100 for butyl acetate. Figures above 100 indicate a faster rate of evaporation than that for butyl acetate, while figures below 100 indicate a slower evaporation rate. For example, the figure for methyl ethyl ketone is 165, for cyclohexanone, 23, and for diacetone alcohol, 14.

News Inks   Tremendous amounts of inks are produced for the printing of newspapers—either by letterpress or by web offset. These are simple, inexpensive inks and involve only a small amount of chemistry. They do not contain any drying oils or drier, and "dry" entirely by penetration of the ink solvent into the newsprint.

The main ingredients in news inks are carbon black and mineral oil. The carbon black is a type called furnace black, produced by burning either natural gas or atomized mineral oil in brick-lined furnaces. It is common to use about 1–2% of a wetting agent, such as gilsonite or pitch, to produce a news ink that has good flow.

Because news ink is very "soupy," and is used on highspeed presses, there is a tendency for the ink to "fly" or "mist." A small amount of anti-misting additives are often incorporated in the ink to prevent or reduce misting. These are materials such as bentonite and silicas. When added, they shorten the ink somewhat, helping to prevent misting.

With the help of an emulsifying agent, it is possible to incorporate from 7–15% water in news inks. This also helps prevent misting. One reason is that the inks with emulsified water are shorter. The other is that the water keeps the ink droplets from acquiring an electrical charge, which would tend to promote misting.

News ink for web offset differs from that for letterpress in being more highly pigmented. Also, web offset news ink usually contains a small amount of a mineral oil-hydrocarbon resin-type varnish to improve the printing property of the ink.

12   Chemistry in the Pressroom

There is more chemistry involved in printing by lithography than in any of the other printing processes. However, some of the topics covered in this chapter also apply to letterpress, flexographic, and gravure pressrooms.

Paper, ink, and printing plates are brought together in the pressroom. When these things come together on a printing press, along with a water fountain solution on lithographic presses, a number of chemical and physical changes occur. Some of these are desirable, while others cause problems.

A particular type of reaction may involve several materials. For example, when ink dries on paper, the rate of drying depends on the formulation of the ink and often on the properties of the paper, the pH of the fountain solution, the amount of fountain solution emulsified in the ink, and the temperature and relative humidity of the pressroom. Reactions of this kind are discussed in whichever section of the following material is the most important one for the particular case.

Ink in the Pressroom

The different types of inks are explained in Chapter 11, "Chemistry of Inks." They are referred to here only by name.

Printing of Process Inks

The various colors in a multicolor subject are produced in the process color system by printing different halftone values of yellow, magenta, cyan, and (usually) black ink. In many areas, one ink overprints another to create the in-between colors of red, orange, violet, blue, and green in various shades.

Pigments that will produce a fairly transparent ink are used in process inks. One way of explaining the color that the eye sees is to say that all of the colors possible are already on the surface of the paper. All that one ink does is to absorb part of the incident light and transmit the remainder. If one ink overprints another, then more of the incident light is absorbed, and a different color is reflected.

The wavelengths of visible light can be considered to consist of three segments: blue, green, and red. The accompanying table shows what happens when white light strikes a white paper on which different process inks are printed.

Effects of Process Ink Overprinting

Color of Ink or Overprints	Absorbs	Reflects
yellow	blue	green and red (equals yellow)
magenta	green	blue and red (equals magenta)
cyan	red	blue and green (equals cyan)
yellow and magenta	blue and green	red
yellow and cyan	blue and red	green
magenta and cyan	green and red	blue

Note that what the eye interprets as yellow is a combination of the green and red part of the visible spectrum of light. Magenta, a bluish red color, results from the reflection of a combination of blue and red light. And cyan, a greenish blue color, is a reflection of blue and green light.

If magenta is printed over yellow, or the reverse, the yellow absorbs blue light and the magenta absorbs green light. This leaves only red light to be reflected to the viewer's eyes. A yellow-cyan combination absorbs blue and red and reflects green. And a magenta-cyan combination absorbs green and red and reflects blue. Printed colors resulting from various combinations of transparent yellow, magenta, and cyan inks may be called *in-between* colors.

The shade of an in-between color depends on the hue and amount of each ink printed and the size of the halftone dots. For example, if the yellow halftone dots are larger than the magenta, some shade of orange results. For dots of equal size, there is an ideal in-between color. This is usually not achieved, as the color depends on how transparent the second-down ink is; and, in wet printing, it depends on how well the second-down ink traps over the first-down. The trapping problem is covered in Chapter 11, "Chemistry of Inks."

While process inks are quite transparent, they are not completely so. Experiments have shown that a transparent yellow ink is the most nearly transparent. Magenta is a little less transparent, and cyan still less. (Black is not included in this consideration, as it is opaque.)

Printers use various sequences of colors in the printing of multicolor subjects. One common printing sequence: cyan, magenta, yellow, black. With this sequence, the overprinting transparent ink is always one that is more transparent than the ink under it.

Process inks, particularly magentas and cyans, vary considerably in their hues and also in how "clean" or "dirty" they are. When one process ink prints over another, the cleanliness of the in-between colors depends in some cases on the cleanliness of the primary color and in other cases on its hue.

Amount of Ink Printed

Usually, the amount of ink printed is judged by the pressman's eye. A good pressman can judge this quite well. In recent years, a reflection densitometer has been used increasingly for greater precision in checking the amount of ink being printed. For this purpose, small solid-color patches must be printed along one edge of the sheet. The density of these color patches is then read at intervals with a reflection densitometer. To obtain maximum accuracy with a reflection densitometer, the operator should read the reflection density of a particular ink through a filter that has a color approximately complementary to that of the ink. Thus the density of a yellow ink is read through a blue filter, that of a magenta ink is read through a green filter, and that of a cyan ink is read through a red filter. The density readings obtained can be used to adjust the ink settings across the sheet and to help keep the ink density on the sheets as constant as possible during the run.

Ink Film Thickness on Press Rollers

Pressmen usually don't worry about the ink film thickness on the press ink rollers. When the sheet or specific areas of the sheet need more ink, the pressman opens the proper keys a little in the ink fountain. But if trouble arises, it may be possible to determine the cause by the use of a wet film thickness gauge.

Such a gauge has a hand-held two-inch-diameter roller that is held against the vibrating steel roller. The gauge reads ink film thickness between 0 and 1.0 mil—0.001" (0.0254 mm). When an ink is printing properly on a lithographic press, the ink film thickness will vary from about 0.25 to 0.60 mil (0.0064 to 0.0152 mm).

An ink density that is low on the sheets while the thickness gauge reads 0.60 mil or more may indicate a piling condition. This might be due to an ink with poor transfer characteristics, or to too much water emulsified in the ink.

Fading of Inks with Iron Blue or Chrome Green Pigments

Occasionally an ink with iron blue or chrome green pigments will fade or change color on the printed sheets. This change usually happens in the center of the sheets and happens more often if there is a large solid in that area. The vehicle in the ink is the culprit in this case. The vehicle needs oxygen in order to dry. But oxygen is limited in the center of the delivery pile. So the vehicle becomes oxidized at the expense of the iron blue pigment or of the iron blue part of the chrome green pigment. As a result, the iron in the pigment is reduced from ferric iron to ferrous iron. This chemical reaction removes most of the color from the iron blue pigment.

The way to prevent this trouble is to wind the sheets while the ink is drying. So doing allows the vehicle to take oxygen from the air and not to react with the iron blue pigment. The ink-fading problem will arise only with inks containing a considerable percentage of drying-oil varnishes.

Factors Affecting the Ink Drying Rate

The following discussion does not pertain to heatset offset or letterpress inks, ultraviolet or electron-beam curing inks, or flexographic or gravure inks. It is concerned with the factors that affect the drying rate of inks containing drying-oil varnishes, and in particular with lithographic inks, which come in contact with water.

If an ink does not dry in a reasonable length of time, the ink is often blamed. However, not only the ink but the paper, the press, and the atmosphere are involved.

The effects of ink characteristics are discussed in detail in Chapter 11, "Chemistry of Inks." Briefly, the major factors related to *ink components* that affect the drying rate are:
- **Pigments.** Some pigments themselves help drying, while others require a considerable amount of drier.
- **Varnishes.** Some varnishes dry much faster than others.
- **Type of drier.** Cobalt, manganese, and zirconium compounds are used. They are not equally efficient as driers.
- **Amount of drier.**
- **Drier dissipation.** Drier dissipation is explained in the "Chemistry of Inks" chapter. To avoid trouble, check the drying rate of an old ink before it is used on a job.

Some *paper characteristics* affecting ink drying are discussed in Chapter 10, "Chemistry of Paper." These characteristics are:
- **Absorbency of the sheet.** Absorbency of the paper does not affect real drying. However, the more absorbent the paper, the faster inks printed on it will set.
- **Paper or coating pH.** The more acid an uncoated paper is, the slower the printed ink dries. The more alkaline a coating is, the faster the ink dries. The coating on coated paper can also be responsible for the chalking of inks.
- **Moisture in the paper.** The more moisture there is in a paper, the slower the printed ink dries. Occasionally a run of carton

board contains so much moisture that the ink-drying problem is serious.

The method of controlling a press is particularly important in lithographic printing. It is necessary to have good ink-water balance for best printing conditions: enough ink should be used to get full color, with only enough water to keep the plate running clean. Important *press factors* are:

- **Water in ink.** The more water that becomes emulsified in the ink, the slower the ink dries.
- **Fountain solution acid.** As the fountain solution is made more acid, inks with drying-oil varnishes take somewhat longer to dry. It is assumed that the acid reacts with the drier, converting it to a state in which it loses its effectiveness as a drier.
- **Kind of form.** If a light form is being run, there is more chance for water to become emulsified in the ink, making the ink dry more slowly.
- **Multicolor wet printing.** On a multicolor sheetfed press, the fourth-down ink may dry more slowly than the first-down ink (assuming that they dry at equal rates on a slab). The slowing of drying rates results from the sheets having picked up some water from the first three units and having more moisture in the areas on which the fourth ink prints.

Temperature and relative humidity also affect the ink drying rate. The higher the temperature at which sheets are stored after printing, the faster the ink dries. An ink that requires twelve hours to dry at 68°F (20°C) may dry in about six hours at 80°F (27°C). But as the relative humidity of the air increases, inks dry more slowly.

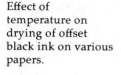

Effect of temperature on drying of offset black ink on various papers.

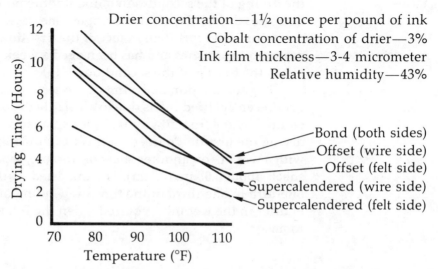

Drier concentration—1½ ounce per pound of ink
Cobalt concentration of drier—3%
Ink film thickness—3-4 micrometer
Relative humidity—43%

Bond (both sides)
Offset (wire side)
Offset (felt side)
Supercalendered (wire side)
Supercalendered (felt side)

Effect of relative humidity on drying of offset black ink on various papers.

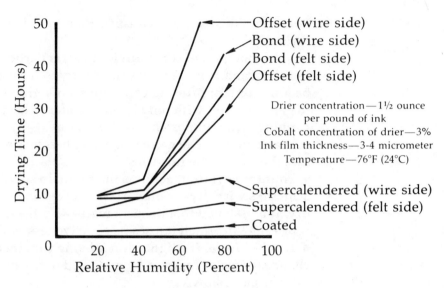

Drier concentration—1½ ounce per pound of ink
Cobalt concentration of drier—3%
Ink film thickness—3-4 micrometer
Temperature—76°F (24°C)

Crystallization of First-Down Ink

When process inks are printed on a single-color press, the second-down ink sometimes does not trap well over the dried first-down ink. It is often stated that the first-down ink has crystallized. The use of a cobalt drier in the first-down ink is often blamed for this trouble. It is argued that, when the first-down ink contains a cobalt drier, the surface of the ink dries so hard that the next ink will not trap properly. This theory explains one possible cause of poor trapping. Another is that greases and waxes in ink come to the top when the ink dries.

Drying of Overprinted Ink Films

When a first-down ink is dried and promptly overprinted, the first-down ink exerts a powerful catalytic effect that accelerates the drying of the second-down ink. But the power of this effect decreases day by day if considerable time passes before the first-down ink is overprinted. In fact, if the first-down ink contains drying-oil varnishes and has been aged a week or two, it will retard the drying of the second-down ink.

The acceleration of drying of the second-down ink printed over recently dried ink is due to a volatile drying accelerator emitted by the first-down ink. This explanation was proved by drying the first-down ink on a sheet of tinplate, then covering it with a wet ink on another sheet of tinplate, separating the two sheets about 0.08 in. (2 mm). The ink dried on the tinplate in one-fifth to one-third of the time (depending on the percentage of drier in the wet ink) required when the ink was exposed to room air.

Gloss Ghosting and Poor Trapping on Second-Side Printing

Suppose that a fairly light-coverage form is printed on the first side of sheets, and the inks are allowed to dry. Then the sheets are backed up with a heavy-coverage form. Occasionally, the ink on the second side will show more gloss, after drying, in those places where it is opposite inks printed on the first side. This effect is called *gloss ghosting*. One explanation is that the volatile drying accelerators from the ink on the first side causes the ink opposite to dry much faster. Thus less varnish soaks into the paper and the result is an area that has more gloss.

But this result doesn't always happen. If fact, gloss ghosting does not occur very often. Whether a ghost will appear on the second side may depend on the amount of drier in the second-side ink (the more drier, the greater the tendency for ghosting), the pH of the paper (more ghosting with a high-pH coating), ink absorbency of the paper (less ghosting as ink absorbency increases), and phase separations in the ink (quickset inks printed on poorly absorbent paper may produce gloss ghosting).

A trapping problem sometimes occurs when four-color printing is done on two-color sheetfed presses. The four colors are printed on one side, two at a time, with no trapping problem. Then the first two colors are printed on the second side, again with no trapping problem. After the first two colors on the second side have dried, the sheets are printed with the last two colors. In such cases, these last two colors sometimes fail to trap properly over the first two colors in only those places where there is heavy ink coverage on the first side. This failure produces a trapping ghost on the second side. It is assumed that under certain conditions the volatile drying accelerator from the first-side inks helps to dry the first two inks on the second side, which become so hard that the last two inks will not trap properly on them.

Water Emulsified in Lithographic Inks

There is always some water emulsified in a lithographic ink when it is being run on a press. The effects resulting from too much water in the ink are discussed in Chapter 11, "Chemistry of Inks." These include piling of ink on the rollers, slow drying, "snowflaky" prints, pigment flocculation, and poor trapping in multicolor wet printing.

Tinting of Lithographic Inks

If sheets run on a lithographic press are covered with a more or less uniform tint of the ink, the pressman is faced with a *tinting* problem. There are a number of possible causes for this condition.

We know that water always emulsifies in a litho ink to some extent: the water breaks up into tiny droplets that are dispersed throughout the ink. This state is called a *water-in-ink emulsion*. A comparison of this with an *ink-in-water emulsion* is illustrated in the sketch on page 238.

If an ink-in-water emulsion is obtained, the fountain solution is said to be "dirty." As a result of this condition, a deposit of the ink droplets is made on the plate's non-image areas from which it is transferred first to the blanket and then to the paper as a tinting on the sheets.

Another cause of tinting may be a surface-active agent in the coating of a coated paper. The agent dissolves in the dampener solution and reduces its surface tension, promoting an ink-in-water emulsion.

In other cases, a small amount of some material in the coating of coated paper may dissolve and deposit on the nonprinting areas of the plate. Thus these areas may gradually accept a small amount of ink, which will transfer to the paper and create tinting. That a coated paper is sometimes responsible for tinting can be proved by changing to another paper, whereupon the tinting disappears.

Antisetoff Powders

Powders to prevent wet-ink setoff are made of different kinds of starch, including that from corn, arrowroot, tapioca, potato, and sago. In general, cornstarch has the finest particles and potato starch the coarsest. Particle diameters vary from about 0.0002 inch (5 micrometers) up to about 0.004 inch (100 micrometers).

By blending two or three kinds of starch, it is possible to produce any desired range of particle sizes. In addition, powders are available that are treated with either a silicone resin or a hydrocarbon wax.

In the past, talc and other mineral powders have been used. Their use has been terminated, as continued ingestion of powder from the air can be harmful to the lungs.

Every antisetoff powder contains particles of many sizes. But the particles can be classified by size into two groups. One group consists of the comparatively larger particles that deposit on the sheets and prevent setoff. The other group consists of the fine particles, about 0.0002–0.0008 inch (5–20 micrometers) in size, which tend to become airborne. These deposit dust on presses and pressroom walls and pipes. Dust collectors can be installed to remove a large part of this "nuisance powder."

A coarse powder, with the majority of particles of size 0.003–0.004 inch (75–100 micrometers), protects ink on sheets very well, but the finished sheets have a rough feel. A compromise must be employed, using as coarse a powder as possible without producing too rough a feel on the sheets.

The use of antisetoff powder on sheetfed presses besides helping to prevent ink setoff, also provides slip between sheets so they jog better. Furthermore, since sheets slip over one another more easily, less static electricity is generated. The use of quickset inks or inks that set rapidly with infrared radiation reduces the need for antisetoff powder.

These powders are also used on web offset presses equipped with sheeters for the same reasons that apply to sheetfed-press use. On flexographic presses printing on film or foil and rewinding, antisetoff powder is used to provide the slip that results in a better-formed roll. The powder is also employed in the converting field, where jobs are laminated and plastic films extruded. In these applications, the powder is used to achieve some purpose other than the prevention of ink setoff.

Silicone Fluids   A dilute emulsion (0.1%–3.0%) of a silicone fluid in water is often applied to one side or both sides of a paper web. The emulsion is applied with a special applicator between the chill rollers and the former folder on a web offset press. The applicator can be a spray device but is now more commonly a roller coater. The thin film of silicone on the web helps to prevent smearing of the ink as the web passes over the former.

Silicone fluids are available with a wide range of viscosities. The fluids vary from very thin, easy-flowing liquids to very high-viscosity, slow-flowing types. In straight-chain aliphatic hydrocarbons, carbon atoms are attached to each other, to create a chain of varying length. Silicones are similar, with the difference that silicon, Si, atoms have replaced some of the carbon atoms. There are also oxygen atoms in the silicone molecules. One silicone fluid, dimethyl polysiloxane polymer, has the following formula:

$$H_3C-\underset{\underset{CH_3}{|}}{\overset{\overset{CH_3}{|}}{Si}}-\left[O-\underset{\underset{CH_3}{|}}{\overset{\overset{CH_3}{|}}{Si}}-\right]_n O-\underset{\underset{CH_3}{|}}{\overset{\overset{CH_3}{|}}{Si}}-CH_3$$

(The symbol "n" indicates that the section of the formula in brackets is repeated.)

The dimethyl silicones have been approved by the U.S. Food and Drug Administration for use in food packaging inks. These silicones are nontoxic, so any spray of a dilute water emulsion of a silicone that is inhaled will not cause any body damage.

Silicones have the property of improving the slip of anything to which they are applied. They can be applied to chutes, collating machines, and the feedboards and back cylinders of presses. They help to prevent the buildup of lead on the molds, magazines, and spacebands of linecasting machines. They minimize ink transfer from sheets to press parts such as delivery tapes and impression cylinder tympan sheets.

Reduction of Air Pollution

Because of more stringent requirements in many areas, printers are using a number of approaches to reduce solvent vapors, smoke, and odors that get into the air from the effluent of web press dryers.

Variations in ink formulation (see Chapter 11, "Chemistry of Inks") include low-order, low-smoke inks, inks with a lower percentage of solvents, inks in which water has replaced part of the organic solvent, and ultraviolet inks.

Afterburners are used in some plants. It is necessary to heat the exhaust gas from the dryer to 1,200–1,500°F (650–815°C), at which temperature level the hydrocarbon solvents in the exhaust gas are burned to harmless carbon dioxide and water.

A catalytic incinerator can be used to achieve the same result. Since it operates at a lower temperature—600–800°F (315–427°C)—less energy is required. The exhaust gas passes through a chamber filled with the catalyst. The catalyst helps induce burning of the hydrocarbon solvents.

Another method for reducing exhaust pollution is to employ electrostatic precipitation. With this method, considerably less energy is required, and only electrical energy is needed. In the hot exhaust gases from a web press dryer, the hydrocarbon solvents are in the vapor state. Electrostatic precipitators will not remove them until they are in a finely divided liquid state.

To get the solvents to form a liquid mist, the exhaust gas must be cooled about 200°F (111°C). This cooling is accomplished by passing the gas through one half of a *heat wheel*. A heat wheel is a device that enables a considerable amount of heat from one stream of gas to be transferred to another, cooler stream. The rotor of the heat wheel is filled with stainless-steel wire mesh. As it rotates slowly, the mesh picks up heat from the exhaust gas. A motor blows cool air through the other half of the rotor to cool the mesh. The result is that the dryer exhaust gas is cooled enough to produce a liquid mist of the hydrocarbon solvents, while the air on the other side of the rotor is heated.

The exhaust gas then passes through an ionizer, where an electric field induces an electrical charge on the tiny liquid particles. Finally, the gas moves through an oppositely charged collecting cell, where the liquid is trapped as the charge on the particles is neutralized.

Ionizer and collecting cell segments of electrostatic precipitator.

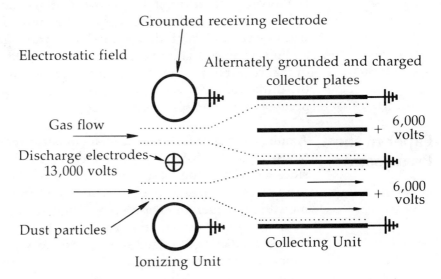

This electrostatic precipitation method does not remove all of the hydrocarbon solvent, but reduces its quantity and eliminates smoke and a considerable amount of odor.

Wet-scrubber units are also being used to a limited extent. They remove the hydrocarbon solvent by passing the exhaust gas through chambers in which it is sprayed with water.

Solvents in the exhaust gas from gravure and flexographic press dryers can be removed by passing the gas through a chamber filled with activated carbon. The solvents are removed by adsorption onto the surface of the activated carbon particles. When no more solvent can be removed from the exhaust, steam is used to strip the solvents from the carbon. While this operation is proceeding, the dryer exhaust gas is transferred to a second chamber, also filled with activated carbon. On cooling, the steam and solvents liquify, separating into two layers. The recovered solvents can be either sold or used on the press as a dilution solvent.

The carbon adsorption system has been modified to achieve removal of hydrocarbon solvents from the exhaust gas of web offset press dryers. These hydrocarbon solvents have much higher boiling points than the solvents used in gravure and flexography. They adsorb readily onto activated carbon, but the carbon cannot be reactivated with steam. The solvent recovery problem has been solved by the use of mild heat—about 200°F (93°C)—and a vacuum of 1 mm of mercury.

One installation of this type of system removes over 85% of the solvents, resulting in the recovery of over 300 pounds (136 kg) of solvents per day. The recovered material is then used as a truck diesel fuel. With this method, no natural gas is required, and it is claimed that the electrical energy cost is only about 6% of that required for the operation of an afterburner. However, the initial capital investment is high, and the equipment occupies considerable space.

Paper in the Pressroom

Among the paper factors that relate to performance on the press (see Chapter 10, "Chemistry of Paper") are these: felt and wire sides; grain, and the reason sheets are printed grain-long on litho presses; appearance of inks on coated and uncoated paper; moisture in paper, the reason paper changes size with a change in moisture content, and the reason this size change can lead to wavy-edged or tight-edged sheets; and the effect of the pH of paper or coating on the drying time of certain types of ink.

Air Conditioning in the Pressroom

Paper will run in a more trouble-free manner if the pressroom is air-conditioned. Air conditioning includes the control of both temperature and relative humidity. Such control helps not only to reduce paper problems but also, in the winter, to reduce static electricity. During humid weather, the lowering of the relative humidity by air conditioning helps to reduce the drying time of some types of ink.

Static Electricity and Its Elimination

Static electricity interferes with the slippage, separation, and normal travel of sheets of paper and plastic films.

When paper moves over a metallic surface, it is possible for the metal to give up some of its external electrons to the paper. When the paper suddenly breaks away from the metal, the transferred electrons are trapped on the paper, giving it a negative charge. It is also possible to get electron transfer when one sheet of paper slides over another sheet. When such sliding happens, one sheet is negatively charged and the other positively charged. Therefore they attract each other, interfering with sheet separation and causing poor jogging at the end of the press.

The best way to eliminate static is to avoid low humidity in the pressroom. Paper falls somewhere between being a conductor and being a nonconductor of electricity. Its conductivity increases as its moisture content increases. Generally, static electricity is not a problem if the relative humidity is above 40%. Since a coating on paper acts as an insulator, static charges remain longer and give more trouble with coated paper.

Because of the presence of moisture on a lithographic press, static electricity is usually less of a problem in lithography than in letterpress. Web presses, partly because of their higher speed, tend to build up more static in paper than do sheetfed presses. Another reason webs are more susceptible to acquiring static charge is that paper loses moisture during passage through web press dryers.

If paper acquires electrons from parts of the press or bindery equipment, then the equipment becomes charged. Unless the equipment is well grounded to neutralize these charges, they can build up and become dangerous.

Static can be reduced by the use of antisetoff powders and also by the application of a silicone solution to a printed web.

Static eliminators are available. In one way or another they neutralize the charge on paper or film. One method utilizes high-voltage electricity to generate an ion cloud. Other units employ radioactive materials that emit alpha particles (positive-charged helium ions). It is customary to refer to the *half-life* of such materials. This is the time required for one-half of the atoms to disintegrate. Some static eliminators use polonium 210, which has a half-life of 138 days. Because of this short half-life, replacement of the radioactive element is required yearly. (After 414 days, only one-eighth of the polonium atoms remain.) Other static eliminators use the radioactive americium 241, which has a half-life of 433 years. With such equipment, yearly replacement is not necessary.

Static electricity is not always detrimental. Use of it is made in *gravure electroassist*. In this case, the electrical charge helps to pull ink out of gravure cells, thus reducing the number of missing dots in highlight areas. It is used also in the creation of lithographic plates by electrostatic imaging.

Chalking of Inks on Coated Paper

It has been said in the past that inks chalk on coated paper because too much of the varnish soaks into the coating, leaving the pigment "high and dry." This explanation has been definitely proven to be incorrect.

Inks may chalk a few hours after they are printed. But usually they will dry to a nonchalking state after a day or two, and sometimes after two weeks or a month. It is now assumed that chalking is caused by the inactivation of part of the drier in the ink by something present in the paper coating. Thus an ink that chalks temporarily is merely a slow-drying ink, made so by loss of part of the drier.

All evidence verifies this explanation. Using the number of days required for an ink to become nonchalking as the criterion, experimenters have found that a particular ink dries in a shorter time as the percentage of drier in it is increased. Inks with drying-oil varnishes become nonchalking in a shorter time on papers with a high-pH coating. But a longer time is required as more water becomes emulsified in the ink. There is no correlation between the number of days to nonchalking of a particular ink and the absorbency of the paper on which it is printed.

To reduce the chalking time, several things can be done, all of which are helpful to obtain drying of an ink that has lost part of its drier. Here are some recommendations:

1. Use a higher percentage of drier in the ink.

2. Use an alkaline fountain solution, so that there will be no retardation of drying due to acid.

3. Add a "drying stimulator" to the fountain solution. This material will add a little more drier to the wet ink film.

4. Run with as little water as possible, so that less water is emulsified in the ink.

Moisture Sensitivity of Paper

Occasionally a paper that shows a good resistance to picking, judged by test results with one of the commercial pick testers, will pick badly on the third or fourth units of a multicolor lithographic press. This unexpected picking is due to the moisture sensitivity of the paper, which absorbs a certain amount of moisture as it passes through the first printing units. This additional moisture lowers the paper's resistance to picking. Some papers are more sensitive to moisture than others.

The coating on many letterpress coated papers is easily loosened with water. In spite of this fact, such papers can often be run on a single-color lithographic press. But trouble usually occurs when these papers are run on a multicolor press.

Blistering of Coated Paper on Web Presses

After a web of coated paper passes through the dryer, blistering of the coating is sometimes produced. The heat of the dryer causes some of the moisture in the paper to vaporize. If this water vapor cannot escape rapidly enough through the coating, the result is a blistering of the coating. Here are some conditions that make blistering more likely to occur:

1. The moisture content of the paper is high.

2. Heavy paper is being printed (more moisture needs to escape).

3. The internal bond strength of the paper is low.

4. The coating is not porous enough.

5. There is heavy ink coverage. This condition is particularly important when the heavy coverage is in the same areas on both sides of the web.

6. The temperature of the paper web is raised rapidly in the dryer, rather than more slowly as is done in a longer dryer.

Blistering of coated paper is not so much of a problem as it used to be. This improvement is due partly to the production of better coated papers and partly to the better designs of web press dryers.

Fountain Solutions in the Pressroom

Some reactions between a litho fountain solution and ink or paper are discussed in other chapters. This section considers the composition of fountain solutions and some of the chemical reactions in which they are involved.

Purpose of Fountain Solution

In lithographic printing it is necessary to keep the non-image areas of a plate moistened with water so that they will not accept ink. During platemaking, these non-image areas are desensitized, usually with a thin absorbed film of gum arabic, so that they prefer water instead of ink. (Some plates are desensitized with a hydrophilic film of gelatin.)

If the desensitized film were able to remain on a plate indefinitely, it would be possible to run plates with nothing but water in the dampening fountain. Water alone can, in fact, be used on sheetfed presses for short runs. However, the desensitized film wears off gradually as a plate continues to run on the press. Eventually it is necessary to use chemicals in the fountain solution to rebuild the desensitized film.

Why a Fountain Solution Is Usually Acid

The two main ingredients in a fountain solution are a desensitizing gum (usually gum arabic) and an acid (phosphoric acid, an acid phosphate compound, or citric or lactic acid).

The acid converts the desensitizing gum to its free acid form in which the molecules contain carboxyl groups, –COOH. It is assumed that these groups help in the adsorption of the gum to the metal plate. Furthermore, phosphoric acid not only acts as an acid but also has desensitizing properties.

Enough acid should be used to convert most of the gum to its free-acid form. Beyond this point, the acid serves no useful purpose. A good way to check acid concentration is to measure the pH of the fountain solution. Aluminum litho plates are being run satisfactorily with fountain solutions of about 4.0–5.5 pH.

Excess acid in the fountain solution is not only useless but may be a disadvantage. If such a solution is emulsified into inks containing varnishes with drying oils, the inks take longer to dry.

Other Materials in Fountain Solutions

Usually, prepared fountain solutions contain ingredients in addition to the basic desensitizing gum and acid. Magnesium nitrate, $Mg(NO_3)_2$, is an example. It serves partly as a buffer and partly to reduce plate corrosion.

When zinc plates were used, fountain solutions usually contained ammonium dichromate, $(NH_4)_2Cr_2O_7$. It helped as a corrosion inhibitor to prevent the acid from reacting with the zinc. Today all litho plates, except those of paper and plastic, are aluminum or anodized aluminum. With these plates, there is no need to use ammonium dichromate. By eliminating it, the danger of chromic poisoning can be avoided.

Fountain Solutions with Alcohol or Alcohol Substitutes

With the introduction of dampening systems that transferred fountain solution to one of the ink form rollers, it became necessary to use about 20% by volume of some kind of alcohol in the fountain solution. Initially denatured grain alcohol (ethyl alcohol) was used, but now isopropyl alcohol is preferred. Some lithographic plants have used normal-propyl alcohol. Experiments at the GATF research laboratory have shown that isopropyl alcohol and normal-propyl alcohol behave practically the same. But normal-propyl alcohol is somewhat less volatile, so the concentration of vapor in the pressroom air is lower than when isopropyl alcohol is used. A temperature control unit for the fountain solution will help considerably to keep the vapor concentration low.

When an alcohol is made part of a fountain solution, it is important to add the alcohol to the fountain solution, with stirring. If fountain solution is poured into alcohol, the gum in the fountain solution may precipitate.

Because of the cost of alcohol and the problem of vapors in the pressroom, many companies have attempted to use some substitute. A few of these formulations are running satisfactorily, but most of them have been inferior to the use of alcohol. New and improved replacements for isopropyl alcohol are being developed.

One reason that an alcohol-water solution is able to wet the surface of the ink and allow the solution to be transferred to the non-image areas of the printing plate is that alcohol reduces the surface tension of a fountain solution. A 20% (by volume) aqueous solution of isopropyl alcohol has a surface tension only about 4/9 that of pure water. On the basis of an extensive investigation of fountain solutions carried out at the GATF research laboratory, it is believed that isopropyl alcohol, because of its miscibility in ink solvents as well as in water, reduces the ink/water interfacial tension. Thus the isopropyl alcohol diffuses across the interface between the alcohol-water solution and the ink and forms a water-receptive surface on the ink. As a result, the alcohol-water solution wets the surface of the ink on the ink form roller, and the roller carries this solution around to the printing plate.

Many surface-active agents are available that will lower the surface tension of water as much as isopropyl alcohol does, and only a small percentage of the surface-active agent is needed to accomplish the lowering. But when a fountain solution is formulated with another agent of this type, generally the performance is very poor compared with an alcohol-water solution.

Consideration of the isopropyl alcohol mechanism suggests that a good substitute substance must meet the following specifications:

1. It must have some solubility in water.

2. It should lower the surface tension of water to 70% or less of the surface tension of pure water.

3. It should have some solubility in nonpolar solvents, such as the hydrocarbon solvents often used in inks.

4. It should not be too volatile.

5. It should not have too high a molecular weight: it must be able to move rapidly into the water-ink interface, since it is being continuously renewed by roller rotation.

As might be expected, only a few chemical compounds fit all of these requirements. It is very likely that continued work will lead to a satisfactory substitute for isopropyl alcohol.

**Alkaline
Fountain
Solutions**

While acid fountain solutions are usually employed on lithographic presses, alkaline solutions are used in some special cases. Their use is not new. Many years ago, an alkaline fountain solution containing a desensitizing gum was used at the GATF research laboratory to help reduce chalking time when inks were printed on a plastic-coated sheet. To give another example: an alkaline solution is advised when printing gold inks made with bronze powders. (Alkaline dampening is not needed when running a silver or an imitation gold ink.)

Alkaline fountain solutions are now being used regularly by offset newspapers. These solutions do not contain any desensitizing gum. They are made alkaline with sodium carbonate or sodium silicate. One of the proprietary solutions contains a substance (called a "sequestering agent") to keep the calcium and magnesium compounds in the water from precipitating. It also contains a surface-active agent that lowers the surface tension to about 4/9 that of pure water.

Several advantages are claimed for the use of an alkaline fountain solution on newspaper offset presses or on letterpresses using the direct-lithography system. There is usually no stripping of ink rollers. Blankets do not become glazed, since there is no gum in the solution. Fungus does not grow in the fountain pan. Aluminum plates run clean and do not need to be gummed up, even for overnight. Although a condition called "ink dot scum" occasionally occurs on aluminum plates run with an acid fountain solution, this problem never arises when an alkaline solution is used.

In spite of these advantages of alkaline solutions for newspaper presses, almost all commercial offset printers use acid fountain solutions. When the use of an alkaline solution is attempted, commercial printers get foaming in the fountain solution, excess water emulsified in the ink, and bleeding of some pigments into the fountain solution, causing tinting on the sheets.

Successful printing of ultraviolet inks with an alkaline fountain solution has been achieved at the GATF research laboratory. It was reported that halftones printed sharp and that no roller stripping was encountered, probably because the special varnishes used in ultraviolet inks do not form soaps with an alkaline material.

**Drying
Stimulator**

A *drying stimulator* consists of a water solution of a compound such as cobalt chloride ($CoCl_2$). The proportion is 1–2 fluid ounces per gallon (8–16 milliliters per liter) of fountain solution.

Cobalt is a metal that accelerates ink drying when the inks contain drying-oil varnishes. As the press runs, the fountain solution containing the cobalt compound becomes emulsified in the ink to some extent. In effect, this adds more drier to the ink, making the ink dry faster.

It is usually not necessary to use a drying stimulator. But it can help when drying conditions are poor, as in the cases of printing when the relative humidity is very high, printing light forms, printing on paper that contains more than the normal amount of moisture, and reducing the chalking time of inks on coated paper.

When a drying stimulator is added to a fountain solution, the stimulator neutralizes part of the acid, and the pH rises. It is generally desirable in this case to use twice as much fountain concentrate as usual in order to keep plates running clean.

Metals for Water Rollers

Most metal water rollers are now chromium-plated. Aluminum or stainless steel can also be used. These are metals relatively easy to desensitize with an acidified solution of gum arabic. Even so, as they continue to run, the metal rollers begin to pick up a layer of ink. When this condition develops, all of the ink should be removed with a good solvent. The rollers should then be treated for about two minutes with a mixture of one fluid ounce of 85% phosphoric acid in 32 fluid ounces of 14° Baumé gum arabic solution (30 milliliters of the acid in one liter of the gum solution). Then the etch should be wiped down and allowed to dry.

Dampening Rollers

Dampening rollers are usually hydrophilic: they prefer water rather than ink. Common dampener surfaces are molleton and a paperlike sleeve.

Most rubber rollers are oleophilic (oil-loving) instead of hydrophilic. A method to make rubber rollers hydrophilic requires three solutions. The first provides an inner bonding layer. The second contains a catalyst to cure the first layer. The third forms an outer hydrophilic layer. The result is a polymerized silicone coating that is hydrophilic.

Lithographic Plates in the Pressroom

Lithographic plates are subject to two main troubles. They scum and they go blind.

The Meaning of Scumming

Scumming occurs when ink adheres to part of the non-image areas of a plate. (Sometimes this is called "greasing.") The term "non-image areas" applies not only to the large areas where there is no image but also to the open areas between halftone dots. Thus, when a halftone begins to fill in, it is said that the plate is beginning to scum.

The Mechanism of Scumming

The non-image areas are *desensitized* during the platemaking operation: they are treated so that they are water-receptive. This treatment is usually accomplished with a thin adsorbed film of a hydrophilic gum, such as gum arabic.

When plates are running clean, the gum film may gradually be worn off the plate, but it is replaced with gum from the fountain solution. If for some reason this process does not occur smoothly, ink varnish molecules may become adsorbed on the nonprinting areas. The result is a scummy plate.

The pigments may also be responsible for plate scumming. For example, blue inks have a greater tendency to scum than do inks of other colors. Also, when certain magenta inks are being printed, it is sometimes difficult to keep the halftones printing clean.

Prevention of Scumming

With the aluminum plates being used today, scumming is not a major problem because aluminum is a metal that is easy to desensitize. There is even less scumming trouble with anodized aluminum plates, since the anodized surface is very easy to desensitize.

To prevent scumming, the plate must be properly desensitized when it is made. Then a good fountain solution must be used, containing about 1 fluid ounce per gallon (8 milliliters per liter) of gum arabic, and having a pH of 4.0–5.5. If a plate on the press is to stand for an hour or more, it should be gummed to protect the non-image areas. If these procedures are followed, a plate should run clean, unless a very greasy ink is being used.

When a plate begins to scum, something should be done at once. If ink becomes firmly attached to parts of the non-image areas, it is very difficult to reverse the process and make these areas water-receptive again. The plate should be treated with a good desensitizing plate etch. Some pressure must be used on the scummed areas to remove the ink so that it can be replaced with the desensitizing gum. Such a plate etch should finally be dried on the plate, since it is known that any desensitizing etch protects better if it is dried. A procedure such as this should be tried at least twice before resorting to the addition of more fountain concentrate to the fountain solution.

Ink Dot Scum on Aluminum Plates

Sometimes aluminum lithographic plates develop a peculiar type of scum, called "ink dot scum." Such scum consists of thousands of tiny, sharp dots of ink. The areas between the ink dots are still well desensitized.

Ink dot scum is associated with the pit corrosion of aluminum. When aluminum corrodes, or oxidizes, the corrosion occurs in many little spots, which become pits. When the desensitizing gum is removed from these pits, they can hold ink.

This type of scum can often be produced by covering a plate with water and allowing it to evaporate slowly. The scum may appear in a band on a plate opposite to a wet dampener roller.

If ink dot scum has not progressed too far, it can be eliminated by treating the plate with a solution of phosphoric acid or oxalic acid. A solution of 5 ounces of oxalic acid per gallon of water (37 grams of acid per liter of water) is usually effective.

Anodized aluminum plates are covered with a hard, adherent layer of aluminum oxide. Such plates are not subject to pit corrosion, so ink dot scum is not a problem with them.

Why Lithographic Plates Go Blind

A plate goes blind when the image areas do not accept ink from the ink form rollers as well as they should. The principal causes for plate blinding are:
1. Original image areas not fully ink-receptive
2. Poor adhesion of image areas to the metal
3. Partial desensitization of image areas
4. Abrasion of image areas
5. Blanket swelling
6. Solvents in the ink or plate cleaner used

Original Image Areas Not Fully Ink-Receptive

The platemaker aims to make plates that are ink-receptive in the image areas. But sometimes things happen such that a plate does not roll up properly at the start of a run. For example, if the platemaker rubs down the developing ink too thin on a surface-type plate, it is possible for the desensitizing etch to cover part of the image areas. Plates in such condition are difficult to roll up on the press.

Poor Adhesion of Image Areas to the Metal

Sometimes a plate starts to print satisfactorily and then begins to go blind as the run proceeds. One reason for this development can be poor adhesion. Depending on the type of plate, more than one material-to-material adhesion can be involved. With surface plates, the light-hardened coating must adhere to the metal; the lacquer, if one is used, must adhere to the coating; the developing ink must adhere to the lacquer.

With copperized aluminum deep-etch plates, the chemically deposited copper must adhere to the aluminum; the lacquer must adhere to the copper; the developing ink must adhere to the lacquer.

If the chemical or physical adhesive bond is poor, the result is a partial blinding of the image areas. Sometimes the pressman can rub up a plate and save it. Otherwise, the platemaker must make another plate, changing either his procedure or chemicals to avoid a recurrence of the problem.

Partial Desensitization of Image Areas

Lithographic plates are gummed up with a solution of gum arabic. Gum arabic or some other desensitizing gum is also used in the water fountain solution. There is a possibility that some of this gum may adhere to part of the image areas of the plate. Then these areas will accept water instead of ink. The result is that the plate is blind in these areas: there is some competition of ink and gum for the image areas. Any change in press conditions that favor the gum may lead to a partial blinding of the image areas. Some of these conditions are as follows:

• **Running with too thin a film of ink.** This condition makes it easier for the gum to break through the ink film and become attached to the material underneath. If the color must be reduced, it is much better to add a transparent extender to the ink and then to print a thicker ink film.

• **Too much water in the ink.** If the ink becomes waterlogged, it is much easier for the gum to replace it on the image areas of the plate.

• **Too much gum in the fountain solution.** The more gum there is in the fountain solution, the more gum will be emulsified in the ink. This gives the gum a better chance to adhere to the image areas.

• **Too much acid in the fountain solution.** The acid makes the gum a better desensitizing agent so that it can adhere more easily to the image areas if it gets a chance.

It is customary to gum plates with a solution of gum arabic if the plates are to be left overnight on the press. The aim is to leave a film of gum arabic on all of the non-image areas of the plate and to leave no gum arabic on any of the image areas. If a film of gum arabic remains on part of the image areas of a plate for several hours, the plate will print with gum streaks when the press is started. The gum arabic adheres to part of the image area over which it is dried and makes that part of the image area water-receptive. Thus gum streaks can be described as one type of blinding of the image areas.

Gum streaks usually occur if there is too thin a film of ink on the image areas when the plate is gummed up, or if the ink is badly waterlogged, or if the gumming solution is not rubbed long enough over the plate to remove it from the image areas. Gum streaks are unnecessary; they can be avoided if the proper procedure is used in the gumming up of a plate that is to be left for any length of time. The correct procedure is as follows:

● **Lift the dampener rollers and allow the ink rollers to roll over the plate for several revolutions before lifting the ink rollers.** During this time, the water in the ink will be evaporating and the ink will pick up tack, leaving a good, greasy lay of ink on the image areas of the plate to repel the gumming solution.

● **Fan the plate as it revolves on the press until the plate is dry.** At this point, the image areas of the plate should be powdered. A mixture of half talc and half powdered rosin is good. The purpose of powdering is to set the heavy lay of ink so that it will not smear onto the non-image areas of the plate during the gumming procedure.

● **Gum the plate.** The image is protected by a good film of ink and the ink is set, so it will not smear onto the non-image areas. Thus the rubbing of the gum can be continued until it is all removed from the image areas and the plate is almost dry. Trouble with gum streaks should never be experienced if plates are gummed this way.

If a plate starts to print with gum streaks, it can often be reconditioned by lifting the ink rollers and allowing sheets to print until completely blank sheets have been delivered. Then the ink rollers are dropped and printing continues. It may be necessary to repeat this process four or five times. This method often cures blinding due to gum streaks.

The reasoning behind this method is simple. When all of the ink is removed from the image areas, the fountain solution can dissolve the film of gum that is dried on part of the image areas. The slight abrasive action of the dampener rollers also helps to soften and dissolve the film of gum arabic. Once the gum arabic has been removed from the image areas, they will accept ink again and the printing will be back to normal.

There is one more way in which the image areas of a plate can be partially desensitized. If press ink is allowed to dry on the image areas of the plate, these areas often do not accept ink properly when the plate is run again. The chemical reason is not known certainly. It is likely that dried ink is not as ink-receptive as it should be—a statement different from saying that the dried ink is not water-receptive. So the image areas are not blinded by being desensitized in the usual meaning of this term.

There is no need to incur this type of blinding. If a plate is to be left overnight or stored for a rerun, the press ink should be removed and replaced with asphaltum. A film of asphaltum will remain ink-receptive for years. Today, many pressmen are avoiding gum streaks by using an asphaltum-gum emulsion as a substitute practice for gumming a plate and then putting it under asphaltum.

Abrasion of Image Areas

If parts of the image area are actually abraded off the plate, then the plate will be blind in these areas. Abrasion is one of the worst causes of blinding because there is little that can be done to remedy the situation. Abrasion of the image areas can be due to excessive pressure between the plate and the blanket. It can also be caused by abrasive particles in the ink. Some pigments are more abrasive than others. In general, inorganic pigments are more apt to be abrasive than others. Opaque white ink with titanium dioxide and metallic inks are especially bad offenders.

Sometimes the pigment particles used in the coating on a coated paper are hard and abrasive in nature. This possibility can be tested by passing a clean, cold electric iron over the paper several times, using moderate pressure. If the coating is abrasive, it will becomes discolored by particles of iron removed from the bottom of the electric iron. Such a coated paper can be responsible for the wearing of the image areas of a plate if the coating is not securely bound to the paper.

Paper fibers, too, can be somewhat abrasive. When newsprint is run on a lithographic press, the fibers often accumulate on the rubber blanket. Such accumulation often leads to blinding of the image areas of the plate, due to the abrasive action of these fibers.

Another source of abrasion is dry antisetoff spray. When sheets treated with this spray for the first color are run through the press again for the second color, the dry spray particles on the sheets can exert an abrasive action on the second color plate.

Blanket Swelling

The causes of blanket swelling are outlined in the subsequent section on "Rollers and Blankets." The increased thickness of a swelled blanket produces in turn an increase in pressure between the blanket and plate that can lead to abrasion of the plate and ultimately to image blinding.

Solvents in the Ink or Plate Cleaner Used

Most light-hardened coatings and the lacquers used over them are highly resistant to the solvents in most lithographic inks and plate cleaners. Alkaline plate cleaners should be avoided with anodized aluminum plates because the alkali attacks the anodized film. Such cleaners should also not be used on positive-working presensitized plates. If these plates have been exposed to light for any length of time, an alkaline cleaner can attack the image areas, causing the plate to go blind.

The light-sensitive materials in ultraviolet inks are polar in nature and will attack the coating on some types of lithographic plates. For this reason, diazo-type presensitized and wipe-on plates cannot be used with ultraviolet inks. But many of the photopolymer plates are satisfactory for the printing of ultraviolet inks.

Rollers and Blankets

Screen printing is the only printing process that does not use rollers in one way or another. In letterpress, offset, and collotype printing, rollers are used to transport the ink from the ink fountain to the form rollers. A simple inking system involving one or two rubber rollers is used in flexographic printing. And a special rubber impression roller is used in the conventional and electroassist gravure process.

Types of Rollers

The material used for a covering on ink rollers depends on the printing process and the type of ink being used. The roller compound must be formulated so the rollers will not swell and become unduly tacky when they come in contact with the materials in a particular ink.

It is common to speak of "rubber" rollers. But rollers covered with natural rubber are used today only on flexographic presses, when certain inks are being printed. For other applications, several organic elastomers, or synthetic rubbers, are employed. Here is a list of the principal ones and the printing processes in which they are used:

Buna-N   (a copolymer of butadiene and acrylonitrile)—letterpress and offset

Butyl   (a copolymer of isobutylene and butadiene)—with ultraviolet inks; flexography

Vinyl   (polyvinyl chloride)—letterpress and offset

Neoprene   (polychloro butadiene)—flexography

EPDM   (ethylene propylene diene monomer)—with ultraviolet inks; flexography

Thiokol   (a polysulfide rubber)—flexography

Besides these, rollers covered with polyurethane (polyester cross-linked with an isocyanate) are used in letterpress and offset. They are tough, and are not affected by the solvents used in letterpress and offset inks. They generally are not suitable for printing with ultraviolet inks.

Offset press rollers are often covered with a mixture of Buna-N and vinyl. Some rollers are covered only with Buna-N and others, only with vinyl.

Rollers for Ultraviolet (UV) Inks

The vehicles and the photoinitiators used in UV inks cause conventional rollers to swell. The synthetic rubber materials used in conventional rollers are affected very little by the hydrocarbon solvents used in heatset and quickset inks. But synthetic rubber generally will not resist the polar type of vehicles present in UV inks.

To make rollers that are satisfactory for use with UV inks, other elastomers, such as butyl or blends of synthetic elastomers, are employed. Some of these blends give fairly good results with both regular and UV inks. But for best results, rollers should be designed either for regular inks or for UV inks.

Rollers for Flexographic Presses

In general, the flexographic roller material and plate material must be compatible, and both depend on the type of ink being used. Here are some examples:

For water- or alcohol-based inks, the plates can be natural rubber, and the rollers can be natural rubber or neoprene.

For inks containing ketones or esters, a butyl plate is used, and the rollers can be either butyl or EPDM.

If the ink contains aliphatic hydrocarbon solvents, then rollers made with Buna-N are used.

If the ink contains a mixture of hydrocarbons and polar solvents, a roller made with thiokol is employed.

A variety of ink types are used in flexography since the process is used to print on different substrates; the ink must be formulated to adhere well to a particular substrate.

Gravure Electroassist Impression Rollers

Gravure is an intaglio process: the ink is held in recessed areas below the surface of the printing cylinder. The paper web passes between the printing cylinder and the impression roller. Before the electroassist process was developed by the Gravure Research Institute, the only way that the ink was transferred to the paper was by pressure and capillary forces. This often resulted in missing dots, particularly in the highlight areas.

It has been found that the creation of an electrical field between the printing cylinder and the impression roller helps to lift the ink from the cells, with a considerable reduction in the number of missing dots. To accomplish this electroassist, it is necessary to use a semiconductive impression roller. This roller is covered with a rubber coating, 1/2 to 1 inch thick. It is made semiconductive by the inclusion of special carbon blacks or a long-chain amino or hydroxyl substance. Many gravure presses are now equipped with electroassist.

Hickeys and Spots

Sometimes matter being printed develops defects of a kind that can be roughly divided into the categories called "hickeys" and "spots." *Hickeys* are small areas that print almost solid in the center and are surrounded by a white ring. They are caused by small pieces of ink skin or other particles that become attached to the plate or, on a lithographic press, to the blanket. They can also be caused by a rubber roller that is starting to crumble. They print dark because ink skin and rubber are ink-receptive. But since the pieces have a certain thickness, the ink can't print around the edges; this circumstance creates the white ring. Also, coating particles may occasionally accept ink and produce hickeys.

Other printing defects (*spots*) can be caused by paper fibers, slitter dust, and fibers from dampener rollers. The resulting spots usually print white or light gray, because such materials are more water-receptive than ink-receptive.

"Hickey rollers" are designed to remove hickeys from lithographic printing plates. In the past, leather rollers have been used, but they were difficult to maintain. Other rollers have been developed that are more or less successful in removing hickeys. Three types of hickey rollers are in use. One is a tacky roller that will pull the hickeys off a plate. Such a roller may work well initially, but will lose its effectiveness if it loses its tack. Another type has a nap finish; it removes particles by a mechanical action. A third type creates an electrostatic effect to pull the hickeys onto the roller.

Steel Rollers

On the inking system used in letterpress and offset, the rollers alternate between rubber (or a rubber substitute) and steel. With letterpress, there is no problem, as both kinds of rollers accept and distribute ink. On lithographic presses, steel rollers accept ink only if the ink is applied before any desensitizing material, such as gum arabic, has had a chance to come in contact with the steel.

While steel accepts ink if ink is applied first, it is a more water-receptive metal than an ink-receptive one. Under certain conditions, the gum in the lithographic fountain solution can become adsorbed onto the steel in places, and then stripping occurs. The steel does not accept ink in these areas. The letterpress newspapers that converted to the direct-lithography process soon became aware of this problem.

There are two methods for preventing ink stripping of steel rollers. One is to use a roller that is covered with a highly cross-linked hard rubber or with a plastic such as nylon. Both are ink-receptive materials.

The second method is to cover the steel with a film of copper. Copper is more ink-receptive than steel. The best way to apply the copper film is to remove the steel rollers from the press and electroplate them with copper.

A thin film of copper can be deposited chemically on steel rollers without removing them from the press. The rollers must first be thoroughly cleaned. Then they are treated with a solution that commonly contains cuprous chloride, CuCl, and hydrochloric acid, HCl, dissolved in a mixture of ethylene glycol and isopropyl alcohol. The cuprous ions of the cuprous chloride react with the iron atoms of the steel and are reduced to metallic copper. The reaction is:

$$2Cu^+ \ + \ Fe^\circ \ \longrightarrow \ 2Cu^\circ \ + \ Fe^{++}$$

The chemically deposited copper is a very thin film because the reaction stops when the steel is completely covered with copper and thus the cuprous ions can find no more iron atoms to react with. Such a film may wear off in a week or two, and the treatment must then be repeated.

Some of the conditions that may result in stripping of steel rollers are as follows:

● **Using too much fountain solution.** Excess fountain solution causes the ink to become waterlogged, making it easier for the gum in the fountain solution to penetrate the ink and become adsorbed to the surface of the steel.

● **Too much gum in the fountain solution.** A fountain solution usually should contain no more than 1 fluid ounce of 14° Baumé gum arabic per gallon of fountain solution (8 milliliters of gum arabic per liter of fountain solution.) If much more than this is used, the chances that the gum will reach the steel are greater.

● **Too much acid in the fountain solution.** Excess acid may cause stripping for two reasons. First, extra acid improves the desensitizing power of gum arabic. Second, the acid is usually phosphoric acid, which itself has the capability of desensitizing steel.

Prevention or Cure of Roller Stripping

If copper plating or a covering of hard rubber is not used on steel rollers to prevent stripping, avoiding the main causes of stripping will help to prevent it: use as small an amount of fountain solution as possible, and do not use an excess of gum arabic or acid.

Besides following these practices, it helps to clean steel rollers occasionally by rubbing them with a mixture of pumice and an acid such as acetic, hydrochloric, or nitric (*not* phosphoric). This pumice-and-acid mixture abrades off any dried ink or film of desensitizing gum, making the steel ink-receptive again.

Steel rollers are not the only ones that have ink stripping. Sometimes there is partial stripping of ink from rubber rollers as well. A thin film of ink often remains after each washup. In time the roller surface becomes hard and glazed and does not accept the ink as well as it should.

To prevent rubber rollers from stripping, the roller train can be cleaned at least three times a week with one of the special two- or three-solution types of roller cleaner. Such cleaning helps to prevent the formation of dried ink films.

If rubber rollers become hard and glazed because of dried ink, they can be rejuvenated by removing them from the press and soaking them overnight in a bath containing about two pounds of lye—sodium hydroxide, $NaOH$—dissolved in five gallons of water (one kilogram of lye in 20 liters of water). This treatment dissolves the dried ink and makes the rollers effective again.

A small area which has stripped can often be made ink-receptive again by treating it with a greasy material in which a fine abrasive is incorporated. (Such preparations are available commercially.) A little of it is applied to the area that is stripping and the press is allowed to idle for a few minutes. The abrasive grinds off the dried ink or desensitizing gum; the greasy material makes the surface ink-receptive again.

Rubber Blankets for Offset Presses

Blankets, like rubber rollers, must be made of materials that will not swell unduly when they are in contact with the ink being used. For example, blankets and rollers must both be made with special elastomers that will resist swelling when ultraviolet inks are printed.

A lithographic blanket usually consists of two, three, or four plies of a textile fabric covered with a synthetic rubber compound. The fabric is woven to strict specifications from either long-staple cotton or synthetic yarn. The textile plies are then coated with about sixty to eighty very thin coats of a rubber compound containing a solvent. Each coat is dried by evaporating the solvent with heat.

Most lithographic rubber blankets use the synthetic elastomer Buna-N. It is mixed with pigments, softeners or plasticizers, accelerators, and curing or vulcanizing agents (usually sulfur, sometimes peroxides). When all coats have been applied, the blanket roll is heated for a length of time sufficient to convert the uncured plastic mass into the final tough, elastic "rubber." This particular polymerization process is referred to as *vulcanization*.

Blankets made with Buna-N are inert to inks made with drying-oil and heatset varnishes. It is desirable to have blankets that do not swell in contact with ink, since a swollen blanket increases the pressure between blanket and plate and can be one cause of plate blinding. Furthermore, if the image areas swell with one job, these areas can create a ghost image when the next job is printed, due to the increase in pressure in the embossed areas.

Sometimes a problem can arise caused by the piling of coating from coated paper onto a blanket. It is reported that this piling can be reduced by adding certain materials, such as ethylene glycol, to the fountain solution.

It is important to store blankets properly. Heat, sunlight, or blue fluorescent light will cause the rubber surface to harden, glaze, and crack. To prevent this result, blankets should be stored in a dark, cool place, preferably in the tubes supplied by the manufacturer. If they are stacked on shelves, they should be placed rubber against rubber and fabric against fabric to prevent the transfer of the fabric pattern to the rubber.

Lithographic blankets can be classified as conventional or compressible. Compressible blankets have gained in popularity; at least half of the blankets used now are of this type, and considerably more than half of web offset blankets are compressible.

Rubber is not truly compressible, but flows under pressure. When a rubber-covered blanket revolves against a metal cylinder, a bulge is formed. The idea involved in making blankets compressible is to greatly reduce this rolling bulge. The reduction is accomplished by introducing a compressible layer between two fabric layers or under the rubber surface. This layer can be a compressible textile material or a spongy material containing thousands of cells filled with air. Besides being compressible, the layer must also be elastic: it must have the ability to spring back after compression. When a blanket has such a layer, the pressure applied is transmitted vertically.

Usually about 0.002 inch to 0.004 inch (0.05 millimeter to 0.10 millimeter) more packing must be used under compressible blankets than under conventional ones to obtain good printing. With compressible blankets, plate life is increased, streaks due to worn cylinder gears are minimized, and there is less chance of blanket smashup caused by web breaks or doubling sheets. On the other hand, compressible blankets must be handled carefully, as they are more fragile than conventional blankets. And some (but not all) have poorer release properties.

Press Washup Solutions

Various solutions or solvents are used to remove ink from rollers, plates, and litho blankets. It is important to choose the proper material. It must do the desired cleaning job, but it should not swell rollers or blankets unduly, or damage the image areas of plates, or be too toxic, or have too low a flash point, or evaporate too rapidly or too slowly. The toxicity and flash points of many organic solvents are discussed in Chapter 4, "Chemistry of the Compounds of Carbon."

It is difficult to find one solvent that has all of the properties listed above. To achieve the desired result, mixtures are often used; many of these are offered by the suppliers of graphic arts chemicals.

It is convenient to divide press cleaners into two categories: one to remove wet ink and the other to remove glaze. One good cleaner for wet ink is a naphtha. It is not toxic, has little tendency to swell rollers or blankets, and has a flash point of 52–53°F (11–12°C). If fire or insurance regulations demand a solvent with a flash point over 100°F (38°C), then a good grade of mineral spirits can be used that evaporates without leaving an oily residue. The flash point of mineral spirits is about 100–110°F (38–43°C). Higher-boiling materials such as kerosene should not be used. In the other direction, gasoline should never be used because of the fire hazard.

Special commercial two- and three-solution cleaners are also used for the cleaning of ink rollers. When such cleaners are used for the first time on a particular press, they not only remove the wet ink but also begin to remove ink of other colors that were run previously. After three or four washups, it is possible to go from black to yellow with one washup.

The best results are usually obtained with a three-solution cleaner. The first solution is usually a hydrocarbon solvent to which a surface-active agent has been added. It removes ink by a dilution process. As more of the solution is applied, the ink which is left is diluted more and more. The surface-active agent helps to keep the pigment in suspension and to prevent its redeposition on the rollers.

After most of the ink has been removed by the first solution, the second solution is applied. It may contain one of the glycols and another surface-active agent. It acts to emulsify the remaining ink. In this way ink is removed from the rollers almost completely.

If the second solution is left on the rollers, they will not accept ink properly when the press is inked up again. So one of the purposes of the third solution is to remove the second solution. The third solution also removes some of the remaining color. In one of the cleaners, isopropyl alcohol is used as the third solution.

With a two-solution cleaner, the first solution is made stronger to do the job of the first two cleaners of the three-solution system. Then the second solution is used to remove the first one.

These solutions will do a good job of cleaning ink rollers. But it is important that enough of the final solution be used to remove the previous solution completely. Otherwise, the rollers will not ink up properly.

While naphtha or mineral spirits are satisfactory for the removal of wet ink, they will not remove glaze from rollers or blankets. To accomplish this task, a stronger solvent or mixture of solvents is required. A commercial glaze remover can be used. If you want to make your own, here are two fairly satisfactory mixtures:

A. 50% butyl alcohol
      50% xylene
B. 10% isopropyl alcohol
      70% high-flash naphtha
      20% xylene

In these mixtures, the xylene is the active ingredient; the other materials are added to retard the action of the xylene on the rubber. Any glaze remover can be used with or without pumice. The mixture should be left on the rubber as short a time as possible, since it has a tendency to swell the rubber. It is best used at shift end so that the solvents can evaporate from the rubber over a period of time, allowing the rubber to return to its normal thickness.

Commercial glaze removers are presumably formulated to be effective without containing any materials that are highly toxic. Highly toxic materials that should never be used include benzene, carbon tetrachloride, and turpentine. In the formulas A and B above, xylene is more toxic than the other ingredients. Care should be taken to avoid inhaling the vapors.

In past years, turpentine was used to wet-wash lithographic plates. It is a skin irritant and should not be used. Turpentine substitutes are available commercially. In general, they consist of a mixture of pine oil and a small amount of castor oil and ester gum added to a larger quantity of naphtha or mineral spirits. The pine oil provides the same solvent properties as those of turpentine. The small amount of castor oil and ester gum leaves a tacky, nonvolatile residue when the other solvents evaporate. This residue is similar to that obtained when turpentine evaporates.

13 Screen Printing, Heat Transfer Printing, and Collotype

Screen Printing

Screen printing is the most versatile of all printing processes. It is used for printing on many kinds of substrates, such as paper, paperboard, wood, glass, metals, plastics, textiles, ceramic products, and leather. The printing is done not only on flat surfaces but also on round, convex, concave, and irregular shapes.

A screen with a fine mesh is used. In most commercial screen printing, the screen is covered with a light-sensitive coating. This coating is exposed through a positive of the subject to be printed. The exposure hardens the coating in the nonprinting areas. The unexposed areas are then washed out, usually with water, opening the meshes of the screen in the image areas.

In printing, a quantity of ink is placed on the top side of the screen (also called the inner side). The material to be printed is placed under the screen. While the screen is in contact with the material, the ink is forced through the openings in the screen with a squeegee.

Screen printing was for a long time entirely a hand-operated process, with the operator inserting a sheet to be printed, lowering the screen, and using a squeegee to force the ink through the screen onto the sheet. It is still often done this way, but now there are also automatic screen printing presses in use that can print on flat stock at speeds of from 400 to about 3,500 impressions per hour.

The process was originally called "silk screen printing," since the early screens consisted of silk bolting cloth. Although some silk is still used, the most popular screens today are polyester and nylon. Metal screens of phosphor bronze and stainless steel are used to a limited extent.

Many years ago, the stencil for a screen was hand-cut. Today, practically all stencils are made by a photographic process. Three methods are used—direct emulsion, direct-indirect, and indirect or transfer. The chemistry involved in each method is quite similar to the others. The main difference is how the coatings are applied to the screen.

In the *direct* method (used as the primary method by about 70% of screen printers), a light-sensitive emulsion is applied to both sides of the screen, first onto the under side, then onto the top side. Often multiple coats are applied, with drying between each one. The emulsion is often a mixture of polyvinyl alcohol and polyvinyl acetate. Before it is applied, the emulsion is sensitized. It can be sensitized by a solution of ammonium dichromate or by a diazo sensitizer, which is being used more and more. A diazo-sensitized emulsion will remain stable for up to three months at room temperature or up to six months if stored in a refrigerator. Screens coated with a diazo emulsion can be stored in a dark room for up to six months before they are exposed. Furthermore, diazo sensitizers are biodegradable and are relatively nontoxic.

In the *direct-indirect*, or "direct-film," method (used as the primary method by more than 10% of screen printers), a sheet of film is employed that is coated on one side, often with a mixture of polyvinyl alcohol and polyvinyl acetate. This film is not light sensitive. The screen is placed on top of the film, which is emulsion-side-up. Then a sensitized emulsion (the same as is used in the direct method) is squeegeed over the top of the screen. This emulsion sensitizes the one on the film underneath and also binds the film emulsion to the screen.

When the emulsions on both sides are thoroughly dry, the film backing sheet is stripped off. Then an exposure can be made through a positive, the same as with the direct method.

In the *indirect*, or transfer, method (used as the primary method by about 20% of screen printers), most of the steps outlined above are performed on a special film before it is applied to the screen. These films are of various types; one of them consists of a thin backing of acetate or vinyl coated with gelatin. In use, a sheet of the film is sensitized by brushing a water solution of ammonium dichromate, $(NH_4)_2Cr_2O_7$, over it and allowing this application to dry.

After the transfer film has been sensitized, it is exposed through a positive. Exposure hardens the gelatin in the nonprinting areas. Then the film is developed with warm water to remove the unexposed gelatin from the image areas. A cold-water treatment is used to harden the remaining gelatin stencil.

The wet film is placed in contact with the under side of the screen, with the gelatin layer next to the screen. The water causes the gelatin to adhere to the screen. After thorough drying, the thin backing is stripped off, leaving the gelatin stencil attached to the screen. The screen is now ready for printing.

The only advantage of the direct-indirect method over the direct method is that the stencil on the bottom side is uniform in thickness and only one coat is required on the top side. The screens print longer than if made with the indirect method, but not as long as with the direct method. The cost of the direct-indirect method is also between that of the other two, with the indirect method being the most expensive.

Heat Transfer Printing

Heat transfer printing is not another basic printing process. The printing is done by gravure, flexography, screen printing, or lithography. It is what happens to the paper after printing that makes heat transfer a special process.

There are two general methods used in heat transfer printing—melt transfer and dry transfer. In the *melt transfer* method, dyes or pigments are incorporated into a thermoplastic binder, and this ink is printed on paper. When the paper is brought into contact with a textile fabric, and heat and pressure are applied, the entire ink transfers to the fabric. This method is used for the printing of cotton and other fabrics. If the ink contains dyes, the dyeing of the fabric is completed by conventional dye fixation methods. If pigments are used (decalcomania process), no fiber dyeing occurs. The pigments are held on the fiber surface by means of the binder in the ink.

The *dye transfer* method is also known as the sublimation transfer process. The following discussion is concerned with this method, and any further reference to heat transfer printing implies dry transfer.

In the dry transfer process, paper is printed with inks that contain sublimable disperse dyes. Any material, including a dye, is said to sublime when it is heated and changes from solid to vapor without first going through the liquid stage.

The printing can be in a single color, in multiple colors, or in process color. The printed paper is placed in contact with the fabric. As heat and pressure are applied to the back of the paper, the dyes in the ink sublime, condense on the fiber surface, and then diffuse into the interior of the fiber.

As the temperature increases, the dyes begin to sublime into the narrow air space between the ink and the fabric. When the air becomes supersaturated with the dye vapor, this condition is relieved by vapor condensation on the surface of the fabric. Then the dyes begin to diffuse into the interior of the fabric. This process continues until the partial dye vapor pressures of the printed paper and of the dyed fabric reach equilibrium.

The efficiency of dye transfer from the ink on the paper to the fabric depends on the pressure applied, the temperature, the dwell time, and the shade of color. The efficiency increases as the pressure increases, up to a certain value; then further increase in pressure has little effect. As might be expected, the efficiency increases as temperature increases, and also as dwell time increases. For certain dyes, the optimum dwell time ranges from 30 seconds at 410°F (210°C) to 20 seconds at 445°F (230°C). The color transfer efficiency varies from about 90%–95% for light shades to about 40%–60% for heavy shades.

Heat transfer printing is not suitable for cotton or wool. It can be used on certain synthetic fibers but not on others. One reason is that the dyes must be heated to at least 390°F (200°C) to obtain adequate sublimation, and this is above the softening point of some synthetic fibers. The softening and melting points of several common fibers are shown below:

	Softening Point		Melting Point	
	°F	°C	°F	°C
Cellulose acetate	375	190	450	230
Cellulose triacetate	435	225	575	300
Nylon 6	340	170	420	215
Nylon 66	455	235	480	250
Acrylic	420–490	215–255	—	—
"Qiana" nylon	about 445	about 230	535	280
Polyester	445–465	230–240	495	255

From this table, it is apparent that cellulose acetate and nylon 6 cannot withstand the required transfer temperatures. Triacetate, nylon 66, and acrylic could be used, but they exhibit poor washfastness when printed by heat transfer. Furthermore, nylon 66 and acrylic do not give as bright colors as can be obtained by the direct printing of acid dyes on nylon 66 and of cationic dyes on acrylic.

"Qiana" nylon is suitable for the heat transfer printing of light to medium shades of color. Polyester has none of the disadvantages mentioned; it is the most suitable fiber for printing by this method.

The sublimable disperse dyes are mostly primary, secondary, or tertiary amines of three main types: amino-azo benzene, amino-anthraquinone, and nitro-diaryl-amine. They sublime in a relatively narrow range—390–420°F (200–215°C). Dyes are available that sublime at lower temperatures, but they generally have poor washability and lightfastness. There are also dyes that sublime at higher temperatures, but they cannot be used because the temperatures exceed the softening point of the synthetic fibers.

Heat transfer printing on paper of seamless patterns for transfer to wide textile rolls is mainly done by rotogravure. It is also done sometimes on rotary screen printing presses, and in increasing amounts by flexography—mostly in England.

Printing on sheets of paper is carried out largely on sheetfed lithographic presses. These sheets are used to make polyester fashion shirts and pictorial T-shirts. A high percentage of such printing uses process color.

Since gravure inks contain solvents and dry rapidly with mild heat, it is possible to print heat transfer gravure inks on relatively nonporous paper. As a result, the dye crystals stay mostly on the surface of the paper, resulting later in maximum dye transfer to the fabric.

In flexography and rotary screen printing, the heat transfer inks are often water-based. Such inks require a more porous paper to prevent puckering and to avoid smearing in multicolor printing. In this case, more dye is absorbed into the paper, resulting in somewhat poorer color transfer to the fabric.

The heat transfer inks look flat and quite dull when printed on paper. When they are transferred to the fabric, the colors become considerably brighter and clearer. There must be close cooperation between the printer and the textile firm to achieve the desired results for a particular fabric.

Besides synthetic textiles, heat transfer printing is being used for the decoration of polyester-surfaced table and counter tops, polyester lacquer-coated metals, wall hangings, and other specialties. Heat transfer at present accounts for only a small fraction of the total textile printing market, but it is predicted that it may capture 20%–25% of the world market by 1980.

Collotype

Collotype is a continuous-tone process. Sensitized gelatin is exposed through a continuous-tone negative. The gelatin is hardened in relation to the amount of ultraviolet light received. When the plate is printed under the proper conditions, it accepts ink in inverse proportion to the amount of hardening of the gelatin. Thus a continuous-tone print is obtained when the ink is transferred to paper.

Originally, the sensitized gelatin coating was applied to a lithographic stone. In modern collotype, the gelatin coating is applied to a grained aluminum plate. The gelatin solution can be sensitized either with ammonium dichromate, $(NH_4)_2Cr_2O_7$, for a fast emulsion, or potassium dichromate, $K_2Cr_2O_7$, for a slow one. A mixture of the two sensitizers is often used, making it possible to control the required length of the exposure.

Besides gelatin and sensitizers, the coating solution may contain chrome alum as a hardener or glyoxal, $O{=}CH{-}CH{=}O$, as a plasticizer.

Exposure time through a continuous-tone negative is critical. It depends on the light source used and the speed of the coating. The gelatin must be exposed correctly in each tonal area. The negatives used have a density range of about 1.1–1.3, and a gamma value close to 1.0.

After exposure, the plate is immersed in water or an alcohol-water mixture at about 50°F (10°C). This immersion removes the dichromates, making the coating no longer light-sensitive. Then the plate is dried and stored for a day. This procedure toughens the gelatin so the plate has a longer press life.

When the plate is to be printed, it is first immersed for about 25 minutes in a tank containing a mixture of three parts water to one part glycerin. After removal from the tank, the plate is blotted with newsprint to remove most of the solution. On the press, it is treated with a mixture of glycerin and formaldehyde. The formaldehyde tans the gelatin, giving the plate the oleophilic nature that it needs to hold ink.

Water causes the gelatin to swell. The more it swells, the more hydrophilic and the less oleophilic it becomes. During printing, a balance must be maintained to keep the gelatin swollen just the right amount. If too little water is present, the plate takes too much ink. If too much water is present, the plate takes too little ink and the prints look washed out.

During printing, the paper gradually removes water from the plate. Therefore, the water must be replenished at intervals. The glycerin helps to hold water on the plate. If the relative humidity of the air in the pressroom is high, the glycerin will remove some water vapor from the air, maintaining the water level on the plate. Another method is to keep the relative humidity of the pressroom at 45%–50% and to use a multiple-spray system when needed to add water containing a little glycerin to the plate.

For collotype printing, a press that has a good inking system and on which plate pressure can be controlled is needed. Presses that have been used for this purpose include a direct lithographic press with eight ink form rollers and a modified sheetfed offset lithographic press.

Inks for collotype are usually made with drying-oil varnishes, often of the alkyd type. They are quite stiff and have a much higher tack than sheetfed lithographic inks. Also, it is essential that their pigments be very finely ground. There is a wide choice of pigments, the only restriction being that they must not bleed into the water-glycerin solution. A manganese drier is most commonly used; a cobalt drier is occasionally employed.

Special papers are required. They must have the proper amount of moisture and have a pH close to neutral. High pick resistance is needed to withstand the pull of the gelatin in the nonprinting areas in particular. Pick resistance is not quite so important when the printing is done on an offset press. Uncoated paper must be used for direct printing; a supercalendered paper is best. Coated paper can be printed if an offset press is used.

To print by collotype requires a high degree of skill on the part of the craftsmen. Because of the difficulties of the process, the number of collotype plants has greatly declined. There are perhaps four in the United States and probably less than a dozen in the world.

Collotype is most competitive with other printing processes in short runs of from 100 to 5,000 full-color copies with an image size up to about 40″ × 60″ (1.0 × 1.5 m). It is used to reproduce fine-art paintings and to produce posters, murals, banners, point-of-purchase displays, maps, ad blowups, etc. Translites for light-box displays are produced by printing both sides simultaneously on opaline paper or vinyl sheets.

If collotype is printed properly, the printing quality is the highest of any printing process. For that reason, collotype is used for the highest-quality reproduction of fine-art paintings.

14 Tables

Chemical Elements

Name	Symbol	Atomic Number	Atomic Weight*	Name	Symbol	Atomic Number	Atomic Weight*
Actinium	Ac	89	(227)	Fermium	Fm	100	(257)
Aluminum	Al	13	26.98	Fluorine	F	9	19.00
Americium	Am	95	(243)	Francium	Fr	87	(223)
Antimony (Stibium)	Sb	51	121.75	Gadolinium	Gd	64	157.25
Argon	Ar	18	39.95	Gallium	Ga	31	69.72
Arsenic	As	33	74.92	Germanium	Ge	32	72.59
Astatine	At	85	(210)	Gold (Aurum)	Au	79	196.97
Barium	Ba	56	137.34	Hafnium	Hf	72	178.49
Berkelium	Bk	97	(247)	Helium	He	2	4.00
Beryllium	Be	4	9.01	Holmium	Ho	67	164.93
Bismuth	Bi	83	208.98	Hydrogen	H	1	1.01
Boron	B	5	10.81	Indium	In	49	114.82
Bromine	Br	35	79.90	Iodine	I	53	126.90
Cadmium	Cd	48	112.40	Iridium	Ir	77	192.20
Calcium	Ca	20	40.08	Iron (Ferrum)	Fe	26	55.85
Californium	Cf	98	(251)	Krypton	Kr	36	83.80
Carbon	C	6	12.01	Lanthanum	La	57	138.91
Cerium	Ce	58	140.12	Lawrencium	Lr	103	(257)
Cesium	Cs	55	132.90	Lead (Plumbum)	Pb	82	207.19
Chlorine	Cl	17	35.45	Lithium	Li	3	6.94
Chromium	Cr	24	52.00	Lutetium	Lu	71	174.97
Cobalt	Co	27	58.93	Magnesium	Mg	12	24.31
Copper	Cu	29	63.55	Manganese	Mn	25	54.94
Curium	Cm	96	(247)	Mendelevium	Md	101	(256)
Dysprosium	Dy	66	162.50	Mercury (Hydrargyrum)	Hg	80	200.59
Einsteinium	Es	99	(254)	Molybdenum	Mo	42	95.94
Erbium	Er	68	167.26				
Europium	Eu	63	151.96				

*The value in parentheses in the atomic weight column is the mass number of the most stable isotope.

**Chemical
Elements
(continued)**

Name	Symbol	Atomic Number	Atomic Weight*	Name	Symbol	Atomic Number	Atomic Weight*
Neodymium	Nd	60	144.24	Silicon	Si	14	28.09
Neon	Ne	10	20.18	Silver (Argentum)	Ag	47	107.87
Neptunium	Np	93	(237)	Sodium (Natrium)	Na	11	22.99
Nickel	Ni	28	58.71	Strontium	Sr	38	87.62
Niobium (Columbium)	Nb	41	92.91	Sulfur	S	16	32.06
Nitrogen	N	7	14.01	Tantalum	Ta	73	180.95
Nobelium	No	102	(254)	Technetium	Tc	43	(97)
Osmium	Os	76	190.20	Tellurium	Te	52	127.60
Oxygen	O	8	16.00	Terbium	Tb	65	158.92
Palladium	Pd	46	106.40	Thallium	Tl	81	204.37
Phosphorus	P	15	30.97	Thorium	Th	90	232.04
Platinum	Pt	78	195.09	Thulium	Tm	69	168.93
Plutonium	Pu	94	(244)	Tin (Stannum)	Sn	50	118.69
Polonium	Po	84	(209)	Titanium	Ti	22	47.90
Potassium (Kalium)	K	19	39.10	Tungsten (Wolfram)	W	74	183.85
Praseodymium	Pr	59	140.91	Uranium	U	92	238.03
Promethium	Pm	61	(145)	Vanadium	V	23	50.94
Protactinium	Pa	91	(231)	Xenon	Xe	54	131.30
Radium	Ra	88	(225)	Ytterbium	Yb	70	173.04
Radon	Rn	86	(222)	Yttrium	Y	39	88.90
Rhenium	Re	75	186.20	Zinc	Zn	30	65.37
Rhodium	Rh	45	102.90	Zirconium	Zr	40	91.22
Rubidium	Rb	37	85.47				
Ruthenium	Ru	44	101.07				
Samarium	Sm	62	150.35				
Scandium	Sc	21	44.96				
Selenium	Se	34	78.96				

*The value in parentheses in the atomic weight column is the mass number of the most stable isotope.

Energy Equivalents

1 British thermal unit = 1,054.35 joules
1 joule = 0.000948 British thermal unit

British Thermal Units/Joules

British thermal units	British thermal unit or joule energy value to be converted	Joules
0.000948	1	1,054
0.001897	2	2,109
0.002845	3	3,163
0.003794	4	4,217
0.004723	5	5,272
0.005691	6	6,326
0.006639	7	7,380
0.007588	8	8,435
0.008536	9	9,489
0.009485	10	10,544

Energy Equivalents

1 British thermal unit = 0.252 kilogram-calorie
1 kilogram-calorie = 3.968 British thermal units

British Thermal Units/ Kilogram-Calories

British thermal units	British thermal unit or kilogram-calorie energy value to be converted	Kilogram-calories
3.97	1	0.252
7.94	2	0.504
11.90	3	0.756
15.87	4	1.008
19.84	5	1.260
23.81	6	1.512
27.78	7	1.764
31.75	8	2.016
35.72	9	2.268
39.68	10	2.520

Length Equivalents

1 foot = 0.3048 meter
1 meter = 3.28 feet

Feet/Meters

Feet	Foot or meter measurement to be converted	Meters
3.28	1	0.305
6.56	2	0.610
9.84	3	0.914
13.12	4	1.219
16.40	5	1.524
19.68	6	1.829
22.96	7	2.134
26.24	8	2.438
29.52	9	2.743
32.80	10	3.048

Length Equivalents

1 inch = 25.4 millimeters
1 millimeter = 0.03937 inch

Inches/Millimeters

Inches	Inch or millimeter measurement to be converted	Millimeters
0.039	1	25.4
0.079	2	50.8
0.118	3	76.2
0.157	4	101.6
0.197	5	127.0
0.236	6	152.4
0.276	7	177.8
0.315	8	203.2
0.354	9	228.6
0.397	10	254.0

Liquid Capacity Equivalents

1 fluid ounce = 29.573 milliliters
1 milliliter = 0.0338 fluid ounce

Fluid Ounces/ Milliliters

Fluid ounces	Fluid ounce or milliliter capacity to be converted	Milli-liters
0.034	1	29.6
0.068	2	59.1
0.101	3	88.7
0.135	4	118.3
0.169	5	147.9
0.203	6	177.4
0.237	7	207.0
0.271	8	236.6
0.304	9	266.2
0.338	10	295.7

Liquid Capacity Equivalents

1 quart = 0.9463 liter
1 liter = 1.0567 quarts

Quarts/Liters

Quarts	Quart or liter capacity to be converted	Liters
1.06	1	0.946
2.11	2	1.893
3.17	3	2.839
4.23	4	3.785
5.28	5	4.732
6.34	6	5.678
7.40	7	6.624
8.45	8	7.571
9.51	9	8.517
10.57	10	9.463

Mass Equivalents

1 ounce = 28.3495 grams
1 gram = 0.03527 ounce

Ounces/Grams

Ounces	Ounce or gram mass to be converted	Grams
0.035	1	28.4
0.071	2	56.7
0.106	3	85.0
0.141	4	113.4
0.176	5	141.7
0.212	6	170.1
0.247	7	198.4
0.282	8	226.8
0.317	9	255.1
0.353	10	283.5

Mass Equivalents

1 pound = 0.4536 kilogram
1 kilogram = 2.2046 pounds

Pounds/ Kilograms

Pounds	Pound or kilogram mass to be converted	Kilo-grams
2.20	1	0.454
4.41	2	0.907
6.61	3	1.361
8.82	4	1.814
11.02	5	2.268
13.23	6	2.722
15.43	7	3.175
17.64	8	3.629
19.84	9	4.082
22.05	10	4.536

Mass of Water Vapor in Saturated Air at Various Temperatures

1 grain/cubic foot = 2.288 grams/cubic meter
1 gram/cubic meter = 0.437 grains/cubic foot

Temperature °F	°C	Grains/ cubic foot	Grams/ cubic meter	Temperature °F	°C	Grains/ cubic foot	Grams/ cubic meter
32	0.0	2.119	4.849	78	25.6	10.39	23.78
34	1.1	2.287	5.234	80	26.7	11.06	25.31
36	2.2	2.466	5.643	82	27.8	11.76	26.91
38	3.3	2.657	6.080	84	28.9	12.50	28.60
40	4.4	2.861	6.547	86	30.0	13.28	30.39
42	5.6	3.080	7.048	88	31.1	14.10	32.27
44	6.7	3.313	7.581	90	32.2	14.96	34.23
46	7.8	3.561	8.149	92	33.3	15.86	36.29
48	8.9	3.826	8.755	94	34.4	16.82	38.49
50	10.0	4.108	9.401	96	35.6	17.82	40.78
52	11.1	4.407	10.08	98	36.7	18.88	43.21
54	12.2	4.723	10.81	100	37.8	19.99	45.74
56	13.3	5.063	11.59	102	38.9	21.15	48.40
58	14.4	5.419	12.40	104	40.0	22.38	51.21
60	15.6	5.798	13.27	106	41.1	23.65	54.12
62	16.7	6.201	14.19	108	42.2	24.98	57.16
64	17.8	6.627	15.17	110	43.3	26.39	60.39
66	18.9	7.080	16.20	112	44.4	27.86	63.75
68	20.0	7.561	17.30	114	45.6	29.40	67.28
70	21.1	8.064	18.45	116	46.7	31.00	70.94
72	22.2	8.605	19.69	118	47.8	32.70	74.83
74	23.3	9.169	20.98	120	48.9	34.46	78.86
76	24.4	9.763	22.34				

Temperature Equivalents Fahrenheit/ Celsius

$1°F = 1.8°C + 32$
$1°C = 5/9(°F - 32)$

°F	°F or °C reading to be converted	°C	°F	°F or °C reading to be converted	°C
−40	−40	−40	86	30	−1.1
−36.4	−38	−38.9	87.8	31	−0.6
−32.8	−36	−37.8	89.6	32	0
−29.2	−34	−36.7	91.4	33	0.6
−25.6	−32	−35.6	93.2	34	1.1
−22	−30	−34.4	95	35	1.7
−18.4	−28	−33.3	96.8	36	2.2
−14.8	−26	−32.2	98.6	37	2.8
−11.2	−24	−31.1	100.4	38	3.3
−7.6	−22	−30	102.2	39	3.9
−4	−20	−28.9	104	40	4.4
−0.4	−18	−27.8	105.8	41	5
3.2	−16	−26.7	107.6	42	5.6
6.8	−14	−25.6	109.4	43	6.1
10.4	−12	−24.4	111.2	44	6.7
14	−10	−23.3	113	45	7.2
17.6	−8	−22.2	114.8	46	7.8
21.2	−6	−21.1	116.6	47	8.3
24.8	−4	−20	118.4	48	8.9
28.4	−2	−18.9	120.2	49	9.4
32	0	−17.8	122	50	10
33.8	1	−17.2	123.8	51	10.6
35.6	2	−16.7	125.6	52	11.1
37.4	3	−16.1	127.4	53	11.7
39.2	4	−15.6	129.2	54	12.2
41	5	−15	131	55	12.8
42.8	6	−14.4	132.8	56	13.3
44.6	7	−13.9	134.6	57	13.9
46.4	8	−13.3	136.4	58	14.4
48.2	9	−12.8	138.2	59	15
50	10	−12.2	140	60	15.6
51.8	11	−11.7	141.8	61	16.1
53.6	12	−11.1	143.6	62	16.7
55.4	13	−10.6	145.4	63	17.2
57.2	14	−10	147.2	64	17.8
59	15	−9.4	149	65	18.3
60.8	16	−8.9	150.8	66	18.8
62.6	17	−8.3	152.6	67	19.4
64.4	18	−7.8	154.4	68	20
66.2	19	−7.2	156.2	69	20.6
68	20	−6.7	158	70	21.1
69.8	21	−6.1	159.8	71	21.7
71.6	22	−5.6	161.6	72	22.2
73.4	23	−5	163.4	73	22.8
75.2	24	−4.4	165.2	74	23.3
77	25	−3.9	167	75	23.9
78.8	26	−3.3	168.8	76	24.4
80.6	27	−2.8	170.6	77	25
82.4	28	−2.2	172.4	78	25.6
84.2	29	−1.7	174.2	79	26.1

Temperature Equivalents Fahrenheit/ Celsius (continued)

°F	°F or °C reading to be converted	°C	°F	°F or °C reading to be converted	°C
176	80	26.7	323.6	162	72.2
177.8	81	27.2	327.2	164	73.3
179.6	82	27.8	330.8	166	74.4
181.4	83	28.3	334.4	168	75.6
183.2	84	28.9	338	170	76.7
185	85	29.4	341.6	172	77.8
186.8	86	30	345.2	174	78.9
188.6	87	30.6	348.8	176	80
190.4	88	31.1	352.4	178	81.1
192.2	89	31.7	356	180	82.2
194	90	32.2	359.6	182	83.3
195.8	91	32.8	363.2	184	84.4
197.6	92	33.3	366.8	186	85.6
199.4	93	33.9	370.4	188	86.7
201.2	94	34.4	374	190	87.8
203	95	35	377.6	192	88.9
204.8	96	35.6	381.2	194	90
206.6	97	36.1	384.8	196	91.1
208.4	98	36.7	388.4	198	92.2
210.2	99	37.2	392	200	93.3
212	100	37.8	395.6	202	94.4
215.6	102	38.9	399.2	204	95.6
219.2	104	40	402.8	206	96.7
222.8	106	41.1	406.4	208	97.8
226.4	108	42.2	410	210	98.9
230	110	43.3	413.6	212	100
233.6	112	44.4			
237.2	114	45.6			
240.8	116	46.7			
244.4	118	47.8			
248	120	48.9			
251.6	122	50			
255.2	124	51.1			
258.8	126	52.2			
262.4	128	53.3			
266	130	54.4			
269.6	132	55.6			
273.2	134	56.7			
276.8	136	57.8			
280.4	138	58.9			
284	140	60			
287.6	142	61.1			
291.2	144	62.2			
294.8	146	63.3			
298.4	148	64.4			
302	150	65.6			
305.6	152	66.7			
309.2	154	67.8			
312.8	156	68.9			
316.4	158	70			
320	160	71.1			

Terminology:
Metric Prefixes

Mathematical Equivalent	Prefix	Symbol
$1{,}000{,}000{,}000{,}000{,}000{,}000 = 10^{18}$	exa	E
$1{,}000{,}000{,}000{,}000{,}000 = 10^{15}$	peta	P
$1{,}000{,}000{,}000{,}000 = 10^{12}$	tera	T
$1{,}000{,}000{,}000 = 10^{9}$	giga	G
$1{,}000{,}000 = 10^{6}$	mega	M
$1{,}000 = 10^{3}$	kilo	k
$100 = 10^{2}$	hecto	h
$10 = 10$	deka	da
$0.1 = 10^{-1}$	deci	d
$0.01 = 10^{-2}$	centi	c
$0.001 = 10^{-3}$	milli	m
$0.000\ 001 = 10^{-6}$	micro	μ
$0.000\ 000\ 001 = 10^{-9}$	nano	n
$0.000\ 000\ 000\ 001 = 10^{-12}$	pico	p
$0.000\ 000\ 000\ 000\ 001 = 10^{-15}$	femto	f
$0.000\ 000\ 000\ 000\ 000\ 001 = 10^{-18}$	atto	a

Index

Abrasion of image   272
Acidity   43
Acids   24
Acids, properties of   25
Activation, energy of   17
Additive plates   147
Air conditioning, pressroom   260
Alcohol (and substitute) fountain solutions   264
Alcohol plate cleaner   158
Alcohols   79, 80
Aldehydes   81
Alicyclic hydrocarbons   72
Aliphatic hydrocarbons   71
Alkali metals   11
Alkalinity   43
Alkyl groups   78
Alkyl halides   77, 78
Aluminum, anodized   129
Anhydrous compounds   22
Anions   55
Anodized aluminum   129
Antisetoff powders   256
Aromatic hydrocarbons   72
Asphaltum   143
Atomic energy   37
Atomic nucleus   7, 11
Atomic number   7, 11, 13
Atomic symbols   13
Atomic weight   12, 13
Atoms   6
Atoms, structure of   7, 11
Automatic film processing   110, 111
Automatic plate processors   145

Bases   26, 97, 129, 194
Bases, properties of   27
Basis weight   206
Benzene and derivatives   86
Blanket swelling   272
Blankets   277
Blinding   269
Blistering of paper   263
British thermal units/joules, table of   293
British thermal units/kilogram-calories, table of   293
Bromide body   100

Carbohydrates   90
Carbon   69
Carbon black   216
Carbon dioxide cycle   71
Carbon tissue   189, 190
Cations   55
Chalking of inks   262
Charcoal   69
Chemical pulp   198
Chemical reaction   1
Coated papers   207
Coating, plate   132, 157
Coatings, multimetal plate   167
Coke   69
Collotype   287
Color sensitivities of emulsions   101
Color temperature   103, 104
Colored inorganic pigments   217
Coloring materials, paper   202
Compounds   4, 16
Conservation of energy   17
Conservation of mass   1
Contact angles   166
Continuing reaction   134, 157
Copolymer   185
Copper relief plates   182
Copperized-aluminum plates   155
Copperizing   160
Corrosion   37
Counteretching   156
Covalent bond   15
Cross-linking   149
Crystallization, ink   254
Crystallization, water of   22

Dampening rollers   267
Dark reaction   133, 157
Deep-etch plates   155
Deionization   59, 60
Demineralization   59, 60
Desensitization, partial   271
Desensitizing   140
Development, photographic   105
Development, plate   158
Diazo compound   147

Diffusion transfer films   123
Diffusion transfer plates   164
Distillation   58, 74
Drier dissipation   227
Driers, ink   226
Dry plates   152
Drying mechanisms, ink   228
Drying stimulators   266
Duplicate plates   187
Dye transfer   285

Electroassist, gravure   261
Electrolytes   33
Electron beam drying   224
Electrons   7
Electrons, extranuclear   8, 11
Electrostatic film   125
Electrostatic plates   172
Electrostatic precipitator   259
Elements   4, 11
Elements, characteristics of common   13
Elements, families of   11
Elements, table of   291
Emulsification, ink/water   238, 255, 256
Emulsions   97, 192, 256
Emulsions, properties of   100
Energy, conservation of   17
Energy equivalents (tables)   293
Energy levels   8, 11
Energy of activation   17
Engraver, electronic   195
Engraving, direct   195
Epoxy resin   196
Equilibrium   30
Esters   85
Etching, powderless   180
Ethers   82
Exposure, photographic   102
Extranuclear electrons   8, 11

Fading of inks   251
Fahrenheit/Celsius, table of   298
Families of elements   11
Fats   90

Feeder driers   227
Feet/meters, table of   294
Felt side, paper   205
Fibrillation   201
Fillers, paper   202
Fixing, photographic   114
Flash point   91
Flexographic inks   240
Flexographic rollers   274
Flocculation, pigment   239
Fluid ounces/milliliters, table of   295
Formulas, molecular   15
Formulas of compounds   22
Fountain solutions   263
Fourdrinier papermaking machine   204
Free radicals   232
Fusion, molar heat of   17

Gases   2
Gases, noble   12
Gloss ghosting   255
Gloss inks   222
Grain in paper   212
Graining, plate   130
Graphite   70
Gravure cylinders   188, 190
Gravure electroassist   261
Gravure impression rollers   274
Gravure inks   243
Groundwood pulp   197
Gum arabic   142

Halides   77, 97
Halogens   12
Hardness of water   55
Heat transfer printing   285
Heatset inks   223, 231
Heatset oils   94
Hickeys and spots   275
Humidity   64
Hydration   201
Hydrocarbons   71, 75
Hydrogen   10
Hydrogen isotopes   10

Hydrogen molecule   15
Hydrolysis   29
Hygrometer   65

Inches/meters, table of   294
Infectious developers   108
Infrared ink setting   230
Ink chemistry   215
Ink drying   212, 213, 234, 252–254
Ink film thickness   216, 251
Ink flying   237
Inks, properties of   234
Inorganic compounds   23
Intensifiers, photographic   121
Ionic solids   19
Ionization of water   43
Ions   18
Ions, negatively charged   21
Ions, positively charged   20
Isomers   88
Isotopes   9
Isotopes of hydrogen   10

Ketones   82

Lacquer application   160
Laser-exposed plates   175, 177
Length equivalents (tables)   294
Length of inks   235
Levels, energy   8, 11
Light sources   102, 103, 137
Light-sensitivity, plate coatings   132
Liquid capacity equivalents (table)   295
Liquids   2

Magnesium plates   179
Mass, conservation of   1
Mass, electron   7, 11
Mass, neutron   7, 11
Mass number   8, 11
Mass, protron   7, 11
Mass equivalents (table)   296
Materials   2
Mechanical pulp   197

Melt transfer   285
Melting points, fibers   286
Metals   5
Metals, alkali   11
Metals, alkaline earth   11
Metals, properties of   6
Metals, relative activity of   34
Metric prefixes, table of   300
Microwave drying   234
Minerals in water   55
Mixtures   3, 16
Modifiers, ink   227
Molar heat of fusion   17
Molar heat of vaporization   17
Mole   27
Molecular formulas   15
Molecular weight   27
Molecules of compounds   15
Molecules of elements   14
Monofunctional acrylate   233
Multifunctional acrylate   233
Multimetal plate classes   168
Multimetal plates   165, 169, 170

Natural gas   73
Negative-working plates   145, 154, 176
Neutrons   7, 11
News inks   247
Noble gases   12
Nucleus, atomic   7, 11

Oils   90
Oligomers   232
Organic acids   83
Organic chemistry   69
Organic compounds   23
Organic pigments   219
Osmosis   61
Ounces/grams, table of   296
Overcoatings   224
Overprinting, process ink   250, 254
Oxidation   23
Oxidation number   23

Paper classes   207
Paper properties   210, 214
Paper refiner   201
Paper sizing   203
Paper stock preparation   201
Papermaking   197, 204
Petroleum   73
pH   43, 45, 46, 212, 213
pH, how to measure   47, 48
Photographic materials   97
Photoinitiator   185
Photopolymer film   125
Photopolymer, gravure   194
Photopolymer plates   148
Photopolymer relief plates   184, 186
Pigments   215, 239
Plastic relief plates   184
Plastic substrate   224
Plate processors, automatic   145
Plates, lithographic   127
Pollution reduction   258
Polyester film base   192, 194
Polymerization   75, 76, 149, 232
Positive-working plates   155, 176
Pounds/kilograms, table of   296
Powderless etching   180
Precipitate   31
Presensitized photopolymer   194
Presensitized plates   147, 161
Press stability of inks   239
Printing, process ink   249
Processing, photographic   105
Products   1
Projection speed plates   173
Properties, chemical   6
Properties, physical   6
Proteins   89
Protons   7, 11
Pulp bleaching   200

Quarts/liters, table of   295
Quickset inks   223, 229

Radioactivity   37
Rapid-access processing   114
Reactants   1
Reaction, chemical   1
Reciprocity, exposure   135
Reducers, photographic   120
Reduction   23
Refiner, paper   201
Relative humidity   64
Relative humidity effects   211, 213
Relief plates   179
Resin, epoxy   196
Resins   149, 151
Reverse osmosis   62, 63
Rollers   273
Roller stripping   277

Safe lights   135
Saturated air, table of   297
Saturated solutions   30
Screen printing   283
Screen printing inks   244
Scumming   267
Sensitivity guide   135
Silicone fluids   257
Silver halides   97, 123, 192
Silver reclamation   116, 117, 118
Silverless films   123
Sizing, paper   203
Sizing, surface   205
Skin sensitivity   144
Soaps   55
Sodium atom (structure)   8, 11
Softening of water   57
Solids   2
Solubility of compounds   32
Solutions   5, 279
Solvents   91, 241, 273
Sponges, treatment   143
Static electricity elimination   260
Stencil scrubbing   161
Substances   3
Subtractive plates   148
Sulfate process   198

Sulfite process   199
Sulfur atom (structure)   9, 11
Supercalender   206
Symbols, atomic   13

Table of British thermal units/joules   293
Table of British thermal units/kilogram-calories   293
Table of chemical elements   291
Table of Fahrenheit/Celsius   298
Table of feet/meters   294
Table of fluid ounces/milliliters   295
Table of inches/millimeters   294
Table of metric prefixes   300
Table of ounces/grams   296
Table of pounds/kilograms   296
Table of quarts/liters   295
Table of saturated air   297
Tack of inks   235
TDS (totally dissolved solids)   55
Temperature conditioning of paper   211
Temperature equivalents (table)   298
Thermomechanical pulp (TMP)   197
Thermoplastic resins   149, 188
Thermoset resins   149, 151
Tinting, ink   255
TLV (threshold limit values)   92, 93
Toxicity   92
Transition elements   19
Trapping   255

Ultraviolet (UV) inks   223, 231, 274

Valence electrons   9, 13
Vaporization, molar heat of   17
Varnishes   220, 224
Vehicles, ink   215, 223
Vesicular films   124

Washing, photographic   118, 119
Washup solutions   279
Waste treatment   161
Water   55
Water in paper   210, 262
Water of crystallization   22

Wet-strength papers   209
White inorganic pigments   216
Wipe-on plates   150
Wire side, paper   205

Xylenes   88

Zinc plates   179